BEING HUMAN IN GOD'S WORLD

An Old Testament Theology of Humanity

J. GORDON McCONVILLE

Baker Academic

a division of Baker Publishing Group
Grand Rapids, Michigan

© 2016 by J. Gordon McConville

Published by Baker Academic
a division of Baker Publishing Group
P.O. Box 6287, Grand Rapids, MI 49516-6287
www.bakeracademic.com

Printed in the United States of America

Library of Congress Cataloging-in-Publication Data
Names: McConville, J. G. (J. Gordon), author.
Title: Being human in God's world : an Old Testament theology of humanity / J. Gordon McConville.
Description: Grand Rapids : Baker Academic, 2016. | Includes bibliographical references and index.
Identifiers: LCCN 2016007736 | ISBN 9780801048968 (cloth)
Subjects: LCSH: Theological anthropology—Biblical teaching. | Theological anthropology—Christianity. | Bible. Old Testament—Criticism, interpretation, etc.
Classification: LCC BS670.5 .M33 2016 | DDC 233—dc23
LC record available at https://lccn.loc.gov/2016007736

16 17 18 19 20 21 22   7 6 5 4 3 2 1

For my wife, Helen

"Far more precious than jewels"

Contents

Preface

To attempt to write a book with "Being Human" in the title may seem uncomfortably close to propounding a "theory of everything." If there is a good reason for doing so, it lies in the fact that, both within and outside communities of faith, we are surrounded implicitly and explicitly by concepts of what being human means. What is offered here, therefore, is not some definitive verdict on the subject, but rather an indication of ways in which a biblical theology might bear upon it. The chief weight of the argument falls on the Old Testament, as the title declares. In my attempt to develop an "Old Testament Theology of Humanity" I take this to have a context in a theology of the Old and New Testaments, and in Christian theology more generally. I hope this will be clear from the pages that follow, though it may turn out to be clearer that I am more at home in the Old Testament than in other branches of theology! Yet I think that my interest in the topic has been born of my study of the Old Testament. Because of its rootedness in the history, geography, culture, languages, literature, and wisdom of a people, it is not only an immeasurable resource for the subject but even forces it upon the reader's attention. By its nature, therefore, I believe it has an indispensable place in Christian theological thinking about being human.

The book has an origin not only in my thinking about the Old Testament in general but also in my particular preoccupation in recent years with "biblical spirituality." What I mean by this will appear below. In the confines of a preface, I will say about it only that I take the scholarly quest for meaning in the biblical text to be inseparable from the personal engagement of the inquirer in the task and its subject matter. This being so, what follows should be regarded as an essay in reading the Bible in pursuit of a greater understanding of oneself, individually and in one's various communities, as a human being. As such it seeks to indicate a certain practice of understanding rather than to say all that might be said. Plainly the volume does not do the latter, and another author might well have selected different specific topics from the ones that make up the argument here. Parts of the argument build on essays and conference papers published elsewhere, and these are acknowledged at appropriate places.

Many people have contributed, in various ways, to the making of this book. If it has strengths, I owe those strengths to them. Its weaknesses will mean that I did not learn from them carefully enough. Its immediate provenance is from a project on "Biblical Spirituality" sponsored by Bible Society (UK) and based in the School of Humanities at the University of Gloucestershire. I am grateful to Bible Society for their sponsorship, and especially to David Spriggs, an Old Testament scholar himself, who participated actively with us in the development of the project. My colleagues Andrew Lincoln and Lloyd Pietersen were my chief comrades over the four years or so of the project. Their stimulus and encouragement have been immeasurably important to me, and I owe them an enormous debt. Sheona Beaumont, as a doctoral student on the project, brought important insights from the interface of theology and art.

Among the numerous colleagues from other universities and nations who participated in the project, I record my gratitude to Pieter de Villiers, who took a leading part in two international symposiums on the subject at the University of Gloucestershire in Cheltenham. These resulted in two publications: *The Bible and Spirituality: Exploratory Essays in Reading Scripture Spiritually* and *The Spirit That Inspires: Perspectives on Biblical Spirituality*.[1]

I am also grateful to members of the Bible and Spirituality research group within the School of Humanities, which was an important venue for sharing ideas not only from within theology but also from other subject areas, especially English and history. As well as those already named, the group included our colleagues Melissa Raphael, Shelley Saguaro, Anna French, and Hilary Weeks. And the Theology Reading Group, with colleagues Dee Carter and Philip Esler, and coordinator Paul Caddle, has left its mark here in ways that they will recognize.

---

1. Andrew T. Lincoln, J. Gordon McConville, and Lloyd K. Pietersen, eds., *The Bible and Spirituality: Exploratory Essays in Reading Scripture Spiritually* (Eugene, OR: Cascade, 2013); Pieter de Villiers and Lloyd Pietersen, eds., *The Spirit That Inspires: Perspectives on Biblical Spirituality*, Acta Theologica Supplementum 15 (Bloemfontein, South Africa: University of the Free State Press, 2011).

Finally, my thanks to Jim Kinney and Baker Academic for accepting this volume for publication (and to Tim West for preparing the manuscript so carefully). Jim has been both enormously patient and encouraging, as well as a stimulating conversation partner in matters theological, over a number of years. And I am delighted to be able to join him in offering the pages that follow.

Cheltenham, July 3, 2015

Abbreviations

AB	Anchor Bible	BZAW	Beihefte zur Zeitschrift für die alttestamentliche Wissenschaft
ABD	Anchor Bible Dictionary. Edited by David Noel Freedman. 6 vols. New York: Doubleday, 1992.	ca.	circa, about
AnBib	Analecta Biblica	CBET	Contributions to Biblical Exegesis and Theology
ApOTC	Apollos Old Testament Commentary	CBQ	Catholic Biblical Quarterly
		CE	Common Era
ATANT	Abhandlungen zur Theologie des Alten und Neuen Testaments	CGLC	Cambridge Greek and Latin Classics
BBB	Bonner biblische Beiträge	ch./chs.	chapter/chapters
BBC	Blackwell Bible Commentaries	e.g.	exempli gratia, for example
BBR	Bulletin for Biblical Research	esp.	especially
BC	Book of the Covenant	ESV	English Standard Version
BCE	Before the Common Era	FRLANT	Forschungen zur Religion und Literatur des Alten und Neuen Testaments
BCOTWP	Baker Commentary on the Old Testament Wisdom and Psalms	HALAT	Hebräisches und aramäisches Lexikon zum Alten Testament. Ludwig Koehler, Walter Baumgartner, and Johann J. Stamm. 3rd ed. Leiden: Brill, 1995, 2004.
BETL	Bibliotheca Ephemeridum Theologicarum Lovaniensium		
BEvT	Beiträge zur evangelischen Theologie		
BKAT	Biblischer Kommentar, Altes Testament	HBM	Hebrew Bible Monographs
BTAT	Beiträge zur Theologie des Alten Testaments	ICC	International Critical Commentary
BWANT	Beiträge zur Wissenschaft vom Alten (und Neuen) Testament	JBL	Journal of Biblical Literature
		JBTh	Jahrbuch für biblische Theologie

JSOT	*Journal for the Study of the Old Testament*	PGOT	Phoenix Guides to the Old Testament
JSOTSup	Journal for the Study of the Old Testament Supplement Series	*PS*	*Political Science and Politics*
		RSV	Revised Standard Version
JTS	*Journal of Theological Studies*	SBL	Society of Biblical Literature
KJV	King James Version	SBLDS	Society of Biblical Literature Dissertation Series
lit.	literally		
LXX	Septuagint	SC	Sources chrétiennes
MS(S)	manuscript(s)	SHS	Scripture and Hermeneutics Seminar
MT	Masoretic Text		
NAC	New American Commentary	SSN	Studia Semitica Neerlandica
NASB	New American Standard Bible	StBibLit	Studies in Biblical Literature
NCB	New Century Bible	THOTC	Two Horizons Old Testament Commentary
NIB	*The New Interpreter's Bible.* Edited by Leander E. Keck. 12 vols. Nashville: Abingdon, 1994–2004.	*TZ*	*Theologische Zeitschrift*
		VT	*Vetus Testamentum*
		VTSup	Supplements to Vetus Testamentum
NIV	New International Version		
NRSV	New Revised Standard Version	WBC	Word Biblical Commentary
ÖBS	Österreichische biblische Studien	WMANT	Wissenschaftliche Monographien zum Alten und Neuen Testament
OBT	Overtures to Biblical Theology		
OTG	Old Testament Guides	ZAW	*Zeitschrift für die alttestamentliche Wissenschaft*
OTL	Old Testament Library		
OTM	Oxford Theological Monographs		

Introduction

On Thinking about Being Human

A Biblical Study of Humanity

The aim of this book is to explore what it means to be human according to the testimonies of the Bible, especially the Old Testament. It is, therefore, a biblical and theological study rather than an "anthropology" in the strict sense.[1] In expressing it thus, I am locating the inquiry about the human condition and experience within a particular context, namely, in a theological tradition in which the Old Testament is taken to be Scripture. As Hebrew Bible, it is Scripture for the synagogue, while for the church it is part of the two-Testament Bible, or differently, the two-Testament witness to Jesus Christ. For myself, the project has its specific context in the Christian theological heritage, as well as in a curiosity that is essentially my own, of which more in a moment.

Theologically speaking, the question about what it is to be human in the context of Christian Scripture is inevitably christological. How can an Old Testament study of humanity relate to the Christian confession of faith in Jesus Christ as the Word made flesh, as God's incarnate Son, in whom there was no sin? Must not any study of humanity, in biblical perspective, be a study of the humanity of Christ? To this one may respond that the New Testament's portrayal of the humanity of Jesus, and the church's confession of Christ as

1. See John Rogerson's distinctions between German and English usage at this point, where the former is about the nature of the human being, while the latter is closer to ethnography (J. W. Rogerson, *Anthropology and the Old Testament* [Oxford: Blackwell, 1978], 9). Hans Walter Wolff's classic *Anthropology of the Old Testament*, trans. Margaret Kohl (London: SCM, 1974), being theological and exegetical, is an example of the German usage.

1

God the Son, do not foreclose explorations of the limits and possibilities of the lived experience of human beings. On the contrary, it is the belief in Christ's humanity that compels us to keep before us the Old Testament's testimony about God's involvement with human beings, both from the creation and in the specific historical experience of Israel. This is the clear implication of the church's historic creedal affirmation of Christ's true humanity, together with everything that connected him with historical Israel. The Old Testament remains the bulwark of Christian theology against dualisms that undermine its incarnational theology. The present work is not a Christology, yet I take it to be christological, because in attempting to understand how the Old Testament helps us think about being human, we may be better able to understand what it means to confess the humanity of Christ.

There are theological entailments in the study, therefore, that should not be underestimated. The basic question concerns the ways in which the ultimate destiny of human beings in Christ bears upon their existence in the present world. There is no straightforward answer to this question. Both the New Testament and strands within historic Christian theology strike notes that seem negative about the Christian's this-worldly existence, yet can also affirm positive aspects of it. This point undergirds H. Richard Niebuhr's classic work *Christ and Culture*. On the negative side, he finds that "the world" sometimes appears to be entirely opposed to Christ, as in the First Letter of John: "If any one loves the world, love for the Father is not in him" (1 John 2:15 RSV).[2] Yet Jesus is also shown to have engaged prophetically and sympathetically with the world. He not only forgives sins but also heals the sick in body; he trenchantly criticizes the abuse of the weak by the strong; he employs illustrations from the working life of farmers and fishermen in his teaching, a life that he shares on a basis of friendship; he respects home and family, and even the due ordering of temple life (as when he instructs a man healed of "leprosy" to go and show himself to the priest; see Mark 1:43–44; Luke 5:14); and he recognizes God-given rights of the ruling authorities (in his answer to the question about taxes in Matt. 22:21, and as interpreted by Paul in Rom. 13). Niebuhr sums up this side of his portrayal thus: "The other-worldliness of Jesus is always mated with a this-worldly concern; his proclamation and demonstration of divine action is inseparable from commandments to men to be active here and now."[3] Christian theology is bound to grapple with this aspect of the legacy of Jesus.

2. H. Richard Niebuhr, *Christ and Culture* (London: Faber & Faber, 1951), 60–61.
3. Ibid., 11; cf. 129–30. The examples taken here from the Gospel reports of Jesus' life are partly his and partly mine.

Niebuhr famously detects five models in the history of Christian thought and practice, on a spectrum ranging from outright opposition ("Christ against culture") to accommodation ("the Christ of culture"). Between these extremes lie three intermediate points, representing attempts to express both the transcendence of Christ's kingdom and the responsibility of Christians to engage with the life of the world.[4] For some there is a paradoxical relationship, in which, while all culture is infected by sin, Christians can nevertheless inhabit the world in which it prevails because of the power of Christ to penetrate to the roots of the human heart and mind and "[cleanse] the fountains of life."[5] For others, while it is admitted that good things have been corrupted, human culture can be "a transformed life in and to the glory of God."[6]

Niebuhr knew that his account was, in some measure, an oversimplification of a complicated reality, a point that has recently been stressed again by D. A. Carson in a reevaluation of *Christ and Culture*. For Carson, the questions raised by the concept of culture today are exceedingly complex and are bound to look different depending on where one stands in the modern world.[7] The point should be taken as a salutary warning against all-encompassing theories. Even so, the question that occasioned Niebuhr's work remains inevitable because it arises from the biblical legacy. And in fact it surfaces in arenas of theological discussion quite different from his, for example in a recent work of Jürgen Moltmann.[8] Moltmann finds four approaches to "eschatology," which are in fact approaches to the challenge of living ethically in the world. His own preferred model is one that he calls "transformative," a basically hopeful orientation to the possibilities of human action in the world,[9] not unlike Niebuhr's fourth model ("Christ the transformer of culture"). Interestingly, Carson points out that Niebuhr too expresses a tacit preference for

4. These are "Christ above culture," "Christ and culture in paradox," and "Christ the transformer of culture."

5. Niebuhr, *Christ and Culture*, 188. Niebuhr's label for this view is "dualist." He associates Paul and Luther with it, yet calls it merely a "motif" (187).

6. Ibid., 197. Niebuhr associates Augustine and Calvin with this perspective.

7. He wonders, for example, whether Abraham Kuyper, had he grown up in the "killing fields" of the Khmer Rouge in Cambodia, would have developed the view of Christ and culture that he did (D. A. Carson, *Christ and Culture Revisited* [Grand Rapids: Eerdmans, 2012], ix). Carson believes an understanding of Christ and culture requires a much more refined analysis than that offered by Niebuhr.

8. Jürgen Moltmann, *Ethics of Hope*, trans. Margaret Kohl (Minneapolis: Fortress, 2012). In preparation for his study of Christian ethics, Moltmann offers an analysis of theological orientations to the possibilities of effective action in the world that has some affinities with Niebuhr's, though using a quite different nomenclature and with no apparent debt to Niebuhr. He identifies four approaches to eschatology—namely, Lutheran (or "Apocalyptic"), Calvinist (or "Christological"), Anabaptist (or "Separatist"), and "Transformative."

9. Ibid., 35–41.

this model, by virtue of his failure to offer any critique of it according to his otherwise customary pattern.[10]

The discussion so far has shown that the challenge bequeathed to us by Jesus and the New Testament calls us to ongoing interpretation of the human condition in the light of the coming kingdom. If analyses of models and approaches must be treated with caution, it is clear that certain false trails are to be avoided. One lies in the danger of allowing our own cultural commitments to overdetermine our view of Christ, who is then wrongly invoked as a sanction for them. And the other is the opposite, namely, the danger of despising God's "good" creation and consigning it to perdition while awaiting eschatological renewal.[11] The task of discerning the truth in the relationship between Christ and culture is not one that can be categorically decided by means of certain techniques. Rather, it is a function, on the one hand, of readers' careful understanding of their own situation and prior commitments, and, on the other, of an appreciation of the nature of the biblical witness as a complex dialogue between the work of Christ as finished and as a prophetic call to live constructively in the world. This can be put in more explicitly theological terms as an openness to the guidance of the Holy Spirit.[12] For my part, I embark on the task ahead in a spirit of cautious optimism, broadly sympathetic with the "transformative" approaches just mentioned, while recognizing that such optimism may be chastened in the process.

Transformation, Transcendence, and "Spirituality"

I said a moment ago that the present inquiry has part of its context in a curiosity that is essentially my own. This is not to claim some special privilege or insight, but rather to name a dimension of it that is inescapable. Any theological question put to Scripture is in some sense a question about the self, self-knowledge being inseparable from the knowledge of God. This is more obviously the case when the human person is, as here, the express object of the inquiry. One can put the point logically, or hermeneutically, as well as theologically, because the object of the inquiry is at the same time the subject of it. If I presume to write about "being human," I do so unavoidably as a human being. This means that the manner of knowing that is assumed here is

---

10. Carson, *Christ and Culture Revisited*, 28–29.

11. Niebuhr, *Christ and Culture*, 124–25.

12. Niebuhr puts it in trinitarian terms, saying that "the Spirit proceeds not only from the Son but from the Father also, and that with the aid of the knowledge of Christ it is possible to discriminate between the spirits of the times and the Spirit which is from God" (*Christ and Culture*, 116).

not that of a subject gaining knowledge of an object by means of techniques that the subject has mastered, rather as a linguist or an archaeologist might do. I cannot break out of the circle in which I myself am part of the inquiry. None of this means that there is no place here for the ordinary techniques employed in biblical studies. The Bible is in one sense a historical document or set of documents, and it follows that the tools of philology, history, literature, sociology, and other disciplines are relevant by definition. Ultimately, however, the Bible invites the reader to undertake an act of self-involvement, a kind of reading that may be called "performative." This is no accident; the hermeneutical conundrum is itself an entailment of a biblical view of the self as known only in relation to God. The project, therefore, has been conceived not primarily as an analysis of the sorts of options available in a study of Christ and culture, but as an engagement of a reader with Scripture in a quest for what it means to be human. Put differently, this can be described as an exercise in "biblical spirituality."

The close involvement of oneself with a work is always true in some measure of anyone who writes. But I want to make a particular point of it. I have used the term "spirituality" in the heading to this section, and I realize that it is a term for which the phrase "scare quotes" might have been invented. For some, it implies a kind of unreality about the tough business of living. But I hope it is clear from the foregoing paragraphs that this is far from what is meant here. I mean it, rather, to refer to the ways in which belief is turned into all the dimensions of the practice of living. Nor is this something that can be worked out in a theoretical way, but rather in the school of life, with its hardships as well as joys. Kees Waaijman, one of the foremost scholar-practitioners of Christian spirituality, sees the discipline of spirituality as addressing "the divine-human relational process as transformation."[13] This idea of "transformation" applies to everything that falls within human experience, and is a key concept for the task at hand. Sandra Schneiders sees it as one of the essential objectives of New Testament interpretation.[14] For writers like these, transformation is not a value in itself, but a factor in the human relationship with God. They point to a conception of the human being that is far from "steady state." Rather, we will reckon with growth and change as of the essence of human being. Such change, furthermore, is not the sort that simply happens, as with age or by accident. Rather it is associated with the orientation of one's life, or with the discipline of a certain "practice."

13. Kees Waaijman, *Spirituality: Forms, Foundations, Methods* (Leuven: Peeters, 2002), 4.
14. Sandra Schneiders, *The Revelatory Text: Interpreting the New Testament as Sacred Scripture*, 2nd ed. (Collegeville, MN: Liturgical Press, 1999), 14.

As David Ford has it: "The dynamics of Christian life are explored primarily through the worship of God and the transformation of the self before God."[15]

Schneiders has also spoken of spirituality as "lived experience," and further defines this as "conscious involvement in the project of life integration through self-transcendence towards the ultimate value one perceives."[16] This definition allows for a range of ultimate values, so that it can apply in principle to the religious and nonreligious alike. Her work as a New Testament scholar, however, is based on a transformative hermeneutic of reading Scripture indebted to Paul Ricoeur. Her idea of "self-transcendence" refers to a person's aspiration to change the condition in which they find themselves.[17] As such it is close to the concept of transformation.

In Christian spirituality, the context within which such concepts become meaningful is the narrative of the Christian life, in which the individual and group participate in the larger story of the church of Christ. The "ordinary" life has thus an eschatological dimension, its transformations experienced in hope as belonging within the ultimate transformation of all things in Christ.

If the present work belongs broadly within spirituality thus understood, it may be thought of as a study of "biblical spirituality" in particular.[18] This is because it will proceed by exegetical and theological study of parts of the Old Testament, within the larger horizon of the Christian Bible. Biblical spirituality, as a self-consciously distinctive aspect of Christian thought, is a relatively recent inquiry into the ways in which the Bible is or may be used in the translation of belief into thought and practice. It draws in principle on all the disciplines of theology and is hospitable to the full range of methods commonly used in biblical studies. It is distinguished from closely related

15. David F. Ford, *Self and Salvation: Being Transformed* (Cambridge: Cambridge University Press, 1999), 2.

16. Sandra Schneiders, "Christian Spirituality: Definition, Methods, and Types," in *The New Westminster Dictionary of Christian Spirituality*, ed. P. Sheldrake (Louisville: Westminster John Knox, 2005), 1.

17. John Macquarrie has used it in the slightly different sense of an apprehension of the sublime (Macquarrie, *In Search of Humanity: A Theological and Philosophical Approach* [London: SCM, 1982], 25–37). "Transcendence" can be used in a variety of senses. In the present study I mean it primarily in the sense defined here by Schneiders. It comprises a belief in the possibility of personal change, together with an understanding that resources for such change come from beyond the self. For more on this, see below, ch. 9.

18. The present volume has roots in a project whose aim is to establish biblical spirituality as one of the disciplines of biblical studies. It has so far resulted in two published volumes, each following an international symposium, namely: Pieter de Villiers and Lloyd K. Pietersen, eds., *The Spirit That Inspires: Perspectives on Biblical Spirituality*, Acta Theologica Supplementum 15 (Bloemfontein, South Africa: University of the Free State Press, 2011); and Andrew T. Lincoln, J. G. McConville, and Lloyd K. Pietersen, eds., *The Bible and Spirituality: Exploratory Essays in Reading Scripture Spiritually* (Eugene, OR: Cascade, 2013).

aspects of biblical study, such as biblical theology, or "theological interpretation," because its specific focus is on the relation between the use of the Bible
and human transformation, whether of individuals or groups.[19] As such it
opens onto every aspect of human life, including religion and ethics, politics
and power, art and science, work and leisure, age and gender. Most of these
topics will find a place in the course of our study.

The work at hand, therefore, draws on multiple sources of inspiration.
The reader will have noticed that the concept of "transformation" occurred
both in the discussion of Christ and culture and in the description of "biblical
spirituality." This may be taken as a guiding motif in everything that follows.
I mean by this that the act of Bible reading is self-involving, in the sense that
it is existentially open to change. The act of writing this book has been, for
me, a performative act of self-involvement, part of my own attempt to discover what it means to be a human being in God's world. The accent here
is on discovery, a pursuit of the possible as well as the mandatory. I believe
this follows a stimulus from within the Old Testament, notably the Wisdom
literature. There is also in it an aspect of the celebration of humanity, not in
a "humanistic" sense, but as a grateful response of the creature for the gift of
creation. I want it to express wonder. Part of this is because of the enormous
possibilities and diversity of human existence. While there are things that are
true of all human beings, and things that are presumably true of all Christian
lives, the apparently limitless potential of human living seems to me to be
implied in God's creative purpose. This claim will have to be elaborated in the
argument of the book and qualified by taking account of human potential for
evil as well as good. But it is an important part of the concept, and in a sense
the act of writing belongs, for myself, to the exploration of human possibility.

The Bible on Being Human

The Bible focuses relentlessly on the human being. In biblical terms, it is
impossible, of course, to think of humanity apart from its relation to God,
just as it is impossible to think about God apart from his relation to humanity. One cannot prioritize one over the other as the true subject of the Bible.
The point is reflected, for example, in the title of Robert Gordis's book on
Job, *The Book of God and Man*.[20] Gabriel Josipovici calls his book on the Bible
The Book of God but writes of its narratives: "The same protagonists, God,

19. So Lincoln, McConville, and Pietersen, *Bible and Spirituality*, xii.
20. Robert Gordis, *The Book of God and Man: A Study of Job* (Chicago: University of
Chicago Press, 1965).

man, and Israel, run through the entire story."[21] The life of the human being, in biblical terms, takes form and meaning in God's world and in relation to him. The study of humanity cannot but be theological. This is entailed in the concept of humanity as "image of God" (Gen. 1:26), to which we shall return.

Yet the human being is everywhere powerfully present to the reader, by virtue both of vivid depiction and the reader's own humanity. The genius of the biblical writers in their portrayals of the human condition has been recognized in a huge number of works on biblical narrative and poetic art.[22] The Old Testament's most brilliant narratives, such as the stories of Joseph (Gen. 37–50) and David (1 and 2 Samuel), have long fed the religious and literary imagination. Yet the terms "narrative" and "poetry" only begin to indicate the full range of depiction. Sagas, fables, novellas, histories, folklore, laws, instruction, wisdom, introspection, speculation, denunciations, visions, praises, lamentations, songs of love, rage, ecstasy—all together form a dazzling, unbridled array of human depiction.

The Bible is indeed art. It is worth pondering this, especially in relation to Christian interpretation of the Old Testament. There are "big picture" concepts that have played important parts in comprehending the significance of the Old Testament as Scripture. One such is "salvation history," with its perception that the Bible tells a story of God's personal involvement in the world, in the life of Israel, and, for Christians, in Jesus Christ as son of David and Messiah. In modern idiom, the related idea that the Bible has a "metanarrative" positions it critically in relation to the "metanarratives" of postmodernity. These wide-angle views of the biblical witness are necessarily part of Christian thinking.

But the broad sweep should not obscure the particulars. It is well known that the forms of the Old Testament can resist being forced into overarching schemes. (The Wisdom literature perennially complicates the concept of the Bible as story.) The writing of the Old Testament is known for what it is when the human experience or perception embodied in it is allowed to be heard. Only by listening carefully to the human voices that speak to us from its pages can we appreciate the profundity of the Bible's depiction of the human. The biblical writers wrote with their own purposes, many of which we cannot know with certainty. But we know that they deployed artistic means in order to probe the deepest reaches of the human heart. They knew how

---

21. Gabriel Josipovici, *The Book of God: A Response to the Bible* (New Haven: Yale University Press, 1988), 12.

22. Robert Alter was one of the pathfinders in this endeavor with his *The Art of Biblical Narrative* (New York: Basic Books, 1981) and *The Art of Biblical Poetry* (New York: Basic Books, 1985).

to lay bare the human soul to their audiences, with all the techniques that critical analysis can name.[23] Their timeless appeal lies in the fact that they do not offer a treatise, but draw the reader into a profound engagement with his or her own humanity.

For at the heart of the Old Testament's depiction of the human is a question, as expressed in the psalmist's cry of wonder, "What is the human being, that you pay attention to them?" (Ps. 8:4[5]).[24] The question comes as part of an act of praise and does not expect an answer. Rather it identifies the nature of humanity as belonging centrally to the subject matter of biblical portrayal, functioning in this context to place the nature and destiny of the human in terms of their relationship with God. The same question recurs in other contexts, and so enters into the rich conversation of the portrayal of humanity. Psalm 144:3–4 also puts it in a context of praise, but now touching the chord of human mortality. And Job has his own version of the question (Job 7:17), as part of his sustained complaint that God has "paid attention" to him in a particularly terrible way (7:11–21).

This triptych of variations on a fundamental question discloses a crucial aspect of our study, namely, that it will not simply be a matter of discovering information. We cannot merely interrogate the Old Testament for some fixed and finished portrayal of the human. Rather, we need to hear it in its own terms, and this means listening sympathetically to its many tones. The voices that characterize humanity are themselves, inevitably, human voices, uttering the human experience rather than describing it from some neutral ground. Their experience has in common their faith in Yahweh, the God of Israel, and their sense of who they are is inseparable from the claims that God makes upon them. This faith is manifested in the numerous ways in which the biblical writers and characters discover it for themselves. We as readers come to the conversation out of our own widely varying experiences, but the search for the meaning of humanity may end not only in an encounter with ourselves but also with the sense of a claim being made upon us.

We have observed that the Old Testament's own recurring question about the nature of humanity ("What is the human being, that you pay attention to them?") receives no definitive answer in the specific contexts in which it is asked. Rather, an answer should be sought within the biblical discourse in

23. The application of categories from Aristotelian rhetoric to biblical literature is a case in point. See, for example, G. A. Kennedy, *New Testament Interpretation through Rhetorical Criticism* (Chapel Hill: University of North Carolina Press, 1984); and for an Old Testament study, J. J. Kang, *The Persuasive Portrayal of Solomon in 1 Kings 1–11* (Bern: Lang, 2003).

24. Where verse numbering differs between English versions and the Hebrew Bible, the English numbering is adopted, with the Hebrew following, as in the reference just given.

its entirety. We will, therefore, work toward an understanding of it through our engagement with that discourse, bringing our modern questions and insights to bear. We are pursuing not so much a "doctrine" of humanity as an understanding of it that rests in our own experience as well as our apprehension of the Bible.

Certain texts are, of course, indispensable for our purpose, notably the creation accounts in Genesis 1–3, to which we shall shortly turn. In the first of these (Gen. 1:1–2:4a), we find the powerful concept of humanity as being "in the image of God" (Gen. 1:26), and in the second (Gen. 2:4b–3:24), the story of the first humans in the Garden.[25] These not only come first in the Old Testament narrative but have also been so influential in Christian thinking about the human condition that they demand a certain precedence. While they are only a part and not the whole of what the Old Testament has to say about the human condition they will lead us helpfully into further exploration of the topic. This will involve consideration of the nature of Old Testament depiction itself; the range of evidence on the nature of the human person, both individually and corporately; and specific issues that arise from our awareness that our own conceptions of the human person are influenced by the modern settings in which we live, an awareness that must play a part in our attempt to hear what the Old Testament has to say. Having thus laid foundations for the inquiry, we will then go on to consider a number of specific topics in the Old Testament's depiction of the human condition (chs. 6–10).

25. I thus adopt the common practice of referring to Gen. 1–3 as consisting of two creation accounts. There is a critical discussion about whether the first of these ends at Gen. 2:3 or at v. 4a, turning on whether v. 4a is a conclusion to the first account, as in most classical versions of the documentary hypothesis, or an introduction to the second, as in Gordon J. Wenham, *Genesis 1–15*, WBC 1 (Nashville: Nelson, 1987), 5–10, 49–55. In my reading of Gen. 1–3, I take it to be important to read the two according to their canonical sequencing, as I will explain further below. In that case, Gen. 2:4a is a hinge between the two sections.

1

Humanity in the Image of God
(*Imago Dei*)

As I indicated in the preceding chapter, the concept of the human being created in the "image of God" has a certain claim to precedence in a study of the Old Testament's view of humanity. It is often observed that the formula recurs very little after its famous use in Genesis 1. This elusiveness, together with uncertainties about its precise meaning in that chapter, makes it precarious to rest an Old Testament anthropology entirely on it. This point is made at length by David Kelsey in his two-volume theological anthropology,[1] where he claims that Genesis 1:26 cannot be used to structure a theological anthropology systematically. There is indeed no "single plot or narrative logic" to a biblical anthropology; rather, the canon has multiple plots and is "systematically unsystematic."[2] In particular, he is unconvinced by renderings of a single, unifying eschatological narrative of the canon in which the "image" is lost, only to be restored through Christ at the end.[3]

1. David H. Kelsey, *Eccentric Existence: A Theological Anthropology* (Louisville: Westminster John Knox, 2009), 2:895–1051.
2. Ibid., 2:896–97.
3. Here he takes issue with, among others, Stanley Grenz, *The Social God and the Relational Self: A Trinitarian Theology of the Imago Dei* (Louisville: Westminster John Knox, 2001); Kelsey, *Eccentric Existence*, 2:902–5.

This basic theological position coheres well with my understanding of the role of the "image" in Old Testament anthropology. Rather than assume at the outset that the "image of God" is the key to unlocking the Old Testament's understanding of the human situation, I propose to consider how far we can understand it in its context, then look for ways in which it might shed light on other facets of the Old Testament's portrayal of humanity, or indeed have light shed back upon it. This in turn should feed into our broader theological understanding. With John Goldingay, I think that "the expression ["image of God"] is a stimulus to reflection as much as a deposit of reflection."[4]

The "Image of God" in the Context of Genesis 1:1–2:4a

We begin, however, by considering the "image" in its context. This brings its own challenges. Kelsey's position, outlined above, rests partly on his belief that the chances of finding firm ground in the exegesis of Genesis 1:26–28 are too slight to allow the text to be used much for theology. For him, the phrase "is so problematic and controversial that the most careful and influential exegeses seem to cancel each other out."[5] Goldingay is hardly less pessimistic: "Neither the expression itself nor the immediate context spells out the phrase's meaning, and answers to the question [wherein lay God's image in humanity] commonly reflect the prejudgments of the circles where they are propounded."[6] We have been warned! Even so, Genesis 1 must be understood somehow, even if only to weigh it carefully as part of the Old Testament's wider testimony.

Let us observe, then, how the "image" takes its place within that first great biblical statement about the creator and the creation and how they relate (Gen. 1:1–2:4a). I offer here a short account of its features, all widely observed, in order to situate verses 26–28 in a discourse and to illustrate the issues for interpretation. It is a highly structured passage. Most obviously it divides God's creative activity into the work of six days, followed by a day of rest. This structuring system is underlined by the repetition of certain phrases: "and God said," "let there be . . . and there was," "and God made," and "God saw that it was good." The seven-day pattern has been analyzed to show how carefully crafted the composition is. In a time-honored and widely followed analysis, the six days are paired, so that days 1–3 correspond to days

---

4. John Goldingay, *Old Testament Theology*, vol. 1, *Israel's Gospel* (Downers Grove, IL: IVP Academic, 2003), 102.
5. Kelsey, *Eccentric Existence*, 2:900.
6. Goldingay, *Old Testament Theology*, 1:102.

4–6 respectively, as the general to the particular. Thus light is created on the first day and the sun, moon, and stars on the fourth. In this structure, the seventh day, with its Sabbath rest, stands outside the pattern and may be seen as a culmination of the whole.[7] In an alternative structure, the fourth day is understood as a midpoint. The effect of this is to throw some weight onto the theme of worship, since the fourth day portrays the heavenly bodies not as the objects of worship that they almost universally were in the ancient Near East but simply as parts of the one God's creative work.[8] These two patterns, which can be regarded as overlapping, have in common that they portray the creation of all things within a context of the worship of the one God who made everything, in the one case by focusing on the Sabbath, which was a vital part of Israel's worship (cf. Exod. 20:8–11), and in the other by means of a repudiation of the worship of anything other than the God of Israel.

In addition to these observations, Gordon Wenham has drawn attention to the preponderance of the number seven in the passage: for example, the phrases "God saw that it was good" and "and it was so" each occur seven times. The phrase "And God said" occurs ten times.[9] Furthermore, the passage is enclosed by statements about God's creation, with Genesis 2:3–4a echoing chiastically the elements of Genesis 1:1.[10] These features draw attention to leading interests of the passage. The sevens echo the seven-day sabbatical structure, and perhaps in addition express something of the wholeness and orderliness of the creation. The prominence of "and God said," together with "and it was so," highlights the powerful, creative speech of God. And the repetition of "God saw that it was good" emphasizes the divine appraisal of the created world as "good."

To these formal points should be added the observation that the account of the sixth day of creation is substantially longer than those of the other days. In narrative terms, the story slows down and becomes expansive, so that it is not adequate to express the structure of the passage as a neat symmetrical framework. Rather, there is a particular focus on the subject matter of the sixth day, on which God creates humans. The humans do not have this day all to themselves, however, but share it with other land creatures (Gen. 1:24–25).

---

7. J. Richard Middleton, *The Liberating Image: The* Imago Dei *in Genesis 1* (Grand Rapids: Brazos, 2005), 74–75. Middleton traces this observation to Johann Gottfried von Herder, the eighteenth-century German poet and philosopher.

8. Gordon J. Wenham, *Genesis 1–15*, WBC 1 (Nashville: Nelson, 1987), 7.

9. Ibid., 6.

10. Ibid., 5. Wenham confines the chiastic relationship to 1:1 and 2:3, but the point can be made so as to include v. 4a, which repeats the verbs *bārā'* and *'āśâ*. On most accounts v. 4a is part of the first creation account, though Wenham prefers to see it as the introduction to the account in the remainder of ch. 2.

In distinguishing the humans from the creatures of both days 5 and 6, one must recognize similarities as well as dissimilarities. As with the humans, God speaks to the creatures of air and sea on day 5, blessing them and commanding them to "be fruitful and multiply" (1:22; cf. 1:28). Humans therefore share the land with the land creatures, and with the nonhuman creatures of the air and sea the capacity both to be addressed by God and to propagate. (It is curious that the latter features occur with the creatures of sea and air, and not with the land creatures, but they are presumably not intended to be exclusive.) In terms of propagation, therefore, humans are part of a created order that is designed for reproduction, as with the vegetation on the third day.

Humanity is nevertheless distinguished from the other creatures in important ways. It is only in the case of the humans that God deliberates with himself before acting, and only the humans are said to be made "in our image and according to our likeness" (Gen. 1:26). They are further marked out, first, by a triple use of the verb *bārā'* rather than the more regular *'āśâ*; second, by being specified as "male and female" (v. 27; this is evidently assumed of the other creatures, since they too "multiply," but passed over in silence); and third, by assigning them "dominion" over the other creatures of both the fifth and sixth days (v. 26b). The command to have dominion is then repeated and elaborated in verses 28–30, extending the vegetable creation to them for food, with the further addition that this was also given to the other creatures. There is a certain progressive structure to the sixth day, which may be expressed as four stages in the development of its thought:

1. Creation of the land creatures (vv. 24–25);
2. Creation of humans in the image and likeness of God (v. 26a); human dominion over the creatures of days 5 and 6 (v. 26b);
3. Creation of humans in God's image, *male and female* (v. 27); *command to multiply* and to have dominion over the creatures (v. 28);
4. Plants as food for humans (v. 29); plants as food for other creatures (v. 30).

The immediate corollary of this structure, itself part of the larger composition of this creation narrative, is both that humanity is unique in certain respects, and also thoroughly integrated within the created order with the nonhuman population of days 5 and 6.

We may draw certain preliminary inferences from this survey of the structure and discourse of Genesis 1:1–2:4a. The idea of humanity as being in the "image of God" has its context in a depiction of the interrelationships of

God and all created things. This depiction is not merely descriptive, but calls for worship of the one God, the creator. The text expresses the activity of God in several important ways. The phrase "and God said" with its regular consequence "and it was so" shows that acts of creation originate in God's speech, or indeed his thought,[11] which has the effective power to produce the world. This effectiveness of God's mere thought belongs to the writer's strategy to demonstrate the unrivaled power of God over against other gods, or indeed the creation itself. It may be called a "fiat" view of creation, which, as Robert P. Gordon has pointed out, is also found, for example, in Psalms 33:6, 9; 148:5–6.[12]

God is also said, however, to "create" and to "make." The verb *bārā'* (to create), as in Genesis 1:1, 21, 27 (3x) and 2:3–4, only ever has God as subject when referring to making something, and so has often been claimed to express the uniqueness of God's creative activity; that is, it is deliberately nonanthropomorphic. However, this may not be its intended effect in the chapter. Significantly, it is used seven times in 1:1–2:4a, of which three occur in the bracketing introduction and conclusion, and three in a single verse (v. 27) of the creation of the humans. It is thus employed overwhelmingly in relation to the act of creation as a whole and that of humanity in particular. This suggests a stylistic, rhetorical purpose, as one of the ways in which the text accords a special status to the humans. (The seventh occurrence in v. 21 relates to the creatures of sea and air.)[13] If the use of *bārā'* has this rhetorical purpose, it may not in itself imply a kind of creative activity unique to God. Indeed, as Gordon points out, *bārā'* can bear the sense of "cut," and a nonanthropomorphic meaning of it may not have been obvious to the biblical writers.[14] Gordon assigns the verb to God's activity in "fashioning" the world, along with the more regular word for "making," *'āśâ*, which is used throughout the passage. This language suggests some commonality between the creative acts of God and human beings.[15] Gordon also points to the analogy

11. Speech and thought are closely associated in the Old Testament; the verb *'āmar* can often be translated either way.

12. Robert P. Gordon, "The Week That Made the World: Reflections on the First Pages of the Bible," in *Reading the Law: Studies in Honour of Gordon J. Wenham*, ed. J. G. McConville and Karl Möller (New York: T&T Clark, 2007), 231.

13. Perhaps this is merely to achieve a sevenfold usage of the term or to distinguish another pressure point on the view of creation advocated—namely, the force of mythological thought behind the great sea creatures.

14. Gordon, "Week That Made the World," 233.

15. A similar point is made by Karl Möller: "It would be a dogmatically inspired overstatement to claim that [the biblical writers'] aim was to portray [God's] activity as Creator as being entirely without analogy (Möller, "Images of God and Creation in Genesis 1–2," in *A God of Faithfulness: Essays in Honour of J. Gordon McConville on His Sixtieth Birthday*, ed. Jamie

between the fashioning work of God in Genesis 1:1–2:4a and the completion of the construction of the tabernacle in Exodus 39:32–43, which reinforces the idea of God as "builder."[16] The language for creation in Genesis 1:1–2:4a, therefore, is not significantly different from 2:4b–25 in this respect, with its use of *yāṣar*, "to form" (2:7–8), as well as *'āśâ* (2:4b, 18), though the two creation accounts have often been thought to differ in precisely this way. The point may appear to run counter to the concept that God produced the world merely by his thought or speech, but it is not necessary to suppose that the two ideas are incompatible. The unity of God's conception and production is one aspect of the total picture, while his "creating" and "making" focus on a kind of purposeful activity; the former speaks of his separation from the world, his being independent of it, while the latter puts him in close and intimate touch with it. For Richard Middleton too, Genesis 1 portrays God as "artisan." The literary structure of 1:1–2:3 testifies to God's forethought, care, and delight in constructing the cosmos.[17]

God not only conceives and constructs the cosmos but also "sees that it is good." God appraises his work by looking at it, and makes a value judgment about it. The verdict of "good" (*ṭôb*) means not only that the finished product is worthy and well executed but also that it is beautiful. The artisan is also an artist who creates something aesthetically admirable.[18] These anthropomorphic aspects of God's creative activity will play a part in our understanding of the meaning of the "image."

Humanity as "Image of God"

So far we have observed the place of humanity as the "image of God" in the conceptual structure of Genesis 1:1–2:4a, but we have not begun to explore what the phrase might mean. We have seen that it is part of the narrative's strategy to focus on the special importance of the humans, a strategy that is put into effect partly by simple expansiveness. For example, God's deliberation (1:26) merely rehearses beforehand what he is then said to do. And the specification "male and female" adds nothing substantive to what was said to the creatures of air and sea, who were also "created" (*bārā'*), blessed, and

Grant, Alison Lo, and Gordon J. Wenham [New York: T&T Clark, 2011], 25). Möller argues also that the verb *bārā'* may be capable of describing human activity.

16. Gordon, "Week That Made the World," 234–35.

17. Middleton, *Liberating Image*, 74; cf. Möller, "Images of God," 27–28, who argues for a nuanced view of God in Gen. 1–2, incorporating aspects of transcendence and immanence.

18. On the aesthetic vision in Gen. 1, see Melissa Raphael, *Judaism and the Visual Image: A Jewish Theology of Art* (London: Continuum, 2009), 43–64.

commanded to "be fruitful and multiply" (1:21–22). Our analysis of the structure of verses 26–30, above, showed that the human creation is deeply involved with the nonhuman. Humanity is by no means unique in all respects, but has a profound fellowship with the other parts of God's total work.

However, by virtue of the same literary structure, it is clear that the trope of the "image of God" also serves the literary strategy of marking out humanity as distinct within the whole picture. The immediate way in which the significance of the "image" is developed in the discourse is in terms of "dominion" over the other creatures. The point is evident not only in the structure of verses 26–28 but in the syntax of verse 26, which should be read, with Wenham: "Let us make [humanity] in our image, according to our likeness, *that they may rule* the fish of the sea . . ."[19] The purpose clause "that they may rule" is supported by the form of the verb *rdh*, "rule" (a simple *waw* followed by the imperfect). In terms of the discourse, this is the only way in which the meaning of the "image" is developed, and it is bound to play a part in how the concept is to be understood.

Yet this does not explain why the specific expression "in our [God's] image [*ṣelem*] and according to our likeness [*dĕmût*]" should be chosen, or what kinds of connotations it may have evoked. The idea that God should have an "image" at all is striking, in view of the Old Testament's prohibition of the making of images of God (Exod. 20:4–5a). The terms there are different (*pesel, tĕmûnâ*), but the word *ṣelem* evidently refers to some physical form, and can denote idols (Num. 33:52). The addition of *dĕmût* ("likeness") in Genesis 1:26 does little to lessen the impact of the strongly physical implication in *ṣelem*, though it has sometimes been taken to do so. The pairing of *ṣelem* and *dĕmût* appears not only in a ninth-century Aramaic inscription relating to the statue of a king[20] but also in Genesis 5:1–3; in 5:1 *dĕmût* occurs alone by way of a back-reference to Genesis 1:26, and in verse 3 the two terms appear in a note that Adam transmitted the "image" to his son Seth, now with *dĕmût* in the first position. This pattern of use makes it unlikely that *dĕmût* is introduced in 1:26 to diminish the physical force of *ṣelem*.

The notion of human "likeness" to God, as postulated by the Genesis narrative, is therefore problematical. One indication of this lies in the further account of beginnings in Genesis 2:4b–3:24, where the notion of likeness to God also plays a central role, namely, in the temptation of the human pair in the garden of Eden to become "like God, knowing good and evil" (Gen. 3:5). The point depends on the recognition that Genesis 2:4b–3:24 should indeed be read as

19. Wenham, *Genesis 1–15*, 3–4.
20. Ibid., 29.

part of an integrated whole along with Genesis 1:1–2:4a.[21] But the echo is un-mistakable and forcefully demonstrates the theological danger that is courted by the notion of godlikeness. The aspiration to it, at least under the conditions in play in Genesis 3, is shown here to be at the root of the human experience of alienation and of mortality itself. Behind the desire for godlikeness lurk the ever-present possibilities of tyranny and idolatry. The sequel to Genesis 1:1–2:4a in 2:4b–3:24 highlights precisely this dilemma of the human condition—namely, how to understand and inhabit godlikeness in a properly human way.

Interpreting the "Image of God"

In early Christian theology, the "image of God" in Genesis was often taken to refer to the spiritual and moral or rational capacities of the human.[22] As generally recognized today, such readings tended to be influenced by prevail-ing philosophical categories and thus have little or no warrant in the text of Genesis.[23] Rather, as has been shown by the exegesis above, the "image" applies to the human as such.

Modern interpretations of the "image" look not only to exegesis of Gen-esis but to the wider context of the ancient Near East as the religious and cultural matrix of biblical thought and imagery. It is by now well known that the book of Genesis, especially in its accounts of the origins of the world, speaks pointedly into a specific world of ideas: Canaanite, Mesopotamian,

21. Karl Möller rightly takes issue with Dale Patrick and Allen Scult, who argue that the Priestly source's view of God as creator in Gen. 1:1–2:4a "forecloses any significant story that might follow" (Patrick and Scult, *Rhetoric and Biblical Interpretation*, JSOTSup 82 [Sheffield, UK: Almond Press, 1990], 117). Möller rejects this on the grounds that it forecloses any interplay between the two accounts ("Images of God," 28). While it may be that Gen. 1–3 comprises originally separate accounts of creation, we have no access to the putative original forms or their contexts. If they do derive respectively from the pentateuchal sources P (Priestly) and J (Yahwist), then it seems that P (or a redactor) has prefixed its account (1:1–2:4a) to the already-extant J account; see Frank Moore Cross, *Canaanite Myth and Hebrew Epic* (Cambridge, MA: Harvard University Press, 1973), 306. As Terence E. Fretheim puts it, "Genesis 1–2 together constitute the only perspective on originating creation of which we can be certain" (*God and World in the Old Testament: A Relational Theology of Creation* [Nashville: Abingdon, 2005], 33).

22. For accounts of theological interpretations of the "image," see Middleton, *Liberating Image*, 17–24. See also Claus Westermann, *Genesis 1–11*, trans. John J. Scullion (London: SPCK; Minneapolis: Augsburg, 1984), 148–49, for early Christian interpretations, and 147–58 for an overview of ancient and modern readings.

23. One version of this was a distinction between "natural" human qualities reflected in the "image" (*ṣelem*) in contrast to the "supernatural" (or "gratuitous") ones denoted by "likeness" (*dĕmût*). This was already seen to be untenable by Calvin. See John Calvin, *Genesis*, trans. and ed. John King (1554; Calvin Translation Society, 1847; repr., Edinburgh: Banner of Truth Trust, 1965), 93–94.

and Egyptian.[24] There is a marked contrast, for example, between the dignity ascribed to humanity in Genesis 1, by virtue of their elevation above other parts of the creation and the "dominion" given to them over their fellow creatures (Gen. 1:28), and the status of humans in the Mesopotamian stories of Enuma Elish and Atrahasis, in which they come low in the creation's pecking order and are little better than slaves of the gods.[25] The idea of the "image of God," or *imago Dei*, as applied by Genesis to all of humanity, is part of a critical dialogue that Genesis is undertaking over against these concepts.

This point has been thoroughly demonstrated by Richard Middleton, who locates the *imago Dei* in the "symbolic world" of Genesis and over against its ancient Near Eastern background. The concept of the "image" in the sphere of the divine-human relationship is known in Mesopotamia and Egypt. In Egypt the idea of the king as the "image" of a god was frequent and applied to a large number of pharaohs in relation to several different gods.[26] In Mesopotamia there are fewer texts, but significantly the Akkadian term *ṣalmu*, cognate of the Hebrew *ṣelem* (image) used in Genesis 1:26, occurs in all but one of them.[27] In both places, while images may have had several symbolic functions, the concept forms part of those nations' respective royal ideologies. In Egypt the king as divine image was a cultic intermediary who guaranteed the cosmic order, natural and social, on earth; in Mesopotamia the concept was that of a more active, functional representative.[28] This could explain the practice of erecting statues of kings in places far from the king's heartland, probably to represent the power of the king, and so that of the god, in the king's absence.[29]

24. See Wenham, *Genesis 1–15*, xlvi–l, 5–10, for mainly Babylonian parallels to Gen. 1; also Victor H. Matthews and Don C. Benjamin, *Old Testament Parallels: Laws and Stories from the Ancient Near East*, 3rd ed. (New York: Paulist Press, 2006).

25. For annotated texts of this Babylonian literature, see Stephanie Dalley, *Myths from Mesopotamia* (Oxford: Oxford University Press, 1991).

26. Middleton, *Liberating Image*, 108–9. He cites the work of Edward M. Curtis in an unpublished dissertation and in "Image of God (OT)," *ABD* 3:389–91. Curtis counts at least eighteen pharaohs, but this may not be the total figure (Middleton, *Liberating Image*, 108n56).

27. Middleton, *Liberating Image*, 111. This point was noted already by Gerhard von Rad in "Vom Menschenbild des Alten Testaments," in *Der alte und der neue Mensch: Aufsätze zur theologischen Anthropologie*, by G. von Rad et al., BEvT 8 (Munich: Lempp, 1942), 5–23; and established by W. H. Schmidt, *Die Schöpfungsgeschichte in der Priesterschrift*, 2nd ed. (Neukirchen-Vluyn: Neukirchener Verlag, 1967), 127–49; and Hans Wildberger, "Das Abbild Gottes: Gen. 1,26–30," *TZ* 21 (1965): 245–59, 481–501. See Middleton, *Liberating Image*, 108n54. I have also noted the connection in McConville, *God and Earthly Power: An Old Testament Political Theology, Genesis–Kings* (2006; repr., London: T&T Clark, 2008), 26n61.

28. Middleton, *Liberating Image*, 110, 119–21.

29. Ibid., 104–7. Middleton notes two Egyptian texts in which the "image" is applied to human beings in general, but thinks these are too early to be relevant to a discussion of the background of the biblical usage (99–104).

These comparisons between Genesis 1:1–2:4a and Egypt and Mesopotamia have introduced the ideas of both "representation" and "rule" to our inquiry. We have noticed above that the function of "ruling" was the only connection with the "image" that could be drawn directly from the text of Genesis 1 because of the syntactical relation between "image" and the verb *rdh* in 1:26.[30] The commission of the humans to "rule" over creation therefore reflects an underlying metaphor in which the creator God is himself king. This is manifested in the ordering and commanding aspects of his creative activity in Genesis 1, which are then conferred upon the humans. The conferral of a ruling function on the humans as such, of course, is what is strikingly different about the vision of Genesis 1:26–30 in terms of the nature and place of humanity in the cosmic order. The ancient Near Eastern royal ideologies enshrine views of humanity as a whole, tending to rigidly hierarchical sociopolitical structures. In Mesopotamia, rooted in myths of creation with life-and-death conflicts between deities, they embody religio-political policies of perpetual war.[31] In this context, the Old Testament's idea that the human being as such is created "in the image of God" is part of the reconceiving of the place of the human expressed by Genesis 1:1–2:4a as a whole. It is not only that, in Middleton's terms, a "genuine democratization" of the image has occurred, conferring enormous dignity on human beings as such, but the whole idea of the human relationship to God and the natural and social orders is transformed, in a way that might be called an "ideology critique."[32] There will be more to say below on what kinds of things this might entail in contemporary appropriation of the idea.

The function of "ruling," however, does not constitute or exhaust the meaning of the "image," but is better regarded as a consequence of it.[33] If the human "represents" God somehow, this too needs to be carefully considered rather than simply equated with "ruling."[34] Does the idea of the "image" point to a kind of representation that is based on some intrinsic likeness to

30. Westermann notes the royal connotations of the verb *rdh* in the OT (*Genesis 1–11*, 152).

31. This is argued by Eckart Otto, with special reference to Assyria, in *Krieg und Frieden in der Hebräischen Bibel und im Alten Orient: Aspekte für eine Friedensordnung in der Moderne* (Stuttgart: Kohlhammer, 1999).

32. Middleton, *Liberating Image*, 121, 185–231. I have explored the idea of the Old Testament as cultural critique, including a consideration of the "image," in *God and Earthly Power*, 12–29. Wenham too thinks that Genesis appears to "democratize" Egyptian and Assyrian royal concepts (*Genesis 1–15*, 31).

33. Westermann, *Genesis 1–11*, 153, 155. Karl Barth also sees dominion as a consequence of the "image" and rejects what he calls a "technical connexion" between the two concepts (Barth, *Church Dogmatics* III/1 [Edinburgh: T&T Clark, 1958], 194).

34. Westermann thinks that the extension of the idea of representation from the king to humanity as a whole was impossible, since humanity was by definition the species as a whole;

God? The question arises from the terms we have been discussing, that is, the use of *ṣelem* in Genesis, with its echo of the Babylonian *ṣalmu*, and also the term *dĕmût*, with its inescapable connotations of "likeness."

Image as Representation

We have seen that the idea of the "image of God" in Genesis implies an aspect of human "rule," whatever that entails. Yet the occurrence of the concept in other passages in Genesis suggests that it cannot be construed in functional terms alone. In Genesis 5:1–3, at the head of the genealogy of Adam, God is said to have created Adam "in his *likeness*" (*dĕmût*). The allusion to Genesis 1:26–28 is evident, especially in view of 5:2, which repeats the terms "male and female," "bless," and "create" (*bārā'*), the last again occurring more than once in specific connection with the creation of the human. In 5:1, however, the idea of "likeness" is led by the expression *dĕmût*, not *ṣelem*, and is not attended by the mandate to "rule." Adam then procreates, begetting Seth "in his likeness, according to his image," thus with both the terms from 1:26, now in reverse order. The distribution of terms in this passage, which tells against any sharp distinction between *ṣelem* and *dĕmût*, suggests that the humans bear the "image" of God not only in terms of a mandated function but in some sense intrinsically.

Genesis 5:1–3, therefore, takes a cue from 1:26–28 but goes beyond it. It affirms not only that Adam, now a named individual following the story in chapters 2–4, bears the likeness of God but also that the next generation inherits the "likeness and image" of Adam. This implies that the "image" of God is now borne also by that generation.[35] It further suggests that the human bearing of the divine "image" entails procreation, the human part of the divine intention to "fill the earth." Here, in addition to "ruling," is another way in which the humans are like God.

The "image of God" occurs again in Genesis 9:5–6, where it is predicated of humanity as such, here too in the context of "being fruitful, multiplying and filling the earth" (9:1, 7). The passage therefore reaffirms this fundamental requirement of the humans after the devastation of the flood, along with a primacy among the creatures, which now inspires the creatures' dread of humans (9:2). The new element in the created order, the availability of animals as food for humans, gives rise to a distinction between the slaughter of animals

---

and he rules out the notion that they are portrayed here as representing God to the creation (*Genesis 1–11*, 153).

35. Cf. Wenham, *Genesis 1–15*, 127.

and that of humans, with the penalty of death for the latter on the grounds that "God made humanity in his own image" (9:6). Once again, the "image" is more than a role, but says something about the very identity of the human.

I have been suggesting that there are aspects of both function ("rule") and intrinsic nature in this likeness of humans to God. In fact, it is difficult to separate these two aspects of the "image," as Middleton has rightly argued. For him, the exercise of divine rule on earth cannot be entirely understood as delegation of a task, but rather supposes an actual likeness of the human to the divine.[36] Human representation of God is to be understood in this sense, that only one who is like God can represent him. Middleton sees not only the function of rule, but also the "artisan" metaphor, as forming this picture of human godlikeness. God has begun a task of artful construction by his twofold activity of separating and filling (the activities of days 2 and 3 in Gen. 1:6–13), and humans are now called to continue both these aspects of his work by procreating—that is, "filling" the earth and "subduing" or "organizing" it (corresponding to God's activity of "separating").[37] Middleton argues that the created world is like a cosmic temple, and just as no ancient Near Eastern temple would be complete without the installation of the image of the deity, so God's creation of the world is not complete without the creation of humanity "in his image." He goes on to draw attention to the work of Bezalel, who was filled with the spirit of God and wisdom in order to accomplish the fine craftsmanship involved in making the tabernacle (Exod. 31:1–11): "Bezalel's Spirit-filled craftsmanship, which imitates God's primordial wise design and construction of the cosmos, is functionally equivalent to the *imago Dei*."[38] The point is, importantly, not only about function, but about imitation.[39]

The human being, as "image of God," may be said to be the place where God is present in the creation. In support of this point, Middleton again turns to the Mesopotamian royal ideology, and especially the practices relating to the consecration of cult images, in ceremonies known as "mouth-washing" (*mīs pî*) and "mouth-opening" (*pit pî*). By virtue of these ceremonies, the statue was ritually transformed to become, in some sense, the god. He expresses carefully the sense in which this should be understood: "The result of the *mīs pî* is that the carefully carved and decorated statue is said to be born of the gods and becomes the living presence of the deity on earth. The mode of this presence . . . was distinct from either a merely symbolic reminder of

36. Middleton, *Liberating Image*, 88.
37. Ibid., 89.
38. Ibid., 87.
39. We return to Bezalel and other dimensions of human creativity in ch. 9 below.

deity, or the actual, literal god."[40] Middleton notes how some attempts to conceptualize the presence of the god in the statue have reached for language from the Christian theology of the Eucharist, such as "transubstantiation" and "real presence."[41] The suggested analogies indicate at least that the ancient attempts to conceive of the relation of the god to the world were theologically sophisticated.

The perception that the Mesopotamian royal ideology had a sophisticated concept of the relationship between the "image" and the divine presence has been strengthened by further recent research. Stephen Herring, in a work on "divine substitution," argues that Mesopotamian conceptions of image and presence are significant for understanding Genesis 1. Genesis 1 does indeed have a polemical thrust in relation to Mesopotamia, since in its case the "image" takes the form of the human being as such, but nevertheless the nature of the polemic requires an understanding of the Mesopotamian concepts.[42] Herring argues that a proper understanding of representation in Mesopotamia is not mimetic; that is, the image does not function by simply picturing a reality outside itself, but rather "the real presence of the entity represented participates in the representation." The image therefore becomes a "mode of presencing" the deity.[43] In a discussion of the human king or priest as divine image in Mesopotamia (*ṣalmu*), he concludes that it does not function as a replica but "is more like a repetition or extension of the referent's [that is, the god's] very presence."[44]

The point is highly suggestive for the concept of the human as image of God, because it offers a way of thinking about the relation between function and intrinsic likeness. The functional aspect of humanity's status as "image" depends here on the "presencing" of the deity. Power and presence belong together.[45] Furthermore, the crucial point that the image is not merely a replica suggests that there is a necessary aspect of freedom, on the part of humanity, to explore and enact what it means. These essential points are also supported

---

40. Middleton, *Liberating Image*, 127–28. Middleton refers here to the work of Christopher Walker and Michael B. Dick, *The Induction of the Cult Image in Ancient Mesopotamia: The Mesopotamian Mīs Pî Ritual*, State Archives of Assyria Literary Texts (Helsinki: Neo-Assyrian Corpus Project, 2001).

41. Middleton, *Liberating Image*, 128.

42. Stephen Herring, *Divine Substitution: Humanity as the Manifestation of Deity in the Hebrew Bible and the Ancient Near East*, FRLANT 247 (Göttingen: Vandenhoeck & Ruprecht, 2013), 21. He also refers for theoretical support to Zainab Bahrani, *The Graven Image: Representation in Babylonia and Assyria* (Philadelphia: University of Pennsylvania Press, 2003).

43. Herring, *Divine Substitution*, 18–19.

44. Ibid., 47. For his description of the "washing of the mouth" ritual (*mīs pî*), see 26–37.

45. Ibid., 48, 124.

by the important recent thesis of Annette Schellenberg on the uniqueness of humans as divine image in Genesis.[46]

Image as Relational/Trinitarian

This approach to the "image" draws attention to the relation of the human being to the divine presence in the creation. Human likeness to God tells us something not only about the humans but also about God. What is it about God that leads him to place his "image" within the creation? The question touches on a strand in the interpretation of the "image" that emphasizes relationality. The idea of the "image" as the human capacity to relate to God is proposed by Karl Barth, who thinks that in humanity "God created the real counterpart to whom He could reveal himself." For him, the point of the "image" language is to express, not inherent qualities of the human or even his superiority over other creatures, but rather the fact that in humanity God created "the future partner of the covenant, the kingdom and the glory of God." This partner exists with him in an "I-Thou" relationship from creation to the end of time.[47] Barth also lays strong emphasis on the human "image of God" as "male and female." God as the free creator relates to a counterpart who also is free and whose freedom consists in his relating with other humans, as instanced in the marriage relationship.[48] The human communion corresponds, further, to a communion within God, signaled in self-deliberation, "let us make."[49] Barth's interpretation thus focuses sharply on the relationship between God and humanity; the embeddedness of humanity in the nonhuman and inanimate creation plays only a small part in his analysis. For him, humanity as part of the creation is "the seeing eye at which all creation aims."[50]

46. She too sees that images in the ancient Near East are not replicas ("Abbildungen") of the form of the god but "Repräsentationen dieser Gottheit selbst," such representation, furthermore, being "powerful" ("machtvollen Repräsentation"). See Annette Schellenberg, *Der Mensch, das Bild Gottes? Zum Gedanken einer Sonderstellung des Menschen im Alten Testament und in weiteren altorientalischen Quellen*, ATANT 101 (Zurich: Theologischer Verlag, 2011), 86. Her question is whether human beings have a unique status compared with other created beings in the ancient world. In the Old Testament, one of the ways in which humans are distinct from animals is in the absence of internal divisions among them, since they are not created "according to their kinds"; rather, the ascription of "brotherhood" to them, in connection with the "image" (Gen. 9:5), signifies that their equality ("Gleichheit") is definitive for their humanness ("Menschsein") (ibid., 141–42).

47. Barth, *Church Dogmatics* III/1, 194–97. See also Middleton, *Liberating Image*, 22–23.

48. Barth, *Church Dogmatics* III/1, 195. Barth acknowledges both Wilhelm Vischer and Dietrich Bonhoeffer as his sources for this interpretation.

49. Ibid., 196.

50. Ibid.

A "relational" concept of creation has been taken up by a number of writers,[51] notably Terence Fretheim, with some differences from Barth. Fretheim sees the issue in interpreting the "image" as the need to understand the manner in which God makes himself present within the created order. Theologies of creation can err either by making God a kind of absentee landlord or by conceiving of his presence in the world as overwhelmingly commanding.[52] There is an issue, then, of divine power in relation to human freedom (thus in a point of contact with Barth). This is evident in the manner of God's creating, for God creates not only in an originary but also in a continuing way, and in doing so he has committed himself to a kind of power sharing with the human creature. God really has entrusted the care of the creation to the human, and he will remain faithful to that decision that he has made.[53] Fretheim's view of relationship in the created order, however, extends beyond the one between God and humanity, to that between the human and the earth. In Genesis 2:15, God puts the man in the garden "to till it" (as the older translations have it). But following Ellen Davis, Fretheim points out that the verb is *'ābad*, which elsewhere in the Old Testament regularly means to "serve" or "worship." The human may thus be said to "serve" the earth, a notion that is entirely in line with the interdependence of the human and the earth that we noticed in Genesis 1:29–30.[54] This view of the human as "image of God" finds deep interconnections among God, the human, and the nonhuman creation. It is a refinement in the understanding of relationship in the creation that corresponds well with the embeddedness of humanity within creation that we observed in our reading of the text.

The concept of relationship is therefore fruitful in our attempt to answer the question put at the outset of this section: What is it about God that leads him to place his "image" within the creation? We now see that the "image" implies the presence of God within the creation through humanity, in a way that affirms his ongoing intimate involvement with it. At the same time, the image depicts the human in a relationship of freedom with the creator and in intrahuman relationships. It also draws in the indispensable third dimension of the nature of humans' presence within the creation. The idea of relationality enables an approach that affirms both godlikeness in itself and a dimension of actualizing this in human living.

51. For an account of some of these, see Westermann, *Genesis 1–11*, 150–51.

52. Fretheim, *God and World*, 13–14.

53. Ibid., 49.

54. Ibid., 53, 274. He refers to Ellen Davis, *Getting Involved with God: Rediscovering the Old Testament* (Cambridge, MA: Cowley, 2001), 192. See also her *Scripture, Culture, and Agriculture: An Agrarian Reading of the Bible* (Cambridge: Cambridge University Press, 2009), 29.

The question about humanity has led back to the nature of God. Indeed, the light on the "image" cast by the notion of relationality also leads to reflections on God as Trinity. This is not by way of God's self-deliberation in the words "Let us make" since those words can be explained in other ways.[55] Rather, there is a trinitarian shape to the theological structure in which God originates all things (God the Father) and also participates in the created world through the one made in his "image" (God the Son). The presence of God the Spirit need not be directly inferred from the reference to the "spirit of God" in Genesis 1:2, which does not necessarily imply a hypostasis. Yet the idea of God the Spirit can be aligned with the sense that the creation now awaits development.[56] This is true in spite of the idea that it is "finished" (Gen. 2:1), for it is a "finished" work that has established a new reality, a world in which a creature has been made "in the image and likeness of God" and charged with being "fruitful" and with having dominion over the creation. What this might mean remains to be unfolded. But there is a tension in the concept that God is present in the world by means of his "image" and the fact that the image-bearing creature is other than God, having freedom and responsibility. God has chosen to be involved with his creation in a way that rests much on this human creature. The nature of God's precarious involvement is illuminated in the preamble to the book of Job, where God delivers to the Satan the challenge: "Have you considered my servant Job, that there is none like him on the earth, a blameless and upright man, who fears God and turns away from evil?" (Job 1:8 RSV). It matters enough to God that a human should be just that he is prepared to expose him to the power of an enemy in order to demonstrate it. The project turns on Job's willingness to bear suffering and yet remain in his innocence. The tension involved in human image-bearing is also unbearably clear in Genesis 3. It is in this space, where the humans discover and live what is entailed in their bearing the "image of God," that the depiction in Genesis 1 has room for God the Spirit.

To put the point differently, godlikeness is not a status that has been achieved and now merely needs to be enjoyed. Rather, it commits both God and humans to a life together, the story of which will occupy the pages of the Old Testament and the New. It includes the narratives about worship, in which God chooses

55. These include self-address itself, in a kind of plural of majesty or "royal we," and God's address to the heavenly council, in accordance with other depictions of God in the Old Testament (e.g., Job 1). The latter is handicapped by its possible suggestion that God did not create alone, which would be out of kilter with the rest of Gen. 1.

56. These intimations of the Son and the Spirit have evident echoes in New Testament texts such as Col. 1:15–16 and Rom. 8:19–23. These have their own christological and eschatological implications, which are absent in the Genesis text, though it lays groundwork for them.

to dwell among his people Israel and to seek their love and devotion.[57] And it includes those strands of the Old Testament that call the human partner to imitate God in his fundamental orientation toward the world—that is, in his justice and righteousness, faithfulness, holiness, compassion, and truth. Prophets and psalmists both attribute these qualities to God and hold them up as true marks of the life of humans.[58] Human godlikeness is also imprinted on the Old Testament's pages in the many anthropomorphic depictions of God, in the gamut of emotions that he exhibits, from compassion to wrath, in his baring of his "mighty arm" to deliver Israel from oppression in Egypt (Deut. 4:34), in his guise as husband or parent (Hosea 1–3; 11), and when he appears in humanlike forms, as "the angel of Yahweh" to Gideon (Judg. 6:11–12), or even as three men to Abraham (Gen. 18:1–3).

This godlikeness is not mere imitation, for in the presencing of God in the human there is also, I believe, an aspect of relationship characterized by desire, or even passion.[59] The passion of God for humans is nowhere more clearly expressed than in Hosea 11, which portrays God's love for humans in strongly emotional terms; his "heart" recoils from coming in anger against his people Israel because of his compassion for them, and this emotional attachment even seems to define his holiness (Hosea 11:8–9). The human partner longs correspondingly for God, as in the vivid physiological metaphors of Psalm 42:1–3.

The basis in Genesis 1 for this dynamic understanding of godlikeness is in God's appraisal of the world he has made as "very good." Now he invites the humans not only to admire it with him but also to share his vision and intention for it. Godlikeness is a commission to accept, with an element of exploration. It is not simply an aspect of being human, nor a fixed quality, nor a (mere) function; rather, humanity both *is* the "image" and finds its true self in living it. It entails an element of the unknown, corresponding to the fundamental fact that God has created one other than himself to be and function in ways resembling God. The account of the creation of humanity in God's "image and likeness,"

---

57. Middleton draws attention to God's indwelling of the cosmos, in which creation is seen as a "cosmic sanctuary" (*Liberating Image*, 81–88).

58. All of these qualities are predicated of both God and humans. An obvious example is the command in Lev. 19:2: "You shall be holy as I Yahweh your God am holy." Note also Deut. 32:4; Ps. 119:137; Jer. 23:5–6. On the imitation of God as one important category in the Old Testament's ethical thought, see John Barton, *Understanding Old Testament Ethics: Approaches and Explorations* (Louisville: Westminster John Knox, 2003).

59. The category of desire is adopted by Sarah Coakley, *God, Sexuality, and the Self: An Essay 'On the Trinity'* (Cambridge: Cambridge University Press, 2013). In my reflections on the Trinity in relation to the "image," I found stimulating her section entitled "A Prayer-Based Model of the Trinity" (111–15).

therefore, invites us to read on, not only into Genesis 2:4b–3:24, but further into the biblical story. The "image" initiates a story of the human participation in the life of God. This involves traits that we have observed in Genesis 1 itself: God's gift of life, his ordering of the world, his delight in it, his labor over it, his requiring refreshment. It also involves the life of humans with each other, not just in coexistence but also in the desire for the other that is most keenly expressed in the sexual relationship,[60] but which spills over into all kinds of human relating. The mutuality enshrined in being "in the image and likeness of God" tells against the fissuring of human community which attends much of human experience and which is adumbrated in the Old Testament's own story. In their longing for such relating, humans know something of their origin in God.

This view of the "image" allows it to be read in conjunction with the rest of the Old Testament witness about the relationship between God, humans, and the world. It leads to an understanding of it that both respects its ancient context and opens onto contemporary reexpressions by means of the theological imagination. Regarding its context, it will pay attention to what Middleton has called the "liberating" characteristic of Genesis's depiction of the "image," so that it is no longer an emblem of inherently oppressive social and political forms, but reinvents godlikeness democratically. This can be extended into contemporary contexts to become a ground for resisting every kind of denial of God-given freedom as a condition of humanity, including slavery, economic exploitation, and the subjugation of women.[61] In this respect Genesis 1:1–2:4a stands squarely with the Old Testament prophets. But the kind of responsibility that thus devolves on the humans by virtue of being "in the image of God" does not stop with interhuman relationships but extends to the nonhuman creation, for it is to this that the command to "have dominion" applies (1:26, 28). The "image" opens also onto modern ethical concern about a right human relationship with the creatures and the planet.

In recognizing these responsibilities, it remains to reiterate that the "image" should not be read exclusively in terms of an imperative to act in certain ways. We saw that in its occurrences in Genesis 5:1–3 and 9:5–6, the concept of the

60. See ibid., 7–11, for Coakley's treatment of this. See also Rowan Williams, "The Body's Grace," in *Theology and Sexuality: Classic and Contemporary Readings*, ed. Eugene F. Rogers Jr. (Malden, MA: Wiley-Blackwell, 2001), 309–21.

61. Phyllis Trible famously makes Gen. 1:26–28 her "center" of an Old Testament theology, with what she sees as its predicate of equality between the sexes (Trible, *God and the Rhetoric of Sexuality*, OBT [1978; repr., Philadelphia: Fortress, 1992], 12). The text probably does not exactly bear that meaning, since as we have seen, the sexual differentiation of men and women functions in the text in terms of procreation. However, equality between the sexes returns in the interpretation of the text because of its general liberating tendency, and its opposition to all forms of overbearing behavior of humans toward humans.

human as "image and likeness" of God was not expressed in terms of the call to "dominion." Rather, it was predicated of humans simply as humans. This is not to revert to a notion of the "image" as a status or inherent quality, but rather to observe that, by virtue of the "image," God views humans differently from other parts of the creation. They are peculiarly the object of his delight and desire. This stands against any temptation to see the "image" in terms of power, achievement, or success, a point that has been made cogently by Jean Vanier, who has found through experience that the variously challenged individuals who have formed part of the communities of L'Arche, which he founded, have given profound insights into what it means to be human.[62]

Conclusion

Several things follow from our observations about the human as "image of God." In virtue of the "image," humans may be said to represent the presence of God in the world. The royal language that attends the depiction of the humans in Genesis 1 might suggest that this representative capacity is characterized primarily by power and privilege. However, since the orientation of this language of "image" and rule is in contention with conceptions of divine presence and royal function in the ancient Near East, it follows that ideas prevailing there should not be inadvertently imported into the Old Testament. The extension of the notion of the "image" to all humans, male and female, is the most obvious sign that something radically different is being offered here. And in fact, the bold gambit that casts humans as the "image" of God is also part of a theological vision in which God too is understood in a way that trenchantly opposes ancient Near Eastern conceptions of deity. To say, therefore, that the human is created in the "image of God" becomes a question not only about the human but about God. We have seen reasons to think that the notion of the human as "image" has an aspect of relationality, implying a longing or desire for the divine as well as a sense of mutuality among the humans themselves and a constructive orientation toward the nonhuman creation. In these relationships, the narrative's hints of power are balanced or countered by notes of service. For these reasons, the powerful statement about humanity that appears on the first page of the Bible tends to open up questions about God and the human being rather than close them down at the outset. It remains to be seen, therefore, how the lines of thought in Genesis 1 feed into the Old Testament's developing portrayal of the human.

62. Jean Vanier, *Man and Woman He Made Them* (London: Darton, Longman & Todd, 1985).

2

"Like God" in the Garden of Eden (Gen. 2–3)

We have seen that the notion of the "image of God" is introduced in Genesis 1 in such a way as to create the expectation both that the story of it will be developed in the biblical narrative and that that story will invite readers' participation in it. The first narrative development of the concept comes immediately, in Genesis 2:4b–3:24. While this account should be read in sequence from 1:1–2:4a, as we have observed above,[1] it offers a new and distinct portrayal of the human situation, which gives a fresh, and disturbing, context to the notion of being "like God."

As in the former narrative, the humans are placed in relationship to God, to each other, and to the nonhuman creation. These interrelationships unfold in a new way, however. First, the creation of the human being (*hā'ādām*) is portrayed in a graphic image, in which God forms him from the earth and breathes life into him (Gen. 2:7). His relationship to the nonhuman world has already been specified as the purpose of "working" it (2:5; cf. 2:15).[2] He is now placed into a "garden" (v. 8), which is characterized by both life and delight (vv. 9–14), in an atmosphere of harmony and mutuality. The terms are

1. See the preceding chapter, n. 21.
2. The verb is *'ābad*, which may also be understood as "serve."

distinct from the leading notion of "dominion" in Genesis 1, though it will be recalled that there too the accent was on mutuality rather than domination.

Two further developments take place in Genesis 2. First, the human relationship with God is specified in the first words that God speaks to the human, which are both a declaration of gift and a command that places a limitation. The human has been given all the fruit of the garden that God has made "to eat," with a single exception—namely, the "tree of the knowledge of good and evil" (vv. 16–17). This declaration has in common with chapter 1 the concept of life as a gift, but introduces the idea that the gift is enjoyed on certain terms. The point is set to become crucially important in Genesis's unfolding of the conditions of human existence.

The second development is a narrative introducing the relationship between the man and the woman. Here too something new occurs. While in Genesis 1 the humans were considered together as a distinct entity, in terms of both their location within the creation and their capacity for relating to it, here the accent is on the man and the woman as distinct from each other within a relationship of mutuality. The force of the narrative depends on a certain ambiguity in the term hāʾādām, which may mean either "the man," or the "human being" (Gen. 2:7). The formation of hāʾādām is in the first instance an act that brings into existence the "human being," as distinct from the other parts of the creation. (It was this double possibility of the term in its context that led Phyllis Trible to translate hāʾādām as "earth-creature" until the point at which the male is differentiated from the female.)[3] However, the figure is evidently presented to the imagination as male, for in verse 18 begins the playful scenario in which the human names the nonhuman creatures as part of his search for "a help suitable for him" (ʾēzer kĕnegdô; 2:18). This "helper" turns out to be one who is not part of the existing zoological repertoire, but who is mysteriously of the same substance as hāʾādām, namely, "woman" (2:22–23).[4] At this point the differentiation between male and female is focused by a change in the term used for the male, who is called ʾîš, for the sake of a wordplay on "woman," ʾiššâ (2:23). This language continues into verse 24, where the male-female relationship is rendered as marriage, and the ʾîš leaves the parental home in order to unite with his wife. The narrative's

3. Trible, God and the Rhetoric of Sexuality, OBT (1978; repr., Philadelphia: Fortress, 1992), 72–143 (75 and throughout).
4. Trible took the concept of "helper" to imply the woman's equality with the man, if not her superiority (God and the Rhetoric of Sexuality, 90). But see David J. A. Clines's critical response to this in Clines, "What Does Eve Do to Help?," in What Does Eve Do to Help? And Other Readerly Questions to the Old Testament, JSOTSup 94 (1990; repr., Sheffield, UK: JSOT Press, 1994), 25–48.

primary use of *hā'ādām* for the man is resumed in 2:25, where we read that "the man and his wife" (*hā'ādām wĕ'ištô*) "were naked but not ashamed." In chapter 1, *hā'ādām* denoted "humanity" as such, sexually distinguished as "male and female" (*zākār ûnĕqēbâ*; 1:27); in chapter 2, the semantic possibilities of *hā'ādām*, alongside other terms for the humans, are explored more fully as part of that text's attempt to express something of the nature of the relationship between the male and the female.

Each of the principal relationships set up in Genesis 1:1–2:4a, therefore (God to human, human to human, human to nonhuman), is developed in 2:4b–25. There is a tendency toward complication in the relationships. The relationship between the human and the earth is entwined with that between the human and God, since the latter is now governed by a limitation ("you shall not"), which operates in the sphere of the relationship between the human and the nonhuman ("but of the tree of the knowledge of good and evil you shall not eat"; 2:17). The complication of the relationship between the man and the woman will be developed in chapter 3, in a way that arises out of this already complex tension in the nature of things. The coda to chapter 2, "the man and his wife were both naked, but not ashamed" (2:25), sets up the next stage of the drama.

The tensions built into the picture of Eden in Genesis 2 are rapidly and sharply exposed in the extraordinarily dense exchanges between serpent, woman, and man in 3:1–7. Alongside the innocence of the man and woman, "naked (*'ărûmmîm*) but not ashamed," there is suddenly the serpent, more cunning (*'ārûm*) than any of the creatures. The ironic echo of *'ărûmmîm* in *'ārûm*, a picture of wide-eyed wonder juxtaposed with one of subtle calculation, fast-forwards into dangerous territory. The narrative simply assumes, without explanation, that there are creatures that are "cunning," that the serpent (but recently paraded before the man for "naming") is merely the chief of these, that such a creature possesses moral and intellectual force that has not hitherto been suspected of the nonhuman creation, and that he can engage the humans in a deeply ominous conversation about their destiny.

The interview between the woman and the serpent, together with the silent acquiescence of the man, has long fed the imagination of readers. It strikes a brilliant balance between what is said and what is not said. How did the disruptive cunning of the serpent enter the peace of the garden? How did he know what God had said to the man? How did the woman know? Why did the serpent approach the woman rather than the man? Why would the humans prefer the serpent's reading of things to God's, with so much hanging on the outcome? Such questions have played an enormous part in the reading of the text, not least in relation to men and women, and in thinking about the origin of evil in the world.

Yet the serpent has put his finger (so to speak) on the single most important question: Why would there be a tree in the garden whose fruit the humans may not eat? And in particular, why would there be a prohibition on a "tree of the knowledge of good and evil"? When the serpent encounters the woman, we realize that the disruptive element in the story was already there in Genesis 2, waiting to be teased into life. The puzzling exclusion of "the knowledge of good and evil" now produces an alternative vision of human possibility to that expressed in chapter 2. Where God said, "You will die" (2:17), the serpent says, "You will not die" (3:4). Where God has apparently given the humans access to all they need for life, including the faculty of sight and the capacity to appreciate goodness and beauty (2:9), the serpent now promises that their "eyes will be opened" (3:5). Where God had made the "tree of the knowledge of good and evil" an integral part of the garden, yet put it off-limits on pain of death, the serpent now offers it as a life-enhancing option. The acute dilemma of the woman, as she tries to interpret the reality before her, is loudly evident in 3:6, with its close verbal similarities to 2:9: the tree is "good for food and a delight to the eyes." Was not this the gift of God? And does this tree not possess something further to enjoy, in the promise that its very name appears to make? The perplexing nature of the dilemma is sharper still in the serpent's claim that, if they eat and their eyes are opened, they will "be like God" (3:5).[5] The serpent's view is even apparently vindicated in the outcome, for when the humans have eaten the fruit their eyes are indeed opened and they know they are naked (3:7). And God himself confirms that they have now become "like one of us [the plural curiously evoking the divine plural of 1:26] knowing good and evil" (3:22). This likeness to God is then the direct cause of the barring of the humans from the "tree of life" and immortality, and they are expelled permanently from the garden (3:22–24).[6]

Here the most jarring juxtaposition is with that first disclosure of the place of the humans in the order of things, that God made them "in his image and likeness" (Gen. 1:26)! Reading Genesis 2–3 after Genesis 1, it is strangely dissonant that the creatures made "in the image and likeness of God" now seek to be "like God," and that such aspiration should have such dire consequences, transforming the very conditions of their existence. Does the narrative in chapters 2–3 call into question what was put in place in chapter 1? When the humans have eaten the fruit, with the consequences of

5. I take *kĕ'lōhîm* to be "like God," rather than "like gods," with most modern versions, on the grounds of context, since the serpent's counterreading of the human condition precisely challenges God's.

6. On these implications of the narrative, see R. W. L. Moberly, "Did the Serpent Get It Right?," *JTS* 39 (1988): 1–27.

this in shame, dissolution of harmonious relationships, and expulsion from the garden, what has changed in respect of their having been created "in the image and likeness of God"?

The "Image" in Genesis 2–3

I began the preceding chapter by taking issue with a rendering of biblical history in which the "image" is "lost" in the actions of the first humans in the garden, and is only to be restored eschatologically. I proposed a view of the "image" in which it has both functional and intrinsic aspects. The functional aspect means that, by virtue of being "in the image of God," humans should behave in certain ways with respect to God, each other, and the created world; the intrinsic aspect means that humans are said to be "in the image of God" simply by virtue of being human. The human as "image," moreover, was a kind of presencing of God in the creation. I now want to take further this idea of the divine presence through the human creature.

This connection between the human as "image" and the divine presence on earth has recently been pursued in relation to Genesis 2–3 against the background of Mesopotamian and Egyptian royal ideology. In the preceding chapter we saw that the "image of God" in Genesis 1 has similarities with the Mesopotamian and Egyptian notions of the king as the "image" of the god, notions that were given form in cult statues, which, in both areas, were consecrated in rituals of transformation. In Mesopotamia (chiefly in Babylon), the rituals were known as *mīs pî* (washing of the mouth) and *pit pî* (opening of the mouth), signifying the presence of the god on the earth in the form of the statue. We saw that these concepts help to clarify the understanding of the human as divine image in Genesis 1. It has also been suggested that there are echoes of the same ceremonies in elements of the narrative in Genesis 2–3, for example, when the human being, *hā'ādām*, receives the breath of life from God (Gen. 2:7).[7] In other words, the human in Genesis 2 corresponds

7. The suggestion was initially made by Edward M. Curtis, "Man as the Image of God in Genesis in the Light of Ancient Near Eastern Parallels" (PhD diss., University of Pennsylvania, 1984), cited in J. Richard Middleton, *The Liberating Image: The* Imago Dei *in Genesis 1* (Grand Rapids: Brazos, 2005), 94 and passim (here 129n133); Curtis, "Image of God (OT)," *ABD* 3:389–91. See also Andreas Schüle, "Made in the 'Image of God': The Concepts of Divine Images in Gen 1–3," *ZAW* 117 (2005): 11–13. It has been developed at length by Catherine L. McDowell (formerly Beckerleg), in "The Image of God in Eden: The Creation of Mankind in Genesis 2:5–3:24 in Light of the *mīs pî*, *pit pî* and *wpt-r* Rituals of Mesopotamia and Ancient Egypt" (PhD diss., Harvard University, 2009), now published as *The Image of God in the Garden of Eden: The Creation of Humankind in Genesis 2:5–3:24 in Light of* mīs pî, pīt pî *and* wpt-r *Rituals of Mesopotamia and Ancient Egypt*, Siphrut: Literature and Theology of the Hebrew

to the Babylonian cult statue as representative of the god on earth, while the imparting of life to the human by the breath of God recalls the Babylonian ceremonies that transformed the statue into a bearer of the divine presence. Other proposed similarities include the fact that part of the ceremony of preparation takes place in a sacred garden,[8] that the statue's eyes and other sensory organs were ritually opened, and that the statue was clothed and crowned. These elements, it is argued, are implicit in the Genesis account, where the giving of life to the man in chapter 2 involves the awakening of sensory powers, and where the motif of clothing the human pair in chapter 3 is related to their aspiration to divine status.[9]

The obvious next question is how these echoes of ancient Near Eastern practices help us understand what this second account of creation, and the human as divine "image," may mean. This also requires an understanding of how the portrayal of the "image" in Genesis 1 relates to the one in Genesis 2–3. For some interpreters, the latter account is a story of the human need to grow and develop in certain ways. According to Andreas Schüle, this means that it actually critiques the concept of the "image" in Genesis 1. He thinks that the Yahwist (as he calls the author of Gen. 2–3) argues against the view of humanity articulated by the Priestly writer in Genesis 1. Against P's view (as Schüle understands it) that humans, as bearers of the "image of God," were like God in certain intrinsic ways and bore his power on the earth, the Yahwist argues in chapter 2 that the *imago Dei* fails to do justice to certain essential features of human life, such as the sexual relationship, the desire for knowledge, and the exertion of free will.[10] Schüle also argues that the Yahwist thinks the garden was an unsuitable place for human development since it denied the humans "the knowledge of good and evil," which was necessary precisely for the kind of creativity mandated to the humans in Genesis 1:28.[11]

This view, now held rather widely in Old Testament studies,[12] poses a challenge to the traditional Christian understanding of Genesis 2–3 as a story of

---

Scriptures 15 (Winona Lake, IN: Eisenbrauns, 2015). I am grateful to Dr. McDowell for providing me with a copy of her dissertation, which is cited here. Middleton notes a paper of hers on the topic given at the Society of Biblical Literature annual meeting in 1999. His discussion is in Middleton, *Liberating Image*, 126–29.

8. Schüle, "Made in the 'Image of God,'" 12; Beckerleg (McDowell), "Image of God in Eden," 207. She also cites Gordon J. Wenham, *Genesis 1–15*, WBC 1 (Nashville: Nelson, 1987), 19, for the garden of Eden as having characteristics of a sanctuary.

9. Schüle, "Made in the 'Image of God,'" 13; Beckerleg (McDowell), "Image of God in Eden," 218–30.

10. Schüle, "Made in the 'Image of God,'" 14–18.

11. Ibid., 17–18.

12. For a short account of the earliest Christian interpretation of the paradise story, see Ellen van Wolde, *Stories of the Beginning: Genesis 1–11 and Other Creation Stories*, trans.

the "fall" of humanity, where the humans, having been made "in the image of God," sin decisively against the creator by eating the fruit of the "tree of the knowledge of good and evil." In its favor, it can be pointed out that "knowing good and evil" elsewhere denotes the attainment of a measure of maturity (Deut. 1:39; Isa. 7:15). The expression, indeed, appears to suggest the capacity to make moral decisions, to distinguish between right and wrong. There is, therefore, something curious about the creator's reluctance to trust the human creatures with what seems to be an essential capacity for living a responsible life. It is a strength of the "maturation" interpretation that the garden of Eden story evidently aims to explain why human beings have to come to terms with the world in which they live and the hardships of life that it presents.

Yet one cannot avoid the sense that it is a story of loss. Whatever "knowing good and evil" means in this context, it is not a simple matter of ordinary human maturing, but is mysteriously bound up with the possession of life itself. The expulsion of the pair from Eden because they have eaten from the tree that bears this name means they have lost any possibility of access to the other tree, the "tree of life." This latter symbol means either that the humans possessed immortality in the garden up to the point where they ate the fruit of the other tree or, as James Barr argued, that they had the possibility of attaining it, which they failed to grasp.[13] It was this powerful sense of loss that embedded itself in the theological tradition, both Jewish and Christian. Catherine McDowell, indeed, points to biblical and postbiblical sources suggesting that the first humans, in their primeval innocence, were endowed with manifestations of the divine glory.[14] In her view, therefore (unlike Schüle), the narrative of the Babylonian rituals is echoed in a negative way. For whereas in the latter the statue-image is transformed into a manifestation of the divine, for McDowell, the human pair's consciousness of nakedness in Genesis 3:7 is a realization of the forfeit of the primeval glory with which they had been

---

John Bowden (London: SCM, 1995), 62–71. She argues that the reading of the story as an account of "original sin" comes to prevail only with Augustine in the fourth century CE; cf. Schüle, "Made in the 'Image of God,'" 16–17. See also Lyn M. Bechtel, "Genesis 2.4b–3.24: A Myth about Human Maturation," *JSOT* 67 (1995): 3–26. She traces the beginnings of a "maturation" interpretation of Gen. 2–3 back to Hermann Gunkel and Umberto Cassuto in their commentaries on Genesis; she also cites Carol Meyers, *Discovering Eve: Ancient Israelite Women in Context* (New York: Oxford University Press, 1988), and van Wolde, *A Semiotic Analysis of Genesis 2–3: A Semiotic Theory and Method of Analysis Applied to the Story of the Garden of Eden* (Assen, Neth.: Van Gorcum, 1989) (Bechtel, "Genesis 2.4b–3.24," 4nn4–5).

13. James Barr, *The Garden of Eden and the Hope of Immortality* (Minneapolis: Fortress, 1993).

14. Beckerleg (McDowell), "Image of God in Eden," 230–33.

clothed.[15] More important, in the element of the "opening of the eyes," the relationship between Genesis and Babylon is one of stark contrast: "In each case, the opening of the eyes was not only an act of animation, but of divinization, or, in Gen 3:5–6, an attempt by Adam and Eve at divinization."[16] In her reading, therefore, the Genesis text, if it is aware of the ancient Near Eastern parallels we have noticed, testifies to a loss of divine affinity rather than an attribution of it.

Here then are two sharply contrasting approaches to understanding Genesis 2–3, either as the gaining of wisdom and knowledge and the satisfaction of certain human aspirations, or as the forfeit of certain possibilities for fuller life. In order to try to resolve this impasse, we have to consider once more the relation of Genesis 2–3 to Genesis 1. Where these are read sequentially, the loss of immortality in the garden is understood against the background of the creation of the humans "in the image and likeness of God" (Gen. 1:26). What happened in the garden, therefore, had some sort of effect on the bearing of the "image." Classical Old Testament criticism subverted this assumption with its postulate that the "second" creation narrative was the earlier, so that it began to be read without regard for its literary setting following Genesis 1. This tendency has persisted into some recent scholarship, not least in the assessment that the Priestly version of beginnings has no knowledge of an entry of sin and violence into the world before the flood. That is, because Genesis 2:4b–4:26, together with 6:1–8, is absent from the Priestly source (P), the assumption has been made that P's view of human origins has no place for sin in the portrayal of the human condition in those sections of the book.[17] This view has been rightly opposed, as we have observed, chiefly on the grounds that it takes no account of the form of the text as it has been handed down. It is significant that Schüle, who argues for distinct theologies of P and JE (the combination of the Yahwist and Elohist sources), recognizes a form of interaction between the two creation narratives, albeit in the sense that the latter expresses dissent from the former. He is aware, however, that this characterization of the relationship between the two is hard to press absolutely. And he concedes that Genesis 2–3 might be understood as *either* explaining how the humans, created

15. Ibid., 229–30.
16. Ibid., 235.
17. Norbert Lohfink has argued that the P account of origins, from creation to Israel's settlement in the land, is entirely peaceful, with violent elements coming only from other pentateuchal sources. See Lohfink, "God the Creator and the Stability of Heaven and Earth," in *Theology of the Pentateuch: Themes of the Priestly Narrative and Deuteronomy*, trans. Linda M. Maloney (Minneapolis: Fortress; Edinburgh: T&T Clark, 1994), 116–35. Cf. William P. Brown, *The Ethos of the Cosmos: The Genesis of Moral Imagination in the Bible* (Grand Rapids: Eerdmans, 1999), 60, 64, 101.

in the "image of God," could turn away from God, *or*, in his own preferred way, as a rejection of the notion of the "image." These readings, he goes on, "certainly do not exclude one another, for they are located on different levels of explanation. The first one relates to the content of the creation narratives, the second to their conceptual framing."[18] This appears to make a distinction between supposed original meanings of the separate texts and their meaning in the combined form that we possess. At the least, this means that the interpretation of the sequence of Genesis 1 and Genesis 2–3 remains open.[19]

The "Image" in the Combined Creation Accounts

The central issue in reading the two creation accounts together is what it means to say that human beings are in any sense "like God." There are reasons, as we have seen, to think that the notion of the "image" is at play in Genesis 2–3 as well as in Genesis 1. And the juxtaposition of the two texts calls, in my view, for a weighing of both discourses together. The relationship has been portrayed as one of sharp contrast, where Genesis 1 offers a picture of completeness, in which the human exercises his power of dominion over God's world, while Genesis 2–3 introduces a new problem in the humans' relationships. Yet there are indications against this.

In recent interpretation of Genesis 1, there has been discussion of this exact point—namely, whether it portrays a finished, undisturbed creation, or whether the account contains within it a residue of the widespread ancient Near Eastern "combat myth" (or *Chaoskampf*). The latter case has been proposed by Jon D. Levenson, who thinks that the idea of a possible resurgence of a subdued Chaos, though stronger in other Old Testament texts, is not absent from Genesis 1; rather, the "forces of Chaos" persist within the created order, and "their persistence qualifies—and defines—[God's] world-mastery."[20] Richard Middleton, in contrast, has argued that Genesis 1 presents a clear alternative to the combat myth, and "signals the creator's original intent for shalom and blessing at the outset of human history, prior to the rise of human (or divine) violence."[21] These contrasting views illustrate the hermeneutical challenge of

18. Schüle, "Made in the 'Image of God,'" 14.

19. McDowell is cautious about the relative priority of Gen. 1 and Gen. 2–3. She thinks that the case may be argued either way, but points to the *tôlĕdôt* formula in Gen. 2:4a as suggesting that the placing of Gen. 2–3 after Gen. 1 has been deliberately effected by a redactor ("Image of God in Eden," 280–83).

20. Jon D. Levenson, *Creation and the Persistence of Evil: The Jewish Drama of Divine Omnipotence* (Princeton: Princeton University Press, 1988), 65.

21. Middleton, *Liberating Image*, 269.

trying to understand the two creation accounts in terms of each other. The difference between Levenson and Middleton recalls the point noticed above, about whether P (Gen. 1) presents a picture of a finished creation, without a record of the entry of any disturbance into the world through human agency.

In my view, while there are important distinctions between the two Genesis accounts of creation, the differences between the portrayals of the human situation in them have sometimes been overstated. We have observed this already in relation to the meaning of the verb *bārā'* (create) in Genesis 1, where we saw that it does not express the exclusive transcendence of God's creative activity as has often been held, but is compatible with the notion of God as an artisan, in ways that have analogies with human creative actions.[22] On these grounds, Karl Möller holds that interplay between the two accounts should not be precluded by an overemphasis on divine transcendence in Genesis 1, nor by a doctrine of *creatio ex nihilo*. Rather, both accounts know that God is immanent as well as transcendent, and on these grounds he does not want to foreclose a notion of what he calls *creatio ex tumulto* in Genesis 1.[23] This move, away from undue polarization of P and JE, seems to me to be in the right direction.

Ultimately, the juxtaposition, or coexistence, of the two texts must be reckoned with as part of the hermeneutics of reading Genesis. John Rogerson has proposed that the Old Testament creation texts, in Genesis and elsewhere, have an element of critique of certain kinds of *status quo*. This is a familiar point in general, often taken to mean that the biblical texts aim critically at mythologies of creation in non-Israelite cultures such as Babylon. Rogerson, in contrast, finds that Genesis 1, by presenting a certain kind of ideal existence, constitutes a critique of conditions experienced in the actual world, which he thinks are portrayed in Genesis 6–9, the story of the flood and its aftermath. He points to the paradox that Genesis 1 and Genesis 6–9 together "ascribe the origin of the world to the God revealed to Israel, but also affirm that the world of human experience is not the world that God intended."[24] Furthermore, he argues that "[this] paradox, expressed in the contrast between Genesis 1 and the compromise world of our experience in Genesis 9, must be maintained at all costs"[25]—that is, in order that the Old Testament's

---

22. See above, ch. 1, nn. 12–17, 21.

23. Möller, "Images of God and Creation in Genesis 1–2," in *A God of Faithfulness: Essays in Honour of J. Gordon McConville on His Sixtieth Birthday*, ed. Jamie Grant, Alison Lo, and Gordon J. Wenham (New York: T&T Clark, 2011), 28–29. *Creatio ex tumulto* means in effect the same as *Chaoskampf*, or primeval battle.

24. John Rogerson, *A Theology of the Old Testament: Cultural Memory, Communication, and Being Human* (London: SPCK, 2009), 48.

25. Ibid., 63.

powerful call to change the world can be heard. In this account, Rogerson has opted to find a counterrepresentation to Genesis 1 in chapters 6–9, rather than chapters 2–3, doing so with a nod to the critical habit of isolating P from J.[26] Yet a contrast between Genesis 1 and Genesis 2–3 can produce the same effect. How can we think of a world that God created "good," when there is much about the actual condition of the world and of humans that is at odds with such a divine intention?

For Rogerson, the relationship between Genesis 1 and the texts that portray the actual world is one of critique. We saw the obverse of this in the thesis of Schüle, who sees Genesis 2–3 as the critique of Genesis 1. In common here is that interpreters are seeing, in different ways, the jarring nature of the juxtaposition of these texts. I think the category of critique is not entirely suitable for the case. Rather, we have in Genesis 1–3 a complex portrayal of the human condition. I suggest, therefore, that Genesis 1 should be read in such a way as to expect a continuation that reckons with the realities of ordinary human existence. It is one thing to have concluded, as we did above, that in Genesis 1 the humans represent the divine presence on earth and carry certain responsibilities in consequence. But this leaves much open in terms of how the humans can bear those honors and responsibilities. In my view, the real issue concerns the "hostage to fortune" that is constituted by the human being as "image of God" in Genesis 1. Against the backcloth of both Genesis 1 and concepts of divine presence in the ancient Near East, the postulate of the human being as the manifestation and agent of God in the world is complicated by the humans' apprehension of themselves. If the "good" creation in Genesis 1 was completed by the advent of the humans, it was also disturbed by the presence in it of this new agency that had delegated to it some of the attributes of God. This seems to me to be the important destabilizing factor in Genesis 1.[27] Much of the Old Testament, in story, prophecy, and wisdom, is predicated on this destabilizing human factor.

Genesis 1–3, therefore, depicts the human condition in its conflicted relation to good and evil, life and death. Its function as a depiction of the world as it is finds resonances in other parts of the Old Testament. The idea of "the knowledge of good and evil" reappears in Deuteronomy, functioning in a positive way in the Old Testament's vocabulary of the ethical life, in

---

26. Ibid., 46.

27. I have made this essential point elsewhere, in "Human 'Dominion' and Being 'Like God': An Exploration of Peace, Violence, and Truth in the Old Testament," in *Encountering Violence in the Bible*, ed. Markus Zehnder and Hallvard Hagelia (Sheffield, UK: Sheffield Phoenix, 2013), 194–206. There is also in that place a fuller account of Isaiah's depiction of Assyria's idolatrous self-deception, offered more briefly here.

some of the final words of Moses to Israel, where he says: "See, I have set before you this day, on one hand life and good, on the other, death and evil" (Deut. 30:15). Here, the terms "good" and "evil" correspond to each other in a carefully constructed correspondence with "life" and "death." In the choice of good there is life; in the choice of evil there is death. The echo of Genesis 3 in these juxtapositions is evident. In this quasi-Edenic command to "choose life" (Deut. 30:19), therefore, Deuteronomy's rhetoric of the moral life is crystallized in a choice between "good" and "evil." The prize is "life," the theme that dominates the peroration in 30:15–20; and the exhortation is predicated on the moral maturity to make decisions leading to it.

A further illustration comes from the book of Isaiah. Isaiah depicts human misjudgment in the moral realm in a series of pictures in which true and false are confused:

> Woe to those who call evil good
>   and good evil,
> who put darkness for light
>   and light for darkness,
> who put bitter for sweet
>   and sweet for bitter! (Isa. 5:20 RSV)

Strikingly, at the head of these polarities is "good and evil"; moral corruption is encapsulated in the inversion of these. Isaiah's rhetorical point is substantiated in the prophecy by its portrayal of bearers of authority. In counterpoint are figures who judge rightly, whether the child born to exercise the royal authority of David with justice and righteousness (Isa. 9:6–7[5–6]) or the "Servant" who will bring justice to the nations (Isa. 42:1–4), and figures who mistake authority for self-aggrandizement.

The theme of human rule runs throughout Isaiah. In the structure of the book, the faith of King Hezekiah is in counterpoint with the faith failure of King Ahaz; whereas Ahaz refused to place his trust in Yahweh and so brought upon himself and Judah overwhelming judgment in the form of Assyria (Isa. 7–8), Hezekiah averted judgment at the hands of the same power by faith and prayer (Isa. 37). It is Assyria itself, however, that becomes the emblem of presumption in its false arrogation of godlikeness. The picture is developed at length in two places in the book, in Isaiah 10 and 36–37. In these places the great empire considers itself not only invincible but also capable of bestowing all the gifts upon subject peoples that the Old Testament (especially in Deuteronomy) attributes only to Yahweh. While for Isaiah "glory" (kābôd) belongs exclusively to Yahweh God of Israel (Isa. 6:3), he assigns it ironically to Assyria: "under his glory a burning will be kindled, like the burning of fire" (10:16). In the prophet's portrayal, Assyria is deeply self-deceived, as 10:15–19 in particular makes plain.[28] A central feature of the portrayal of human rule in Isaiah is the striking contrast between, on the one hand, Assyria's self-attribution of wisdom (10:13), fantasy of irresistible power, and vacuous promises of peace (36:16–17) and, on the other, the wisdom, peace, justice, and righteousness predicated of the ideal human ruler (e.g. 9:6–7[5–6]; 11:1–9).[29]

The book of Isaiah thus bears a complex witness to the problem of human power that we found to be articulated in Genesis 1–3. The pretensions of Assyria correspond vividly to the portrayal there of the human propensity to take to themselves a "godlikeness" defined by self-aggrandizement and violence. Yet Assyria's false self-exaltation contrasts not only with the exalted Yahweh but also with portrayals of just human rule, which too entail the forceful suppression of opposition (e.g., Isa. 11:4).

In the biblical story, Isaiah's Assyria stands alongside Genesis 3 as a paradigm of godlikeness misconstrued. Yet in the space between the ruthless tyranny of Assyria and the righteous judgment of the Davidic scion, or even of Cyrus, is a suggestion that by wise judgment a true rule may also be discerned.

Conclusion

I have proposed in these two chapters on humanity "in the image of God" that its meaning has to be understood by reading Genesis 1 along with other texts, initially Genesis 1–3 as a whole. Our reading of the two creation accounts (as Old Testament criticism has typically seen it) has yielded a story not of a "loss" of the image in Genesis 3—since the image was not a property that could be lost—but of one in which the idea of humanity bearing the image of God was developed in terms of the reality of the human condition. The result was somewhat paradoxical: humans are entrusted with presencing God in the world yet are subject to a fatal misreading of what this means as subjective reality.

While Genesis 2–3 has aspects of loss that have led to the traditional reading of it as a narrative of a "fall," the reading offered here is concerned rather

---

28. There is, incidentally, a telling turn of phrase in the prophet's appraisal of Assyria as failing to grasp God's purpose in the events in which it is involved: "he does not so intend, and his mind [*ûlēbābô*] does not so think [*lō'-kēn yaḥšōb*]" (Isa. 10:7 RSV), which echoes the characterization of human wickedness in Gen. 6:5: "every imagining of the thoughts of their hearts [*maḥšēbōt libbô*] was only evil continually."

29. This is heightened by the structure of Isa. 9–12, with its alternating pictures of true and false rule. Note also the failure to discern divine judgment (9:8–12[7–11]), judgment on a leadership that was founded on lies and folly (9:13–17[12–16]), and "iniquitous decrees" (10:1–4).

with an exploration of what is entailed in the idea of the human as divine image in the world as it is. I have proposed too that the exploration continues beyond Genesis 1–3. In fact, both the ideas of godlikeness and of "knowing good and evil" appear at other places in the Old Testament story. The language of divine image recurs a couple of times in Genesis after chapter 3 (5:1–3; 9:5–6), but godlikeness is expressed in other forms too, as when Moses is said to be "like God" to Pharaoh (Exod. 7:1),[30] or when the Davidic king is characterized as "son of God" (Ps. 2:7), or when the standards of behavior enjoined on human beings correspond mirror-like to attributes of God. The latter include holiness (Lev. 19:2), faithfulness (*'ĕmet, 'ĕmûnâ*), steadfast love (*ḥesed*), and righteousness (*ṣĕdāqâ*), all of which are predicated of both God and humans. The last of these qualities, *ṣĕdāqâ*, is most strikingly attributed to Noah, the survivor of the flood: "Noah was a righteous man [*'îš ṣaddîq*], blameless among his contemporaries; and Noah walked with God" (Gen. 6:9). Here is an early hint that the project of human godlikeness is not lost or ended in Genesis 3. On the contrary, the presencing of God on earth in the human being implies an intention, carried by the Old Testament's narrative and rhetoric of persuasion, that it should be reflected in the conduct of human life together.

Similarly we saw that the motif of discerning between "good and evil" persisted in the Old Testament. In Genesis 1–3, it is charged with a sense of the danger that the exercise of fundamental judgment about things is in reality a divine prerogative, and thus the mystery of how this can be devolved upon humans. Yet the obligation of human beings precisely to exercise such discernment occurs both in relation to ordinary human maturing (as in Deut. 1:39; Isa. 7:15) and to the life of moral responsibility in covenant with God (as in Deut. 30:15–20; Isa. 5:20).

It follows that the portrayal of the human condition in Genesis 1–3, together with what follows it in the Old Testament, shapes expectations for the actual conduct of human life. Those expectations are predicated on the assumption of real human agency, since this is entailed in the human presencing of God on earth. Because it corresponds to divine agency, it has important aspects of both rule and creativity. In this respect, the human as divine image is deeply paradoxical. The real and present danger in the human apprehension of what it is to be "like God" is everywhere apparent in a world in which the abuses

---

30. For this as an echo of the idea of the "image of God," see John T. Strong, "Israel as a Testimony to YHWH's Power: The Priests' Definition of Israel," in *Constituting the Community: Studies in Honor of S. Dean McBride*, ed. John T. Strong and Steven S. Tuell (Winona Lake, IN: Eisenbrauns, 2005), 89–106, esp. 94–96. For Strong, Moses functions like a testimonial stele to Pharaoh (or in reality, postexilic Judah to Persia).

of God-given authority seen in the pharaoh of the exodus, Isaiah's king of Assyria, or the Rome of the New Testament have all too many counterparts, and in a world where the greatest good is construed as the investment of ultimate value in human persons, states, or institutions. This deeply affects the character of societies and those who compose them, and the power in general to distinguish right from wrong, often resulting in the use of violence to pursue goals or to consolidate interests.

Yet the Old Testament (whether taken by itself or in conjunction with the New) does not succumb to pessimism about the human condition or its destiny; on the contrary, there is a glory that properly attaches to it, for which perhaps Psalm 8 can serve as text and motto. I take Genesis 1–3, in its highly nuanced depiction of humanity in God's world, to mandate a further exploration of the Old Testament's conception of human possibilities and limitations, in respect of both rule and creativity. This will be our concern in the remainder of the present study.

3

The Human "Constitution" in the Old Testament

Our guiding question since the beginning of this book has been the psalmist's "What is the human being, that you give attention to them?" (Ps. 8:4). In the preceding pages, we have laid some foundations for an answer to this question. We began by observing that it has contexts not only in biblical texts but also in both theological tradition and the orientation of the reader to the question. We went on to consider the key opening chapters of Genesis and the concept of the human as "image of God." In doing so we have found that the human being was created to embody the presence of God on earth, in such a way as to incorporate the various aspects of human existence (ch. 1). And in chapter 2 we saw that this entailed a capacity to grow and develop in the moral life and in relationships both between people and with the earth. In all of this we have been alert to the possibility of certain potentially misleading oppositions creeping into our understanding of the human person, as between emotional and intellectual, bodily and psychological, personal and social, spiritual and pragmatic.

In the present chapter, I want to pursue these lines of thought exegetically by considering a number of aspects of the human condition in relation to a range of Old Testament texts. The quest is in a sense about the nature of human nature, to put it slightly quirkily. By this I do not mean to suggest "doin' what comes naturally" (since that kind of "nature" is almost certainly subject to all kinds of variation), but rather what Terry Eagleton calls the "species-being" in which humans participate.[1] That there is such a thing is not simply to be taken for granted. It is distinct from the idea that all humans are "irreducibly particular," or indeed that the notion of human nature is simply a cultural construct.[2] An implication of our study so far, especially of the human as "image of God," is that there are indeed things that can be said of human nature as such that cannot be said about other beings.

There is in the Old Testament a certain anthropological language. This can be examined lexically, key terms being *nepeš* (often "soul"), *rûaḥ* ("spirit"), and *lēb* or *lēbāb* ("heart").[3] However, the Old Testament does not operate like a lexicon, nor do these key terms have neatly matching English equivalents. We will therefore understand its anthropological language best by reading texts, that is, by observing actual linguistic usage in theological and rhetorical contexts. No single text can say all that might be said about this. Rather, we learn by immersion in a story, with its various images.[4] We now turn, therefore, to consider some texts which shed light on the nature of the human being, and in particular to the idea of love or desire for God.

Language and the Human Constitution

The "Heart" (Lēbāb)

One of the Old Testament's crucial texts for understanding the human being is the exhortation to Israel in Deuteronomy to "love Yahweh your God

1. Terry Eagleton, *The Event of Literature* (New Haven: Yale University Press, 2012), 8.

2. Ibid.; cf. Mark Elliott, "Human Embodiment," in *The Dynamics of Human Life*, ed. Mark Elliott (Carlisle, UK: Paternoster, 2001), 101. Elliott cites certain feminist critiques of the idea of a fixed human nature. Daphne Hampson, for example, finds differences between boys and girls in terms of a sense of self, girls being naturally more prone to think relationally than in terms of an individuated self (Hampson, *Pure Lust: Elemental Feminist Philosophy* [London: Women's Press, 1984], 119–20). Elliott thinks such oppositions too simplistic ("Human Embodiment," 101).

3. In Hans Walter Wolff's classic treatments of these concepts, he takes the chief terms and assigns them separate aspects of the human constitution. Thus *nepeš* is "Needy Man," *rûaḥ* is "Man as he is Empowered," *lēb(āb)* is "Reasonable Man" (Wolff, *Anthropology of the Old Testament*, trans. Margaret Kohl [London: SCM, 1974], 10–58). The approach taken here differs from Wolff's in the sense that these anthropological terms are not assigned systematically to separate parts of the human constitution, but each is seen to have a range of potential and overlapping meanings according to context.

4. The search for the human may be compared with the search for God, since in biblical thought the two are inextricably linked. In this sense, Elliott's insight on the knowledge of God is apposite: "We are too much like God to know him metaphysically, in concepts; instead we need images held together by story, and thus contingent yet connected by narrative intentionality" (Elliott, "Human Embodiment," 80).

with all your heart, with all your soul, and with all your might" (Deut. 6:5). This is the usual translation of the Hebrew,[5] though each of the terms requires examination. It is part of the famous passage, closely following the giving of the Ten Commandments, which begins: "Hear, Israel, Yahweh your God, Yahweh is one" (6:4), and goes on to call upon Israelites to make the words of Moses a decisive part of their lives, both by the inculcation of teaching and by outward practice (vv. 6–9). While it is an outstandingly important Deuteronomic text, it is also typical of the pedagogy of the book and its highly distinctive rhetorical style, which is based on the premise that intellectual and moral perception are in principle inextricably united.

The term *lēb* and its variant form *lēbāb* are traditionally translated by the English "heart." While both the Hebrew and the English terms broadly express something about the core of the human being, one cannot assume that the connotations that belong to "heart" will always carry over to the Hebrew *lēb/lēbāb*. In some Old Testament texts it seems best to translate the Hebrew term with "mind" rather than "heart." An example is Deuteronomy 29:4[3], in which it is closely associated with "knowing," leading some standard translations to adopt "mind" (RSV, NIV), though some, such as ESV, retain "heart," perhaps to signal the connection with Deuteronomy 6:5. This dilemma was also known to the translators of the LXX and the authors of the New Testament.[6] The apparent viability of these different options shows that in translation we only approximate to the original meaning, and either way lose something of its force. The point holds for translation generally. But in this case it may suggest that the Hebrew writers were working with a kind of unitary understanding of the human that modern readers may not immediately recognize.

The point can also be illustrated from other Old Testament usage. The translators' dilemma appears, for example, in Psalm 73. The psalm opens (v. 1) with the affirmation that God is good to "those who are pure in heart" (*lēbārê lēbāb*).[7] The language of the psalm goes on to record the psalmist's

5. *Wĕʾāhabtā ʾet yhwh ʾĕlōhêkā bĕkol-lēbābĕkā ûbĕkol-napšĕkā ûbĕkol-mĕʾōdekā.*

6. Deuteronomy 6:5 LXX [A] has ἐξ ὅλης τῆς καρδίας σου (*ex holēs tēs kardias sou*), but LXX [B] has διανοιας (*dianoias*). Cf. Moshe Weinfeld, *Deuteronomy 1–11*, AB 5 (New York: Doubleday, 1991), 338, who apparently overlooks the A reading. Both Matt. 22:37 and Mark 12:29–30 have forms of καρδία (*kardia*), but also διάνοια (*dianoia*) instead of "might." Luke 10:27 adds διάνοια (*dianoia*) after "strength." Other texts where *lēb* or *lēbāb* is taken as "mind" include: Num. 16:28 (KJV; NRSV paraphrases to "of my own accord"); 24:13 (KJV; NRSV has "will"). In Neh. 4:6[3:38]; Ps. 31:12[13]; Isa. 46:8; 65:17, NRSV has "mind," in agreement with KJV.

7. There is a textual question concerning the first half of this line—namely, whether to read "Israel" with MT, or to amend, as frequently, to something like "the upright" (RSV, NRSV). It does not affect the present point.

confession that he had fallen prey to a complete misapprehension of the true nature of things. He describes this lapse in verse 21, where he says that his "heart" (*lĕbābî*) was embittered (*yithammēṣ*), then in parallel with *lĕbābî* employs another term, *kilyôtay* (lit., "my kidneys"), to fill out the picture of his inmost being. Most translations retain "heart" for *lĕbābî* in the first line, and some other expression for inwardness for the latter term: NASB has "I was pierced within," and NIV "my spirit." RSV, NRSV, and ESV take a different route, offering "soul" for *lĕbābî* and "heart" for *kilyôtay*! The meaning of verse 21 is illuminated by the continuation of the thought in verse 22, where the psalmist compares his former state to the ignorance of the brute beast: "I was senseless [*ba'ar*] and did not know [*wĕlō' 'ēdā'*]." The latter phrase is telling because it shows that the psalmist's problem had as much to do with knowledge and understanding as with his moral state. There is a further parallel in the psalm in verse 26 between *lēbāb*, which occurs twice, and a term meaning "flesh" (*šĕ'ērî*), conveying something like "will" or "courage," and drawing the embodied life of the psalmist into the picture. The psalm therefore uses a range of language to express an experience that encompasses the intellectual, moral, and even physical life of the psalmist. English translations once again make the point that one cannot analyze the biblical view of the person according to an anthropological lexicon. The nature of the human being is conveyed in a narrative, in this case the first-person account of the psalmist who has come through a profoundly disturbing experience.

The "Soul" (Nepeš)

What is true for *lēb/lēbāb* is also true for another key anthropological term—namely, *nepeš*, often translated "soul" in Deuteronomy 6:5 and elsewhere. *Nepeš* does not designate some separable part of the human being, but is capable of bearing various meanings, including physical ones, such as "throat" (Ps. 105:18; Jon. 2:5[6]) and the person simply as an individual (as one among a number: Gen. 46:15–27, several times, but not always translated; Num. 31:28), as well as denoting the person's innermost or essential being. The range of meanings, notably "throat," suggests that the idea of the person's essential being is not separable from one's physical being, so that it can be hard to decide in some contexts whether to translate with a physical term or with the familiar "soul."[8] The psalmist's habit of addressing himself as *napšî* ("my soul"), as in Psalm 103:1–2, is indeed an address to

8. A case in point is Ps. 63:5[6], where *nepeš* is taken by *HALAT* as "throat" (*Kehle*), but NRSV has: "My *soul* is satisfied as with a rich feast" (emphasis added).

the whole self, and can even suggest something of the depths and unknow-ability of the person.[9] In the usage of the Psalms, it can suggest the person in their full being or indeed one who is not yet a finished product, but in the process of formation.[10]

The "Spirit" (Rûaḥ)

The Old Testament also knows of the human "spirit" (rûaḥ), a favorite term of the psalmists as they seek to express what is most profound about human being. It can also have a physiological sense, meaning "breath," and this indeed corresponds to the natural phenomenon of "wind." The attachment of the term to human life therefore rests on an imaginative link between the unseen but powerful force of the wind and that which animates human life itself. The "spirit" can indeed connote the very life of the person (Ps. 31:5[6]), and it can also be the seat of the disposition or will (Pss. 32:2; 51:10–12[12–14]). To this extent, it has much in common with lēb/lēbāb or nepeš. It does, however, have its own particular semantic potential. It has the capacity to characterize a quality of a person, as in the phrase "your spirit of holiness," or indeed "your holy spirit" (rûaḥ qodšĕkā) (Ps. 51:11[13]). This text illustrates the added dimension that the term rûaḥ is also applied frequently to God (Pss. 104:30; 139:7; 143:10). Famously, at the creation it was the "spirit" of God that brooded like a mother bird over the earth as it took form (Gen. 1:2). In that "spirit" can be predicated of both God and human beings, the life of the human has something in common with the life of God. This is brought out in the language of praise, as in Psalm 51:10–12[12–14]. In these verses the "spirit" is in parallel with the "heart" (lēb), so that these terms together convey the person's basic disposition. Then the rûaḥ of the psalmist is made to correspond to that of God:

> Create in me a clean heart [lēb],
>   O God,
>   and put a new and right spirit [rûaḥ] within me [bĕqirbî—in my
>   midst].

9. Note the parallel in v. 1 between napšî and the expression "all that is within me" (kol-qĕrābay), which is all-embracing yet indeterminate.

10. I have made this point more fully in "'Keep These Words in Your Heart' (Deut. 6:6): A Spirituality of Torah in the Context of the Shema," in For Our Good Always: Studies on the Message and Influence of Deuteronomy in Honor of Daniel I. Block, ed. Jason S. de Rouchie, Jason Gile, and Kenneth J. Turner (Winona Lake, IN: Eisenbrauns, 2013), 139–40. The discussion of lēb/lēbāb is also partly based on that essay. The final term in the triad of "heart, soul, and strength," mě'ōd, denotes the person's full resources, which may be personal or extrinsic, such as one's power and wealth.

> Do not cast me away from your presence,
>   and do not take your holy spirit [spirit (*rûaḥ*) of your holiness]
>   from me.
> Restore to me the joy of your salvation,
>   and sustain in me a willing spirit [*rûaḥ*]. (Ps. 51:10–12 NRSV)

The prayer that God should not take his "holy spirit" from him exploits the semantic potential of the term in order to portray the life of the psalmist as having a close relationship with the life of God. God's "holy spirit" here is not the Third Person of the Trinity, but means rather that it is the nature of God to be holy. The prayer of the psalmist, therefore, is that he too should have a "holy spirit," that it should also be his character to be holy. The prayer sheds a clear light on the way in which the human is known in the Old Testament, not as a self-existent composite of faculties or parts, but in the context of seeking and worshiping God. The life of the human is always contingent on the dynamic relationship with God. This is also manifest in the important creation statement in Genesis 2:7, where God is said to breathe or blow (*wayyippaḥ*) the breath of life (*nišmat ḥayyîm*) into the *ʾādām*, so that he became a living being (*nepeš ḥayyâ*). In this picture of the animation of the human, the breath of God (*nĕšāmâ*) is similar to the *rûaḥ* in its physiological connotations. And the human who is formed is described with the term *nepeš*, not a "soul," but simply a living being whose life derives from God. Finally, in the spirit language of Psalm 51, there is an echo of that godlikeness that we observed in our discussion of the "image of God," and which Genesis 1–3 revealed to be a potentially continuing reality, though severely complicated by the human capacity to misapprehend it. It is in worship that we see how it may take shape.

Heart, Mind, Love, and the "Social Body"

One question raised by these observations is whether there is such a thing as a biblical concept, or theology, of "mind." Michael Carasik has argued that Deuteronomy represents "the first coherent attempt to understand the mind."[11] He argues that, both in Deuteronomy's emphasis on learning, knowledge, and memory, and in other Old Testament writings, there was a "psychology of knowledge," by which he means that, for the biblical writers, there was a state of awareness, or inner attitude, distinct from intention and action, though related to these.[12] For him, the "heart" (*lēb*) is a way of speaking about the

---

11. Michael Carasik, *Theologies of the Mind in Biblical Israel*, StBibLit 85 (New York: Lang, 2006), 215.
    12. Ibid., 75–80; cf. 47.

inner life, which has a particular character, whether "crooked" (Ps. 101:4), "proud" (Ezek. 31:10), or "upright" (Deut. 9:5).[13]

While Carasik is intent on demonstrating a distinct human function called "mind," he concedes that there is in Deuteronomy an integration of the intellectual and the emotional in what he calls "psychological commands."[14] Deuteronomy's rhetoric is highly rational, in the sense that it regularly offers reasons for its commands: Israel is to serve Yahweh because he liberated them from bondage to another master in Egypt (Deut. 5:15); they are to keep the commandments because Yahweh disciplines them as a father disciplines his son (8:5), or again, because he has made them as numerous as the stars of heaven (10:22); they are to love the "stranger" (*gēr*) because they were themselves "strangers" in Egypt (10:19). They are also to release debt slaves at the due time and with generous hearts (15:12–15), ensure justice for the needy (24:17–18), and indeed provide at all times for the poor (24:19–22), on the grounds that they were *slaves* in Egypt. They should act with compassion beyond the call of justice, so that the "poor man" will bless you and "you will be in the right [lit., it will be righteousness (*ṣĕdāqâ*) to you] before Yahweh your God" (24:12–13).

This is reasoning rhetoric. Yet it is also emotive. The classic text for this is once again the command to "love" Yahweh. As Yahweh is "one" (Deut. 6:4), so his people are to love him with their whole being (6:5). This is fundamental to all the commands that follow, both the general exhortations in Deuteronomy 6–11 and the more specific ones in chapters 12–26. The point is driven home by its reappearance in 11:13, in an extended passage (11:13–21) that echoes the language of Deuteronomy 6:4–9. And so the whole section between the Decalogue (in ch. 5) and the law code (chs. 12–26) is framed by the call to "love Yahweh."

This "love" language has its home, formally speaking, in the treaty terminology of the ancient Near East. A subordinate king or people was to "love" the more powerful king with whom it was making the treaty. "Love" in this context means neither more nor less than loyalty, and it would be given under duress and with threats of reprisal for breach of it. Because of the well-known parallels between Deuteronomy and the forms and concepts of treaties, it was proposed, in a famous article by William L. Moran, that Deuteronomy's command to love Yahweh lacked emotive content.[15] However, this view overlooks the pervasiveness of emotive language in Deuteronomy's art of persuasion.

---

13. Ibid., 10–11.
14. Ibid., 199–201.
15. William L. Moran, "The Ancient Near Eastern Background of the Love of God in Deuteronomy," *CBQ* 25 (1963): 77–87.

Israel is repeatedly commanded not only to "love" but also to "rejoice" (Deut. 14:26; 16:11, 13–15), and in the sphere of social and economic relations, they are to go beyond the demands of lawful action by doing what is right with glad and willing hearts (Deut. 15:7–11). The logic in the latter context is that as God habitually treats Israel generously, so they too should be generous. This is an appeal to the person that cannot be encompassed by rationality alone.

It is because Deuteronomy's rhetorical appeal is made to persons in the entirety of their being that Carasik and others have departed from Moran's monochrome view of the meaning of love in the book. For Jacqueline Lapsley, "loving God with all your heart and with all your soul" (Deut. 6:5) involves passion and desire as well as obedience.[16] In this conception of the human, there is an intimate connection between the inner life and outward act.[17] Jonathan Burnside, in a major study of biblical law and its influence on modern law, shows that "commanding kindness" is fundamental to the Deuteronomic conception of the human situation.[18] Burnside rightly sees a profound relationship between Deuteronomic Torah and the person's life in the round, so that he can speak of Torah as "spiritual jurisprudence," having the purpose of forming and changing people and society. For him, the shaping of biblical law by "narrative," specifically the narrative of the life of Israel with God, is crucial to an understanding of its formative nature.[19] Much more than "law," therefore, Deuteronomy's program is based on a deep understanding of humanity, to which its rhetorical strategy is designed to correspond.

In this strategy, indeed, Deuteronomy is exhibiting something of a biblical anthropology. How is it that it can, in effect, command love, joy, and kindness? If there seems to be a tension in this it may be because the sharp distinction

16. Jacqueline E. Lapsley, "Feeling Our Way: Love for God in Deuteronomy," *CBQ* 65 (2003): 350–51; Jeffrey Tigay, *Deuteronomy*, JPS Torah Commentary (Philadelphia: Jewish Publication Society, 1996), 77. Lapsley cites, in addition, Walter Brueggemann, *Theology of the Old Testament* (Minneapolis: Fortress, 1997), 420; Dennis T. Olson, *Deuteronomy and the Death of Moses: A Theological Reading*, OBT (Minneapolis: Fortress, 1994), 51. Lapsley's point recalls our discussion of the relational aspect of the "image of God," which could be expressed in similar terms (above, ch. 1, at nn. 47–51).

17. See on this Mark K. George, "Yhwh's Own Heart," *CBQ* 64 (2002): 442–59. Compare Elliott: "To speak in terms of eros means that the body and its desires (if not its needs) are to be taken seriously: there is not a bit of us to be left out in our 'spiritual worship'" ("Human Embodiment," 75–76).

18. Jonathan Burnside, *God, Justice and Society: Aspects of Law and Legality in the Bible* (Oxford: Oxford University Press, 2011). He cites Deut. 15:12–15 and 24:19–21, and also points to the case of Boaz, who acts in a way that comports with the laws of Deuteronomy, and in his actions toward Ruth (Ruth 2:14–15) shows that he "has gone beyond the requirements of social welfare" (238).

19. Ibid., xxix, 1–2, 11–14. I have dealt with Burnside's thesis at greater length in "Biblical Law and Human Formation," *Political Theology* 14, no. 5 (2013): 628–40.

that is sometimes made between the intellectual and affective aspects of the human constitution is overdrawn. Karl A. Kuhn, citing modern cognitive psychology, finds a close relationship between emotion and intellectual judgment. Many emotions, he argues, derive from conscious appraisals related to our values. And he cites Deuteronomy as a prime biblical illustration of the point.[20] In the memorable phrase of Pascal, "The heart has its reasons that reason does not know."[21]

This fusion of the intellectual and the emotional has enormous significance for understanding the nature of Deuteronomy and much else in the Old Testament's rhetoric of persuasion. For the book in its entirety is a pedagogy, based on a deep understanding of the human constitution and aimed at the formation of people as individuals and as a whole community. Many features of Deuteronomy can be explained on this basis. Its surface insistence on "learning" is matched by the provisions it makes for the laws and commands to be practiced and inculcated. In two places it commands the appointment of those who are wise, experienced, and who love justice to be responsible for interpreting and applying the laws and commands in Israel (Deut. 1:9–18; 16:18–17:13). Both passages show a perception that there will be hard cases to resolve (1:17; 17:8), implying that written statute has inbuilt limitations; merely giving commands cannot compel right comprehension and practice of them. Rather, there must be maturity of understanding, together with a love of what is right. And this is what the book as a whole aims to achieve. Far from being simply a law code, it is conceived as a means of bringing a society to maturity in its understanding of what makes for a good life. While it speaks with the authority of law, it shows a keen awareness that right action, and in Israel's case covenant faithfulness, can be guaranteed in the end only by human agents who are dedicated to the understanding and practice of

20. Karl Allen Kuhn, *The Heart of Biblical Narrative: Rediscovering Biblical Appeal to the Emotions* (Minneapolis: Fortress, 2009), 8, 23–27. Kuhn recognizes that there is a debate among cognitive philosophers about whether all emotional responses are related to conscious judgments and values, or whether emotions are essentially pre- or noncognitive, but he concludes that both of these views can be upheld to some degree. He cites in support of his argument Martha Nussbaum, *Upheavals of Thought: The Intelligence of Emotions* (New York: Cambridge University Press, 2001).

21. More fully: "We know the truth not only by reason but by the heart; it is in the latter way that we know first principles. The heart has its reasons that reason does not know" (Blaise Pascal, *Pensées*, ed. L. Lafuma [Paris: Garnier-Flammarion, 1973], 21). The translation is that of John Macquarrie, who cites it and adds his own comment: "There is what we might call a 'logic' of the emotions" (Macquarrie, *In Search of Humanity: A Theological and Philosophical Approach* [London: SCM, 1982], 56). This is, of course, in striking contrast to that other French philosopher Descartes, famed for his *cogito ergo sum*, which privileges the intellectual faculty in human apprehension.

what is right. The metaphor of the "circumcision of the heart" (10:16; 30:6) expresses the point vividly. The mark of the covenant in the flesh has no force apart from the thoroughgoing engagement of the person.

Even well-known critical issues in relation to Deuteronomy can be explained in terms of this perception of the nature of the book. The differences between it and the analogous parts of the book of Exodus can be explained along source-critical or redaction-critical lines. Its variations from the Book of the Covenant (BC) in Exodus 20–23 attest certain "Deuteronomic" interests most commonly associated with the movement that culminated in the religious and political reforms of King Josiah (2 Kings 22–23). Deuteronomy can be thought either to elaborate on or deliberately to replace the older provisions of BC.[22] At the least, the differences between the two corpora require some account of a reasoning process on the part of the Deuteronomic authors.[23] This seems to me to be in line with its own concern for an educated and educating people, where education is understood to embrace the rational, moral, emotional, social, and religious sensitivities that can all be ascribed to the "heart."[24]

Two points remain to be made in connection with Deuteronomy's conception of the human constitution. First, there is an evident theological aspect in its discussion of the "heart," to be placed alongside the linguistic usage that ascribes it to the whole person. The Deuteronomic rhetoric may be said to operate anthropologically in the sense that it understands the intellectual, moral, and affective constitution of the person. The accompanying theological question concerns Israel's covenantal relationship with Yahweh and whether they have the moral capacity to be formed as the people of God according to the standards of the laws and commands. The rhetoric operates on this level also, showing an acute awareness of the human propensity to lapse from best intentions. A parade example is Deuteronomy 8, which lays out the dangers to integrity that are posed by the sufficiency that the promised land is sure

22. Bernard Levinson argues that Deuteronomy aimed to replace BC in his *Deuteronomy and the Hermeneutics of Legal Innovation* (New York: Oxford University Press, 1997). A more traditional critical view is represented by Bill T. Arnold, "Deuteronomy 12 and the Law of the Central Sanctuary *noch einmal*," *VT* 64 (2014): 246–48.

23. For Eckart Otto, the process of ethical deliberation is evident in the growth of the Old Testament law codes, traceable by critical analysis, in response to Israel's historical experience. Deuteronomy's extension of the idea of justice for the poor to the family solidarity of all Israel is a case of this. For him, therefore, law, ethics, and growth are inseparable. See Otto, *Theologische Ethik des Alten Testaments* (Stuttgart: Kohlhammer, 1994), 264.

24. I have elsewhere argued that in its relation to other Old Testament laws Deuteronomy embodies a hermeneutic; that is, it exemplifies in its own variations from those laws a capacity for expansion and interpretation. See McConville, "Metaphor, Symbol, and Interpretation in Deuteronomy," in *After Pentecost: Language and Biblical Interpretation*, ed. Craig G. Bartholomew, Colin J. D. Greene, and Karl Möller, SHS 2 (Grand Rapids: Zondervan, 2002), 346–47.

to bring.[25] The reprise of the golden calf episode in 9:4–10:11 turns for its force on the premise that the people are habitually faithless. The double occurrence of the metaphor of "circumcision of the heart" seems to show an understanding that if such a thing is to become a reality it will depend on some dramatic intervention on Yahweh's own part.[26] And the Deuteronomic subtext of a recalcitrant people, utterly dependent on Yahweh's mercy, seems to be rehearsed again in the Song of Moses (Deut. 32:15–18, 34–43).

However, the Deuteronomic rhetoric also appears, by its nature, to be predicated on the possibility of covenant faithfulness. This is implied in its rhetorical habit of placing its hearers before "two ways," the way of life and the way of death. (In this respect it has affinities with the book of Proverbs.) The culmination of this appeal is in Deuteronomy 30:15–20, which we have noticed before because of its linguistic and conceptual affinities with Genesis 2–3.[27] The text can hardly be understood apart from its assumption of the active possibilities of life and death. It belongs, therefore, in common with Deuteronomy at large, to the Old Testament's invitation to construct the "good life," albeit in the most acute awareness of the moral dangers that attend the attempt.

The second point, in closing the present section, is that the "heart" is predicated both of individuals in Israel and of the people as a whole. This key point is also true of the "image of God," which applies to humanity as such, but by the same token is borne by individuals (Gen. 9:5–6). The rhetoric of Deuteronomy is perfectly tailored to express the inescapable interplay between the one and the many. One of its devices (obscured in English translation) is the alternation between singular and plural address. This used to be thought of as a sign of different sources in the composition of the book, but is now generally recognized as a function of its persuasive discourse.[28] The alternation of singular "thou" and plural "you" allows all Israel to be conceived variously as a unified body and as the individuals who make up the collective. The singular is sometimes thought to evoke the unified people, while the plural more readily denotes the individuals, but the effect is more subtle than this. The point can be illustrated from our base text, Deuteronomy 6:4–9, with its opening

---

25. See Walter Brueggemann, *The Land: Place as Gift, Promise, and Challenge in Biblical Faith*, 2nd ed., OBT (Minneapolis: Fortress, 2002), 43–65, for an insightful exposition of this text.

26. This is because, while in 10:16 the people are exhorted to circumcise their hearts, in 30:6 it is Yahweh who is the agent of the same action.

27. See above, ch. 2, the section entitled "The 'Image' in the Combined Creation Accounts."

28. Georges Minette de Tillesse, "Sections 'vous' et sections 'tu' dans le Deutéronome," *VT* 12 (1962): 56–63. Those who tend to see the change of form of address as having a literary or rhetorical function include Georg A. Braulik, *Die Mittel deuteronomischer Rhetorik: Erhoben aus Deuteronomium 40,1–40*, AnBib 68 (Rome: Biblical Institute Press, 1978); and A. D. H. Mayes, "Deuteronomy 4 and the Literary Criticism of Deuteronomy," *JBL* 100 (1981): 23–51.

call for attention, "Hear, O Israel," which is in the singular throughout. This means that it is the collectivity of Israel who is called to love Yahweh with all its "heart, soul, and strength," and that the obligation to teach his commands to each new generation also belongs to the people constituted as a single entity. Yet as the speech of Moses continues, it is clear that the individual is in view in the sequence "your children . . . your house . . . when you walk by the way . . . your hand . . . your eyes" (vv. 7–9). The language slides easily from one pole to the other, from the collective to the individual, almost without being noticed. But the effect is to portray the individual as possessing his or her being and purpose by virtue of being caught up in the being and purpose of Israel.

The point is manifest throughout the book. The repeated formula "You shall remember that you were a slave in Egypt" is also couched in the singular (Deut. 5:15; 15:15; 16:12; 24:18, 22), yet, while it was the collectivity of Israel that was a slave in Egypt, the command to remember and the action required in consequence are plainly directed to the individual Israelite. Thus the creditor who has rights to the labor of a debt slave must remember that "you were a slave in Egypt" as the motivation for releasing the debt slave in due time and doing so with generous provision (15:12–18). The individual addressed, down the ages, was in fact not a slave in Egypt; nevertheless, the burden of being "Israel" falls upon him, and "Israel" takes its full meaning in the fabric of his existence.

We have been placing some emphasis hitherto on the unity of the human person. To this must now be added the factor of the individual's relation to a collectivity. Both poles are essential to an understanding of the human constitution. The individual is the irreducible center of human consciousness,[29] for which the individual human body is "the condition of possibility."[30] Yet it is equally impossible to conceive of an entirely isolated individual, so much are we bound into social histories and practices. As James K. A. Smith has it, "The 'I' that perceives is always already a 'we.'"[31]

Conclusion

In the present chapter we have considered some of the ways in which the Old Testament conveys what may be called the human "constitution." We

---

29. For John Macquarrie, "there could be no normal human experience, no freedom, responsibility or transcendence, but for the *hegemenikon*, the leading edge which finds expression in the pronoun 'I'" (*In Search of Humanity*, 39).

30. James K. A. Smith, *Imagining the Kingdom: How Worship Works* (Grand Rapids: Baker Academic, 2013), 49.

31. Ibid., 84.

found that its characteristic vocabulary, often based in physiology, does not map onto separable components of the human life but rather functions in nuanced ways within the Old Testament's discourse. English translations, such as "heart," "soul," "mind," and "spirit," were always approximations and cannot be applied consistently to the given Hebrew expressions. The Old Testament's language for the human being, rather, confirms the point that they are portrayed in the complexity of their wholeness.

There is, furthermore, an interplay between the individual and the "social body,"[32] such that neither the "heart" nor the "soul" can be simply equated with the individual's inner life, nor with the notion of individual religion or spirituality in contrast with external or corporate facets of the religious life.[33] The point also shows an intersection between the unity of the human constitution as applied to the individual and the embeddedness of the individual in "social bodies." For ancient Israel, loving Yahweh "with all your heart, soul, and strength" was the foundation for the full range of Deuteronomic provisions, social, economic, and political. The human person is thus twice embodied: as the individual in his or her totality, and within the society to which she or he belongs. The point is not just about the human constitution; rather the double embodiment of human persons is inseparable from their call to realize the full potential of the human in God's world, a call that Deuteronomy couches as a choice between the "two ways" of life and death (Deut. 30:15).

32. The phrase is Smith's (ibid., 75).
33. It was once common to interpret Jeremiah's "new covenant" as a watershed in the development of Old Testament religion, when the prophet discovered the profound reality of the individual's personal piety over against external, national religion. The classic in this regard was John Skinner, *Prophecy and Religion* (Cambridge: Cambridge University Press, 1922). The polarizations of external and internal, corporate and individual, are not countenanced in the Old Testament writings generally, nor Deuteronomy in particular.

4

The Situated Self

The Self, Now and Then

In the preceding chapter we saw that the Old Testament has some distinctive answers to its own question, "What is the human being, that you pay attention to them?" These answers are inseparable from its particular language, concepts, and theology. Its range of vocabulary, such as "heart," "soul," and "spirit," far from depicting discrete components of the human being, serves to explore it in its complexity, both inward and embodied. The picture includes a certain unity of mind, emotion, and will, as well as a pervasive orientation of the individual toward others, both God and fellow humans. In our search for what makes the human, therefore, we have begun to find that the answer is bound into wider views of reality and meaning.

This is true as much for modern understandings of the self as for ancient ones. One cannot think in a detached way about "who I am." Ideas of human identity and meaning vary according to cultural and intellectual environments. The heading of this section, "The Self, Now and Then," is intended to convey this point about diverse conceptions of the person. Such diverse conceptions even coexist within what we may think of as "our" time and culture, and it is important to carry an awareness of this into our examination of what it means to inquire of the Bible for an answer to our question.

The point has been pursued in an influential work by the philosopher Charles Taylor, who has given a penetrating analysis of the rise of the "secular age" in the modern West out of its roots in late medieval religious apprehension of reality.[1] The broad thrust of his thesis is that versions of modern thought, notably what he calls "exclusive humanism,"[2] have developed their character not by simply shedding belief in God and the sacred, but in dialectical relationship with the medieval Christian construction of reality in which belief in God and the sacred was largely unquestioned. Modern secularism is thus itself a specific construction of reality with recognizable religious and intellectual ancestry, rather than the self-evidently value-free position, finally rid of the hindrances of superstition, that it often purports to be. If the medieval synthesis was undergirded, in Taylor's terms, by a certain "social imaginary," so also are modern apprehensions of reality, which have their own unexamined preconceptions about what is self-evident.[3]

The construal of the human person is a crucial aspect of the series of shifts that Taylor charts. People understood themselves differently then and now because they imagined themselves differently in relation to the external world. In the medieval "imaginary," the meanings apprehended and accepted by people were givens, fixed by the nature of the external reality that was accepted by all. The world so conceived was "enchanted"—that is, governed by forces that were beyond observation but that powerfully influenced people and events. In this world, demons and angels were vividly present to the imagination. People believed that they might become demon-possessed and hoped for protection from the "good magic" represented by the church.[4] The individual in this imagined world is what Taylor calls "porous,"[5] being unavoidably open to penetration by such influences.

By contrast, in what may still be the dominant modern "imaginary," the human person is conceived more individualistically, in a way that separates him or her more definitely both from society and from the external world. No longer "porous," this individual may be described as "buffered." That is, they think of themselves as more or less independent of influences either from

1. Charles Taylor, *A Secular Age* (Cambridge, MA: The Belknap Press of Harvard University Press, 2007). For a full analysis of Taylor's thesis, see Andrew T. Lincoln, "Spirituality in a Secular Age: From Charles Taylor to Study of the Bible and Spirituality," in *The Spirit That Inspires: Perspectives on Biblical Spirituality*, ed. Pieter de Villiers and Lloyd K. Pietersen, Acta Theologica Supplementum 15 (Bloemfontein, South Africa: University of the Free State Press, 2011), 61–80.

2. Taylor, *Secular Age*, 42.

3. Taylor's idea of a "social imaginary" is his way of describing the complex range of unspoken, precognitive assumptions that operate in any society; see the chapter entitled "Modern Social Imaginaries" in ibid., 171–76.

4. Ibid., e.g., 32, 42.

5. Ibid., 35; see also 42 ("the enchanted, porous world of our ancestors").

society or the external world. For them, meanings are no longer given and inescapable, but arise within the mind, and they can choose to protect themselves from unwanted external influences by the exercise of choice and will.[6]

"Social imaginaries" are not absolute in any time or place, however. If the Enlightenment appeared to set a new standard for understanding humanity in the supreme value of Reason, this was offset by an emerging awareness that the self and its relation to the universe had darker, mysterious aspects. The growing understanding of the vastness of the universe was one element in this, as was the advance of the belief in evolution, as well as a perception that the human consciousness itself had hidden depths. These elements were somewhat linked, in the sense that evolution gave to humans an unknown and impenetrable past, which left a legacy in the unconscious mind.[7] One effect of this was, for some, to rediscover profound connections between themselves and the external world.[8]

My point in observing this is to present the conception of the human person as a question, a challenge both to the understanding and to the practice of living. The intention of the modern reader to engage with the Bible in order to understand the nature of humanity turns out to have dimensions that might not be grasped at first. This is because, first, I may carry with me, unawares, notions of selfhood that I have imbibed from the common culture and that I have not yet sufficiently named and interrogated. And second, issues of the meaning of the self are in fact being openly contested in the wider cultural environment, in ways that bear directly on our modern attempt to allow the Bible to speak to us.

The chief areas of contention over the meaning of the person have already been encountered in our reading of Genesis 1–3. These include the nature of the human as both individual and relational, and the several aspects of the human's relationships, that is, between human persons, with God, and with the earth. They also include the matter of how human beings may be said to apprehend the truth about reality. In Genesis, this is at the heart of the humans' situation, as exposed in their desire to have their "eyes opened," to be "like God," and to "know good and evil." Knowledge of reality is thus entwined with the readiness to be accountable in God's world for the responsibilities

6. Ibid., 37–38, 41–42.
7. Ibid., 322–51, esp. 343–51.
8. Taylor cites Coleridge, Wordsworth, and the German Romantic Johann Gottfried von Herder, among others, and characterizes the kind of sentiment they represent thus: "As creatures who come to be who we are out of animal nature, which in turn rises from the non-animate, we cannot but feel a kinship with all living things, and beyond them with the whole of nature" (ibid., 344).

bestowed upon them in virtue of their creation "in the image and likeness of God."

In what follows, we consider these topics in the context of modern understanding and debate.

Individuality and Relationship

We are deeply habituated, in modern Western society, to the idea that as human beings we are individuals. There is a sense in which individuality is an irreducible aspect of the human experience. As Raymond Van Leeuwen puts it: "No matter how close humans come to knowing one another, even in the one flesh that is marriage, we remain individual persons, unique centers of consciousness and responsibility, each with his or her own hiddenness."[9] Yet we recognize that the way in which individuality is conceived in relation to groups varies across societies. Arguably, there is always a concept of individuality even in societies that place a strong emphasis on group identity. Biblical Israel had a strong sense of group identity. When individuals behaved badly in Israel their whole "house" might be held guilty, as in the case of Achan (Josh. 7), or at least shamed. The latter possibility explains why families were involved in careful negotiations in matters of sexuality and marriage (as in Deut. 22), or indeed in bringing their own rebellious children to public justice (21:18–21). As John Rogerson has shown, however, it is hard to prove that this strong solidarity derives from some kind of primitive mentality.[10] And criminal responsibility in the biblical laws is generally borne by individuals, and this is even established as a principle in one of them (Deut. 24:16; cf. Jer. 31:29–30; Ezek. 18).

Modern individualism has roots in ideas that pit individuals rather more radically against society and each other, and is usually traced to Thomas Hobbes (1588–1679).[11] In his thesis about the place of the individual in society he argued that the individual's interests are in principle at odds with the interests both of others and of society as a whole, in a "war of all against all."[12] The remedy against the chaos that must surely result from this natural way of

---

9. R. Van Leeuwen, "The Book of Proverbs," *NIB* 5:140. John Macquarrie uses the term "egoity" to refer to "the condition of being an ego or a self" (Macquarrie, *In Search of Humanity: A Theological and Philosophical Approach* [London: SCM, 1982], 38, 39). This is in connection with his point, already noted, about the *hegemenikon*, or "leading edge," that is expressed by means of the personal pronoun "I." See also ch. 3, n. 29.

10. John Rogerson, *Anthropology and the Old Testament* (Oxford: Blackwell, 1978), 55–58.

11. Thomas Hobbes, *Leviathan* (1651; repr., London: Dent, 1931).

12. Mary Midgley, *The Solitary Self* (Durham, UK: Acumen, 2010), 117.

things is in the relationship between the individual and the ruling power. The individual makes certain sacrifices of personal freedom by way of a "contract" in which they receive in exchange the benefits that government can provide, in the form of security. His thesis had a specific context and purpose—namely, to protest, in the context of seventeenth-century wars of religion, against the shocking waste of life on the part of people who were being "conned by pious nonsense into fighting battles that didn't concern them and ending up dead."[13] As a piece of writing, it has strong rhetorical and pragmatic features.

Routes from Hobbes to modern forms of individualism are charted by Mary Midgley. For her, the idea that the individual's interests might be at odds with those of others, or society at large, has modern echoes, for example, in the belief that we are fundamentally, indeed genetically, selfish. This understanding of individuality has gained iconic expression in Richard Dawkins's idea of the "selfish gene."[14] Midgley shows that Dawkins, while claiming the intellectual inheritance of Darwin, is indebted rather to T. H. Huxley, who painted a picture of early human development as a story of the internecine struggle for survival.[15] Darwin had a quite different understanding, actually rejecting "selfishness" as an explanation of conventional morality and finding rather a tendency to sociability and cooperation in human and animal history.[16] Midgley goes on to draw attention to the tendency of modern research to find interdependence and cooperation at the genetic level, and indeed that natural selection, with its implication of perpetual struggle, cannot be the only mechanism of evolution.[17]

Midgley wages war against all forms of reductionism in the attempt to explain human nature. The notion of deep-seated selfishness is one such reduction, because it fails to account for actual complexity in human development and motivation. Other forms of reductionism are found in Nietzsche and Freud, with their fixation on overriding motives for behavior in power and sex.[18] These have value in drawing attention to characteristics of ourselves that we find it hard to confront, but they fail as totalizing explanations.

In general, those explanations of human nature that lay heavy stress on the individual's ultimate solitariness, or selfishness, fail to explain significant aspects of human existence. Midgley's interest in factors of interdependence

---

13. Ibid., 117–19, esp. 118.

14. Richard Dawkins, *The Selfish Gene* (London: Granada, 1976).

15. Midgley, *Solitary Self*, 41–53; citing T. H. Huxley, "The Struggle for Existence and Its Bearing upon Man," *Nineteenth Century*, February 1888, 165.

16. Midgley, *Solitary Self*, 10–12; cf. 15–33, 83–86.

17. Ibid., 97–108, esp. 102. She chronicles modern offshoots of such thinking in radical individualists such as Ayn Rand (ibid., 127–28).

18. Ibid., 119.

and cooperation at fundamental levels of human development and being has consequences for her understanding of society and culture. And in observable experience, people often act in ways that belie a doctrine of radical selfishness, as when they live sacrificially, or even die, for the benefit of others. She is well aware here of reductive deconstructions of such behavior, for example in the extreme individualism of the political theorist Ayn Rand, who preached "the gospel of laissez-faire capitalism" in mid-twentieth-century America.[19]

Marilynne Robinson too, in her extensive critiques of modern forms of human reductionism, has shown how these ideas continue to exert a powerful hold on the popular Western imagination, finding them in the dominant version of capitalism in America (and the UK could be included in the point). When economic well-being is judged in terms of the relative success and failure of "competitors" and "rivals," when our gain is secured only by their loss, the spirit of Darwin is at work.[20] "Austerity" has assumed the form of an ethical imperative that gives a veneer of rectitude to what is in reality an antipathy to the concept of a cooperative society: "Whatever can be transformed from public wealth into private affluence is suddenly an insupportable public burden and should and must be put on the block. . . . There is at present a dearth of humane imagination for the integrity and mystery of other lives."[21] At stake in this relentless reduction of the human is, for Robinson, a hatred of civilization itself, that is, of the beneficial effects of institution and tradition that have nurtured countless lives over many generations and have been the cradle of "all the arts and sciences and philanthropies."[22]

For both Midgley and Robinson, radical individualism has distorted social and political life. The valuable concept of the freedom of the individual can become self-defeating if it is absolutized into radical independence from claims upon us by others or our own claims upon them.[23] The proper state

---

19. Ibid., 127–28. She quotes Rand: "The man who speaks to you of sacrifice, speaks of slaves and masters. And intends to be the master" (*The Fountainhead* [New York: Signet, 1943]). There are echoes of both Hobbes and Nietzsche in this analysis.

20. Marilynne Robinson, "Austerity as Ideology," in *When I Was a Child I Read Books* (London: Virago, 2012), 41–42. Robinson, therefore, may regard Darwin in a slightly less favorable light than Midgley (see above, n. 15).

21. Ibid., 45.

22. Marilynne Robinson, "Darwinism," in *The Death of Adam: Essays on Modern Thought* (1998; repr., New York: Picador, 2005), 61–62.

23. Midgley, *Solitary Self*, 123–34. She refers in this context to the topos in Romantic literature of the young person who strains to be free from parental control and other social conventions (121–24). A celebrated example of the desperation of this Romantic urge was J. W. von Goethe's early novel, *Die Leiden des jungen Werthers* (1774; English: *The Sorrows of Young Werther*), where the hero commits suicide as the only escape from the pain of an

of a human being is one in which persons are understood in their wholeness, "being aware of their various motives and being able to bring them all together,"[24] and in doing so to be open to influences from the surrounding world of which we form a part. This is wholly different from a view in which the individual retreats within himself or herself, into a self-preserving carapace. Such openness can have only benign consequences for civilized living and worthwhile human endeavors such as science and art. It also chimes with the biblical picture in Genesis 1–3 more than with a model of the individual's radical selfishness. Selfishness is of course an inescapable fact of experience. In biblical perspective, however, it is not defined by biological determinism, but always lies under the prophetic call to repent.

Implications of a Relational View of Personhood

Health

This view of the person as both unified and relational has implications in various kinds of practice. The point is illustrated by certain strands of modern thinking about medicine, where there is a recovery of the importance of understanding the whole person in the delivery of successful treatment. One influential advocate of this was the Swiss doctor Paul Tournier, with his concept of *médecine de la personne*,[25] who recognized the importance of understanding the patient as an individual, with their various beliefs and commitments, including their religious ones, since such commitments are inalienably part of them and therefore inseparable from their sense of well-being. Tournier's seminal work has been taken up by a number of scholars in academic medicine, notably in mental health.[26] For example, Thierry Collaud writes about the individual who is encountered in a medical context: "Every relationship with others is surrounded and conditioned by multiple third parties."[27] Citing Emmanuel Levinas, he continues:

---

impossible love affair. The publication of *Werther* reputedly triggered an epidemic of copycat suicides throughout Europe.

24. Midgley, *Solitary Self*, 143; see also 131–32. For the metaphor of life as a dance in a Jewish context, see also Melissa Raphael, *Judaism and the Visual Image: A Jewish Theology of Art* (London: Continuum, 2009), 150–79.

25. See his book of that name: *Médecine de la personne* (Neuchâtel: Delachaud et Niestlé, 1940).

26. See John Cox, Alastair V. Campbell, and Bill (K. W. M.) Fulford, eds., *Medicine of the Person: Faith, Science and Values* (London: Kingsley, 2007).

27. Thierry Collaud, "Beyond the Solitude for Two: Justice, Theology, and General Practice," in Cox, Campbell, and Fulford, *Medicine of the Person*, 157.

We can never entirely take in the person we meet. . . . There will always be something in him that opens out towards the infinite beyond, not least the world of other people. . . . [The patient] is there before me with the life he has lived and with the life that opens up before him, with his beliefs, his values, his hopes and his fears.[28]

He goes on to affirm a link between a person's health and their will or decision making, which may even involve "a fundamental reorientation of one's way of life"; and he goes further, putting health care in the realm of the search for well-being, or the "good life," "with and for others"—that is, observing the sense in which the human person's well-being cannot be abstracted from the various relationships within which he or she exists.[29]

A similar argument has been advanced by the theologian John Swinton. In a work on spirituality, Swinton writes of the intersection of five aspects of personhood, namely, the physical, intellectual, emotional, social, and spiritual—where "spiritual" includes notions of transcendence, meaning, value, hope, and purpose.[30] These five aspects are united by "the movement of the spirit" between them, so that they cannot be separated. Asserting the fundamentally spiritual nature of healing, he sets this against models of health care that see it chiefly on the technological plane. He cites N. N. Wig:

The dominance of techno-medicine has resulted in a redefinition of the issues which once preoccupied philosophers: What is human nature? How is happiness achieved? What is a good life? These questions have been restated as: What is normal? How can it be measured? What conclusions are generalizable?[31]

In Swinton's special concern with mental health, the challenges to the well-being of a person appear sharply as he documents cases of depression, in which the sufferers testify frequently to loss of meaning, abandonment, the disappointment of hopes, and the failure of relationships.[32] Healing was often associated with a renewed sense of connectedness with others, with

28. Ibid., 158–59.
29. Ibid., 161, 163. On the latter point, he cites Paul Ricoeur, *Oneself as Another* (Chicago: University of Chicago Press, 1995), 169–202 (172).
30. John Swinton, *Spirituality and Mental Health Care: Recovering a "Forgotten" Dimension* (London: Kingsley, 2001), 36–37. The five dimensions of personhood are based on Hildegard E. Peplau, *Interpersonal Relations in Nursing* (New York: Putnam's Sons, 1952).
31. N. N. Wig, Mary Hemingway Rees Memorial Lecture (World Federation of Mental Health, Trinity College, Dublin, 1995), 291 (Swinton, *Spirituality*, 51). He also cites, in a similar vein, Thomas Moore, *Care of the Soul: A Guide for Cultivating Depth and Sacredness in Everyday Life* (New York: Harper Collins, 1992), 206 (Swinton, *Spirituality*, 50).
32. Swinton, *Spirituality*, 112–22.

the relationships involved in the healing process themselves tending toward healing. And liturgy and worship could play a part in sustaining a sense of meaning in the face of intellectual difficulties and doubts. In his report of patients' accounts of their experiences of depression, some cited the Old Testament's psalms of lament as having enabled them to feel their problems were understood and identified with.[33]

These approaches to health share a concern for the broader concept of what is often called "well-being." In their attempts to understand a person's health, they draw attention to the question of how the person relates to the world she or he lives in and how these relationships bear upon one's capacity to live a full and flourishing life. It is significant that they emanate from both theological and nontheological sources. The growing literature on "positive psychology" or "positive philosophy" further illustrates the modern recovery of perspectives on the person that are recognizably biblical, even where the psychology in question is not expressly religious.[34]

Ecology

The healing sciences have furnished one example of ways in which the existence of human persons is deeply involved with the world external to them, chiefly in regard to God and other people. Another vital human connection is with the nonhuman world in which we live. Human beings are inevitably "placed," that is, their possibilities for life take shape in places.[35] The land as gift, and life-giving, is a central topic of Old Testament thought, developed at length in Deuteronomy. The psalmist spoke of blessing in terms of being brought out of distress into "a broad place" (Ps. 18:19[20]; cf. 16:6).

33. Ibid., 125–28. On the Psalms and the human person, see below, ch. 10.

34. C. Robert Cloninger, a practicing psychiatrist, interestingly refers to his enterprise as "positive philosophy," a category applied somewhat schematically from the biblical prophets and Plato through to Hegel, Gandhi, and the American Transcendentalists, such as Henry David Thoreau, for their transcendence of dualism and their awareness of what Freud called "oceanic feelings." See Cloninger, *Feeling Good: The Science of Well-Being* (Oxford: Oxford University Press, 2004), 68–69; cf. 106. "Negative philosophy," in contrast, is represented by, among others, William James, David Hume, and Machiavelli (ibid., 9–19). Martin Seligman is aware that religion may have a reinforcing effect on a person's sense of well-being, but thinks it is only one potentially positive influence among many. See Seligman, *Flourish* (London: Brealey, 2011), 90–92; also 259–62, where he chooses to avoid the term "spirituality," preferring "transcendence" to designate a "cluster of strengths" that are important, but in his view not necessarily religious.

35. The land as theological topic was brought to prominence by Walter Brueggemann, *The Land: Place as Gift, Promise, and Challenge in Biblical Faith*, 2nd ed., OBT (Minneapolis: Fortress, 2002); and on "place," see Craig Bartholomew, *Where Mortals Dwell: A Christian View of Place Today* (Grand Rapids: Baker Academic, 2011).

The topic of human "placedness," on its broadest canvas, leads to the generally acknowledged threats that are currently posed to the earth's biosystem, evident in what appear to be the increasing frequency and severity of catastrophic events. It is by now commonplace to recognize that the many parts that make up our world, including ourselves, are closely interconnected. Rachel Carson sounded the alarm on our failure to understand the extent to which human behavior could dramatically alter the planet, with serious implications for all of life. She exposed the damage inflicted by the extensive use of pesticides up to the 1960s, with shocking examples of their power to cause illness and death. But quite apart from individual tragedies, she showed how chemical interventions in agricultural processes intended for specific purposes could interfere drastically with nature's finely balanced interdependencies, with far-reaching and unpredictable effects.[36]

The way in which we think of our relationship with the biosystem has been affected, like other areas of human life, by our cultural and philosophical heritage. Pierre Hadot has written of two sharply contrasting approaches to scientific knowledge, which he labels Promethean and Orphic. In the former, with its echo of the myth of Prometheus, who stole fire from the gods for the benefit of humanity, the role of science is to wrench knowledge from a reluctant Nature. This concept may be associated with the early modern scientist Francis Bacon, who spoke of "torturing" Nature to force her to yield up her secrets.[37] Hadot repeatedly assigns the inspiration of such thinking to Genesis because of its alleged subjection of the created world to human control. He is not alone in thinking that Genesis, with its demythologization of ancient Near Eastern myths, robbed the created world of its mystery.[38] And in a celebrated essay, Lynn White argued that the divine command to humans in Genesis 1:28 to "subdue" the earth (KJV, NRSV, NIV) and "have dominion" over its creatures contributed to a mind-set in which the earth's natural resources were simply available for exploitation in the interests of commercial development and growth.[39]

Fifty years after Rachel Carson, there is widespread recognition that we face massive environmental challenges. There is also a realization that these cannot be disentangled from a sense of who we are as human beings. It is

---

36. Rachel Carson, *Silent Spring* (Boston: Houghton Mifflin, 1962; London: Penguin, 1965).

37. Pierre Hadot, *Veil of Isis: An Essay on the History of the Idea of Nature* (Cambridge, MA: The Belknap Press of Harvard University Press, 2006), 121.

38. The point was lamented by the poet Friedrich Schiller in his poem "Die Götter Griechenlands" (The Gods of Greece).

39. Lynn White Jr., "The Historical Roots of Our Ecologic Crisis," *Science* 155, no. 3767 (1967): 1203–7.

not just that we must be more careful with a world conceived as a living space with limited resources; it is also that we have an unalterable relationship with the planet that belongs to our nature as humans. James Lovelock, in his influential "Gaia theory," proposes a kind of remythologization or "reenchantment" of the earth, in which it is seen as a living organism with the capacity to preserve its necessary balances by regulating itself.[40] This is one way of reimagining the world in response to the destructive imaginings that have been implicated in the current crisis. The Gaia hypothesis may overstate the earth's self-regulating capacity. Yet the dangers of interfering with the delicate balances and profound interdependencies in the "Goldilocks zone" that is our world are all too clear.[41] If Prometheus provided an icon for masterful exploitation, Hadot's alternative icon is Orpheus, whose music was so beautiful that it could charm nature. By invoking it, he advocates an approach based on an understanding of the limits of the human capacity to know and control. At the same time, he expresses a perception that the world, or Nature, resists being subjected to instrumental use. Hadot grounds his thought in philosophical sources, yet the theme of the dangers of knowledge is clearly also biblical, the story of the garden in Genesis 2–3 standing like a sentinel against Promethean readings of Genesis 1.[42]

The earth crisis now exerts an enormous influence on human consciousness, affecting every sphere of life, and may rightly be regarded as a spiritual issue. Ursula King has addressed the relationship between spirituality and global issues in several places.[43] For her the crisis facing humanity is not a matter of ecology in the narrow sense, but rather "a deep spiritual crisis" that calls for "a new vision, a new global order."[44] In this crisis many areas that pose challenges to us in the twenty-first century are interrelated, including matters of justice, economics, gender, racialism, religion, war and violence, health, population, poverty, and hunger. Human beings are being forced, perhaps for the first time, to face up to the oneness of humanity, with the moral and spiritual challenges that that entails. The spiritual nature of the crisis is being recognized within a

40. James Lovelock, *Gaia: A New Look at Life on Earth* (Oxford: Oxford University Press, 2000).

41. The term "Goldilocks zone," where it is "not too hot, not too cold, but just right," is sometimes used for the habitable zone around a star—that is, the space in which conditions are right for supporting life.

42. See above, ch. 2, on Gen. 2–3.

43. Ursula King, "Can Spirituality Transform our World?," *Journal for the Study of Spirituality* 1 (2011): 17–34; King, *The Search for Spirituality: Our Global Quest for Meaning and Fulfillment* (Norwich, UK: Canterbury Press, 2009).

44. I am quoting here from a paper given by Ursula King in a Bible and Spirituality seminar at the University of Gloucestershire, which was based on the works cited above.

range of academic disciplines, such as health and education, in a rediscovery that spirituality is not just something pursued inwardly by individuals. She cites the *Earth Charter*, published in 2000, following at length on the Earth Summit at Rio de Janeiro in 1992, accommodating voices from across cultural and religious perspectives, expressing the awareness that the earth is home to a great diversity of peoples. And she speaks of a new "earth-consciousness," manifest in a sense of wonder toward the planet engendered in media such as television, with its power to observe the living planet in unprecedented ways. Such consciousness has also made its mark in new academic methodologies, such as "ecocriticism."[45]

In King's advocacy of a new vision for a humanity that takes seriously its inalienable commonality and its integral relationship with the planet, she invokes Christian thinkers across a wide spectrum. She cites, for example, Hans Küng and Karl-Josef Kuschel:

> Limitless exploitation of the natural foundations of life, ruthless destruction of the biosphere, and militarization of the cosmos are all outrages. As human beings we have a special responsibility—especially with a view to future genera- tions—for Earth and the cosmos, for the air, water, and soil. We are *all inter- twined together* in this cosmos and we are all dependent on each other. Each one of us depends on the welfare of all. Therefore the dominance of humanity over nature and the cosmos must not be encouraged. Instead we must cultivate living in harmony with nature and the cosmos.[46]

Christian responses to the need to alter the way we live have come from scientists and theologians. In science, Sir John Houghton has had a leading role in international thinking about climate change.[47] Ellen Davis has made the human relationship with the environment a key term for biblical exegesis and theology, in a move that has become influential and irrevocable.[48]

45. See, for example, Greg Garrard, *Ecocriticism* (Oxford: Routledge, 2012). I am grateful to my colleague Shelley Saguaro for introducing me to Garrard's work.

46. Hans Küng and Karl-Josef Kuschel, eds., *A Global Ethic: The Declaration of the Parlia- ment of the World's Religions* (London: SCM, 1993), 26 (emphasis original). She also endorses Teilhard de Chardin's concept of a deep connectedness between humans and planet, encoded in their long history together, such that biological, social, cultural, and spiritual evolution are closely interrelated.

47. Sir John Houghton was Director General (later Chief Executive) of the UK Meteorological Office (1983–91) and cochaired the Intergovernmental Panel on Climate Change (1988–2002). His writings for nonscientific audiences include: *Does God Play Dice?* (Leicester, UK: Inter-Varsity, 1988); *Global Warming: The Complete Briefing*, 3rd ed. (Cambridge: Cambridge University Press, 2004). He has also chaired the John Ray Initiative, a Christian organization dedicated to furthering Christian and scientific thinking about the environment.

48. Ellen F. Davis, *Scripture, Culture, and Agriculture: An Agrarian Reading of the Bible* (Cambridge: Cambridge University Press, 2009). Her observation that the final phrase of Gen.

One of the interesting factors in Davis's work is the influence on her of Wendell Berry, farmer, poet, and novelist. Berry writes of the responsibility of poets to work with their communities in order to reimagine, or "re-member," their own membership "in the wholeness and the Holiness of creation."[49] Here, as in other contexts that we have noticed, the category of the imagination comes strongly into play. Berry attributes to the biblical prophets a "tragic imagination." The idea of the imagination is similar to the Old Testament's concept of the "heart" (*lēb*), variously taken as "heart" and "mind" in translations. Jeremiah describes the human "heart" as "deceitful above all things" (Jer. 17:9), and for Berry the prophets "seek to restore the heart to its proper function, which is often to assess the depth, scope, and causes of the tragedies that grip our world," or to put it differently, to restore the "tragic imagination," by which we have a capacity to reckon with loss so that it can be survived.[50]

The account of the environmental crisis and responses to it has shown, again, how the human being is interrogated with existential questions that place him or her inevitably within a nexus of relationships, both with other people and with the external world. These questions are not just theoretical. While specific problems may have specific solutions, as when a physical disease may be cured by a suitable medical treatment, the totality of the human condition raises unavoidable questions about humanity itself. These have a ring about them that may be called "prophetic," and therefore are such as to call for a response. And the nature of the response has several strands, which include the intellectual, the moral, and the spiritual. This takes us to our next question, how we apprehend the reality of which we are a part.

How Do We Know?

If we as persons are deeply connected with both society and the external world, how does this bear upon that other contentious modern question concerning how we have knowledge of ourselves and our world? In the premodern Christian world, knowledge was inseparable from the revelation of God. But the story of our changing view of ourselves since Christendom is closely bound

---

2:5 could carry the connotation of the human *serving* the needs of the soil (29) was taken up, for example, by Terence Fretheim in his own *God and World in the Old Testament: A Relational Theology of Creation* (Nashville: Abingdon, 2005). See also Hilary Marlow, *Biblical Prophets and Contemporary Environmental Ethics* (Oxford: Oxford University Press, 2009); Arthur Walker-Jones, *The Green Psalter: Resources for an Ecological Spirituality* (Minneapolis: Fortress, 2009).

49. Wendell Berry, "Writer and Religion," in *What Are People For?* (New York: North Point, 1990), 78; cited in Davis, *Scripture, Culture, and Agriculture*, 16.

50. Davis, *Scripture, Culture, and Agriculture*, 16.

up with knowledge. Descartes's dictum "I think, therefore I am" posed a challenge to the belief that humans know themselves by means of the word of God. In the thought of Kant, the limits of human knowledge are determined by the limits of Reason, so that what lies beyond such limits is a matter of speculation. These moves provided a context for all subsequent discussion of the possibilities of knowledge. Such debate is not uniform, of course. Some of it is expressly theological, and some more generally philosophical.

Faced with the widespread modern belief that we cannot have true knowledge of anything that lies beyond our natural powers of observation, we are seeking instead a distinctively theological response that situates true knowledge of self, God, and the external world in the realms of worship and practice, in which knowledge is inseparable from wisdom and the "knower" is personally committed and open to transformation. This kind of answer avoids engaging modern epistemology on its own cerebral terms, but embraces the capacity to know within a distinctive version of the human person.

Such a view of knowledge confronts modern thinking on a broad front. One boundary dispute concerns the nature of scientific knowledge.[51] Not surprisingly, there are modern scientists who are influenced by that philosophical strand in post-Enlightenment thought that is skeptical about the possibility of metaphysical knowledge. What is interesting is the contentious way in which this is sometimes expressed. Peter Atkins, for example, is convinced that science has the exclusive capacity to unlock the secrets of the universe. He contends that "scientists, with their implicit trust in reductionism, are privileged to be at the summit of knowledge, and to see further into truth than any of their contemporaries. . . . While poetry titillates and theology obfuscates, science liberates."[52]

This huge claim proposes a model of knowledge and truth in which only a kind of processing of information has any validity. The disqualification of theology on principle is characteristic of a certain branch of modern science[53]

---

51. The term is almost tautologous, since "science" (Latin *scientia*) originally meant simply "knowledge."

52. Peter Atkins, "The Limitless Power of Science," in John Cornwell, ed., *The Frontiers of Scientific Vision* (Oxford: Oxford University Press, 1995), 123; cited in Midgley, *Solitary Self*, 91. See Midgley, *Solitary Self*, 91–92, for further examples; also Midgley, *The Myths We Live By* (London: Routledge, 2011), 18–29. See also Northrop Frye on the capacity of poetry to keep alive a connection with "the primitive and archaic," understood not as something that civilization outgrows but rather as a witness to fundamental perceptions about reality (*The Great Code: The Bible and Literature* [San Diego: Harcourt Brace Jovanovich, 1982], 22–23, 37).

53. Classic examples are Richard Dawkins, *The God Delusion* (London: Bantam, 2006), and Christopher Hitchens, *God Is Not Great: How Religion Poisons Everything* (London: Atlantic, 2008).

because it regards theology as a rival claimant in the area of understanding. It is noteworthy, even in the short passage from Atkins cited above, how exclusive rights are asserted for science in areas in which theology also makes claims, namely, in access to "truth" and in the capacity to "liberate." Remarkable too, and perhaps less expected, is the dismissive aside on poetry. But this also is telling, for poetry makes its own claim, by virtue of its powerful presence in human history and culture, to express truth about reality. For Atkins, such ideas must be refuted in the name of the "one way" of science.

Claims for the power of science, then, can take on a metaphysical quality, where it is seen as the key to the unlocking of everything worth knowing. For Terry Eagleton, this kind of faith in reason as the supreme arbiter of truth fails to understand the way in which reason functions as part of a person's whole being. Reason is indispensable, but "it is only if reason can draw on energies and resources deeper, more tenacious, and less fragile than itself, that it is capable of prevailing."[54] Believing in God is not the same as believing in some object within creation, nor in a theory or a proposition. Rather, "faith is for the most part performative rather than propositional."[55] This is not intended to undermine creedal statements. Rather it points to the centrality of practice in the knowing of God. And it does so on the basis of a conception of the human being as a complex mix of capacities, all of which operate in their apprehension of the world to which they belong.

The realization that knowing God is of a different order from knowing other things lies behind the testimonies of believing scientists. John Polkinghorne, with an allusion to Anselm's dictum *credo ut intelligam* (I believe in order to understand), makes the point that scientific thinking depends on some initial view about the nature of reality.[56] Polkinghorne also reflects on the nature of language. For him, metaphor and poetry are necessary modes of discourse for speaking about certain kinds of reality: "Metaphor is the poet's indispensable way of expressing what is on the edge of inexpressibility."[57] Here he is thinking about biblical language and language about God, with reference

54. Terry Eagleton, *Reason, Faith, and Revolution: Reflections on the God Debate* (New Haven: Yale University Press, 2009), 110. See also Keith Ward, *Why There Almost Certainly Is a God* (Oxford: Lion, 2008). Ward's title takes a cue from a chapter heading in Dawkins's *The God Delusion*. Ward shows, among other things, that Dawkins's idea that he is propounding an alternative to the "God hypothesis" fails to distinguish among a wide range of philosophical options concerning the nature of reality (Ward, *Why There Almost Certainly Is a God*, 11–14).

55. Eagleton, *Reason, Faith, and Revolution*, 111.

56. John Polkinghorne, *Reason and Reality: The Relationship between Science and Theology* (London: SPCK, 1991), 6. On the back cover of *Reason and Reality*, he is said to be "the only ordained member of the Royal Society." The citation is from the *New Scientist*.

57. Ibid., 31.

to Paul Ricoeur and others.[58] The point is telling in view of the remark of
Atkins about poetry, cited above, and crucial to a biblical understanding of
the human situation and experience.[59] Francis Collins too, one of those who
deciphered the human genome, argues (citing Aquinas) that faith can have
rational foundations and deplores attacks on faith that caricature it as essentially irrational. For Collins, the study of genomes, animal as well as human,
furnished "elegant evidence of the relatedness of all living things" and led him
to embrace a belief in theistic evolution.[60] What these and others recognize is
that there is more to knowing than the processing of information, and that
there is more than one way to know. Furthermore, this is a function of the
nature of the human being.

Mary Midgley has also protested against the "tyranny" and "imperialism"
of exclusive science.[61] She uses the illustration of the different maps that answer
to different kinds of questions: a road map will help you get from London
to Cheltenham, but a walker will need a physical map to show the nature of
a terrain. The deeper point is that the way we know is complex. Intellect,
emotion, desire, and imagination are not at odds with each other, but unite
in thought and action.[62] And in her work on understanding John's Gospel,
Sandra Schneiders speaks of understanding as "the object of *ontological*
inquiry": "For humans as humans, to be is to be-in-the-world participatively,
which is what we call understanding."[63]

The topic of knowledge can be put within a more expressly theological
context. The work of Karl Barth marked one kind of response to radical
skepticism about the possibility of knowing God. His reassertion of such a
possibility through God's own act of self-disclosure in his Word came at the
expense of "natural theology" and remains a reference point for much modern theological discourse. After Barth theology is divided. Sarah Coakley has

58. He refers to Ricoeur's concepts of "surplus of meaning" and symbolism. See Paul Ricoeur,
Discourse and the Surplus of Meaning (Fort Worth: Texas Christian University Press, 1976).
Polkinghorne also cites Janet Martin Soskice, *Metaphor and Religious Language* (Oxford:
Oxford University Press, 1985); and Frye, *Great Code*, on the same topic.

59. We return to the topic of language at several points in the present study, especially in
chs. 5 and 9.

60. Francis Collins, *The Language of God: A Scientist Presents Evidence for Belief* (London:
Pocket Books, 2007), 198–99. He finds that Darwin's own sense of wonder about the harmony
of things led him, on one occasion, to pronounce himself a theist (ibid., 99).

61. Midgley, *Myths We Live By*, 18–29, 178–80.

62. Ibid., 30–41. Note also her admiration of the Gaia hypothesis in Midgley, *Science and
Poetry* (London: Routledge, 2001), 237–49, 285–88. Jürgen Moltmann has also written positively
about Gaia in *Ethics of Hope*, trans. Margaret Kohl (Minneapolis: Fortress, 2012), 109–11.

63. Sandra Schneiders, *The Revelatory Text: Interpreting the New Testament as Sacred
Scripture* (Collegeville, MN: Liturgical Press, 1999), 18 (emphasis original).

attributed forms of liberal theology to what she calls "Kantian nescience," where claims to have direct knowledge of God are held to be philosophically impossible. Theology here becomes "'imaginative construction,' God-in-Godself being radically shrouded in 'mystery.'"[64] Coakley's account of the self in relation to the knowledge of God is instructive.

For Coakley, lines to recovery cannot simply be a matter of turning the clock back to a premodern era, nor can they ignore contemporary claims to knowledge in the areas of the social sciences and moral philosophy. Theology, pursuing its vocation to know and speak about God, must listen to modern voices that enter caveats about the validity of knowledge, because these necessarily chasten and sharpen the theological endeavor.[65] Coakley identifies three specific modern challenges to theological knowledge, or in her terms, "systematic theology." These are the claims, first, that systematic theology makes God the object of human knowledge and is therefore idolatrous; second, that it entails a hegemonic, totalizing bid for power, which necessarily excludes marginalized voices; and third, from a certain brand of feminism, that it is "phallocentric"—that is, that it is shaped by male modes of thought, which aim at mastery and suppress the imagination.[66] These challenges go beyond the empiricism of a critic such as Peter Atkins (noted above) to interrogate the ways in which theology conceives its own task.

The relevance of such challenges to any attempt to think biblically about what it is to be human is clear, however. The danger of idolatry attends the theological enterprise by definition; and modern versions of what it means to be human (as in Freud) readily draw attention to the barely apprehended seductions of various forms of power. Coakley's response to such reductionist moves involves a conception of theology as inseparable from the practice of seeking God. The biblical idea of "seeking God's face" is a key expression of this, with its aspiration toward close and intimate encounter, yet it recognizes that such encounter is by its nature profoundly disturbing.[67] Old Testament writers and characters are troubled by the belief that one cannot "see God's face and live" (Exod. 33:20). The vision of God is of the essence of worship and even an imperative, offering life (Ps. 42:2; Amos 5:6). The trope is regularly undermined by the narratives in which it is set (as in Exod. 33:11; Isa.

---

64. Sarah Coakley, *God, Sexuality, and the Self: An Essay 'On the Trinity'* (Cambridge: Cambridge University Press, 2013), 63, 77–78. She cites two works by Gordon D. Kaufman as examples of such a reading of Kant: *God the Problem* (Cambridge, MA: Harvard University Press, 1972) and *In Face of Mystery: A Constructive Theology* (Cambridge, MA: Harvard University Press, 1991).

65. Coakley, *God, Sexuality, and the Self*, 17–18, 66–99.

66. Ibid., 42–43.

67. Ibid., 21. She cites Exod. 24:10–11; Ps. 27:8; and Matt. 5:8, among other texts.

6:5–8; Judg. 13:22–23). Yet the vision retains its capacity to disturb. There is no human power or mastery in this depiction.

The answer, therefore, to reductive readings of human aspiration to knowledge of God is in terms of an orientation of the self to God in contemplation, prayer, and practice, in readiness for personal transformation in ways that are not foreseen or subject to one's own control. This theology is woven into the fabric of life, or in Coakley's terms, "on the way" (*in via*), a *théologie totale*. It is a road of discovery that is thoroughly engaged with the world but that is forearmed against temptations to idolatrous certainties. The way to truthful knowledge of God and self is through what she calls "un-mastery." It is allied with the apophatic strain in Christian theology, a "knowing in unknowing."[68]

The latter formulation needs to be distinguished from the "Kantian nescience" that she opposes. The notion of "unknowing" is by no means alien to biblical theology. For the psalmists, the felt absence or hiddenness of God is a recurrent theme, especially in the psalms of lament, as in the book of Lamentations.[69] The Wisdom literature too steers a course between the invitation to explore the creation in the personified voice of Wisdom (Prov. 8:1–21) and a strong sense of human limitations (Job 28; 38–41).[70] The limits and dangers of "knowing" are heralded on the threshold of the biblical canon in the story of Eden, with its guarding of the "tree of the knowledge of good and evil" and its portrayal of the desire for knowledge as potentially idolatrous (Gen. 2–3). Coakley's concept of "unknowing" is in line with this. Her formula "knowing in unknowing" aims precisely to guard against idolatry, even as the possibility of knowing is affirmed.

She appeals here also to the category of imagination. This is a vital element, both in her recasting of systematic theology and for our attempt to understand a biblical view of the human. The faculty of imagination can be called in aid of that skeptical version of theology typified by Gordon Kaufman's "imaginative construction."[71] In Coakley's treatment, however, the imagination has the dual power either to carry forward the project of the person's transformation or to subvert it into idolatry.[72] The training of the imagination, therefore, is involved in that seeking of the divine face that characterizes the theological enterprise. This is to recognize the aesthetic dimension in the

---

68. Coakley, *God, Sexuality, and the Self*, 44–46. For theology *in via*, see 15–20; for *théologie totale*, see 34–35 and nn. 66–69.

69. See Samuel E. Balentine, *The Hidden God: The Hiding of the Face of God in the Old Testament*, OTM (Oxford: Oxford University Press, 1983).

70. See further below on this, in ch. 9.

71. See above, n. 64.

72. Coakley, *God, Sexuality, and the Self*, 20.

human experience of God's world, a dimension that is not peripheral, but enmeshed with the life of worship and practice.[73]

The imaginative aspect of human being, moreover, is not a function of the mind only, but is also allied with the theological purpose of reframing human desire. Central to Coakley's thesis is the belief that all human desire, including the "erotic," has its origin in the desire for God, a perception that is shared by some modern biblical interpreters.[74] Her attention to this topic is part of her concern not to pursue theology as a cerebral, intellectual exercise, but to set her account of the historic doctrine of the Trinity "within a constellation of considerations—spiritual, ascetic, sexual, social . . ."[75] Her point, therefore, is to resist the particular Platonic development in which sexuality is relegated to the world that must be left behind in the spiritual ascent, a development that had one deposit in the church's glorification of celibacy and the denigration of particularly feminine forms of human experience such as childbirth.[76] Desire, far from being simply a synonym for sex, is a sign of humanity's condition in relation to God. Indeed, *desire is more fundamental than 'sex.'* This idea involves turning Freud on his head: "It is not that physical 'sex' is basic and 'God' is ephemeral; rather it is God who is basic, and 'desire' the precious clue that ever tugs at the heart, reminding the human soul—however dimly—of its created source."[77] The aim of theology, viewed in this way, is "to examine, and chasten, its own desires, and to draw all dimensions of the self transformatively into that quest."[78] In accordance with her declared intention to explore God as Trinity, the Holy Spirit plays an indispensable role in this.[79]

Conclusion

In the foregoing, there have been two pervasive guiding themes. The first is that there is no universal concept of the human person, or in modern parlance, the self. All notions of personhood are culturally conditioned, and any attempt to understand it needs to be aware of the potency of such conditioning. We

73. We return to this topic also in ch. 9.

74. See below, ch. 8, on sexuality, and especially Ellen Davis's reading of the Song of Songs in Davis, *Proverbs, Ecclesiastes, and the Song of Songs*, Westminster Bible Companion (Louisville: Westminster John Knox, 2000).

75. Coakley, *God, Sexuality, and the Self*, 5.

76. Ibid., 8–9.

77. Ibid., 10 (emphasis original).

78. Ibid., 66.

79. Ibid., 13–15, 21–22. Coakley's project, as her title suggests, is essentially trinitarian.

saw that certain modern versions of the human condition, though widely held to be value-free and unassailable, stand in fact on deep-lying theoretical foundations. There is, moreover, a strong tendency in modern constructions, whether scientific, economic, or more broadly cultural, toward a reductionist view of the human person.[80]

Second, there are modern recoveries of notions of the self that are akin to biblical ones. These recognize especially the themes of relatedness to others and the environment, the role of personal engagement in the process of understanding anything, and the deep connection between human self-understanding and various forms of policy and practice. There are self-consciously theological forms of expressing such connections.

Our guiding question—"What is the human being, that you should pay attention to them?"—is now seen to have a context in our attempt to understand concepts of the self both in the biblical world and in our own. Because such understandings are always located in history and experience, they are always subject to change. We turn now to see how the biblical writers themselves came to terms with the need constantly to rethink who they, and "Israel," were.

80. The concept of reductionism is variously employed by Midgley, Robinson, and Coakley. See also the perceptive essay by Dee Carter, "Unholy Alliances: Religion, Science, and Environment," *Zygon* 36, no. 2 (2011): 357–72. She writes: "Perhaps the single most important move in raging against the dying of the light is to rage against the reductionist account of what it means to be human in this world" (369). Against such views she places the biblical concept of the human created in the "image of God." She has in mind in particular the ways in which the operation of grace and redemption in the created order establishes a "commonality of focus within which the goods of the human and the nonhuman might be considered together" (ibid.).

5

The Old Testament's Transformations and the "Spiritual Sense"

In the preceding chapter, we have been considering some of the ways in which our understanding of what it is to be human is deeply affected by the specific environments in which we live, with their various cultural and cognitive characteristics. As modern people have their symbols and narratives, so too did the people of the Old Testament, and some attention to this important factor is indispensable to our task of interpretation.

The Old Testament: Metaphor and Re-presentation

Our first proposition is that biblical language has the capacity to transcend specific situations in life and become relevant to readers and worshipers generally. The metaphorical quality of the Bible's discourse is indispensable to its depiction of the human. By "metaphor," I mean not only the figure of speech, as when Yahweh's speech is expressed as a lion roaring (Amos 1:2), but also in a sense closer to "typology"—that is, where events, stories, and characters undergo re-presentation in new situations and take on new meanings. It is this quality that enables the human experience that is relayed by the Old

81

Testament to be mediated through the story and life of a particular people, which we may provisionally call ancient Israel.

The Old Testament had its genesis and development in the history, language, and culture of this people. I have said they may be provisionally named ancient Israel because, in fact, the people of the Old Testament is not precisely equivalent to this, and the point is important for our present purpose. By the Old Testament's own account, the kingdom that bore the name Israel, with its capital in Samaria, ceased to exist in 722 BCE (2 Kings 17:1–18:12), a victim of the perpetual political and military ferment in the region. It had existed alongside its sister kingdom of Judah, which incorporated Jerusalem, since the division of the older Davidic-Solomonic kingdom in about 930 BCE. The kingdom of Judah remained for a little over a century, when it fell in turn in 587 BCE, and many of its people were taken into exile in Babylon (2 Kings 25). Thereafter, people from Judah retained and developed their identity in a variety of places, including Babylon, Persia (according to the book of Esther), Egypt, and indeed Judah. Exiles gradually returned to Judah following the decree of the Persian king Cyrus in 539 BCE (Ezra 1:1–4), and on some accounts, many had never left in the first place.[1] Under Persia, Judah became the province of Yehud. In turn the people of Yehud fell under the power of Greece, and finally Rome. Jewish (or "Judean") identity was shaped in all these places, as the great deposit of Jewish law and learning, the Babylonian Talmud, testifies by its name. The Old Testament emerged in the course of this fractured history, in a process that cannot be wholly accounted for. Its unifying factors are its language (Hebrew, apart from a few chapters of Aramaic)[2] and the continuous thread of a story that goes back to the deliverance of a people enslaved in Egypt.

This outline of Israel's history implies many questions about its actual course and how it may be reconstructed. There continue to be major issues about the origins of Israel, now widely thought by scholars to have arisen indigenously in Palestine rather than to have come out, fully formed, from Egypt. And at the other end of the period, a lively school of thought attributes the writing of the Old Testament to a very specific setting within the story sketched above, namely, through the work of an elite group in Persian Yehud.[3] I make no attempt here to settle or contribute to such questions.

1. On the myth of the "empty land," see Hans M. Barstad, *The Myth of the Empty Land: A Study in the History and Archaeology of Judah in the "Exilic" Period* (Oslo: Scandinavian University Press, 1996).

2. Dan. 2:4b–7:28; Ezra 4:8–6:18.

3. So Philip R. Davies, *In Search of "Ancient Israel,"* JSOTSup 148 (1992; repr., Sheffield, UK: Sheffield Academic, 1995).

However, our brief history draws attention to two things. First, it means that any reading of the Old Testament has to try to understand as much as possible about the cradle of this Hebraic literature. When the prophet Isaiah says:

> Let me sing for my beloved
>   a love song concerning his vineyard:
> My beloved had a vineyard
>   on a very fertile hill . . . (Isa. 5:1 RSV)

and continues with his famous Song of the Vineyard (Isa. 5:1b–7), a good deal of knowledge is presupposed beyond the surface meaning of the text, knowledge that first hearers were presumably expected to have in order for them to get the point of the poetic rhetoric. Broadly, it encompasses a historical experience and an understanding of its meaning already in place, not to say something about ancient vineyards. The point can be extended across the entirety of the Old Testament.

However, there is an important sense in which the meaning of the texts cannot be contained by this ancient "Israelite/Judean" matrix. In fact, an essential aspect of the process by which a highly disparate literary deposit came to form what we know as the Old Testament, or Hebrew Bible, was precisely an extraction of texts from "original" situations and their re-placement into new ones, both historical and literary. Canons incorporate and invite interpretations and reinterpretations, and the very differences between the Jewish and Christian canons speak eloquently of this point. So successfully has the literature been reassigned that the quest for "original" situations has to a large extent become a matter of guesswork.

Here then is a factor in reading the Old Testament that is both complicating and liberating. When the leading voice in Psalm 124 invites others to join him in thanksgiving with the words "Let Israel now say" (v. 1), we immediately face the question, what is meant here by "Israel"? Commentators suggest that the phrase implies that a song of thanksgiving, originally by an individual or a small group, came to be used by the worshiping community as a whole.[4] But this community can only be defined in the most general terms, as the (postexilic) cultic community centered on Jerusalem. We know very little about the setting of the psalm. It celebrates a deliverance from enemies, which might have had any number of occasions. And the group that is singing it is

---

4. E.g., Leslie C. Allen, *Psalms 101–150*, WBC 21 (Waco: Word, 1983), 165; cf. Hans-Joachim Kraus, *Psalms 60–150*, trans. Hilton C. Oswald (Minneapolis: Fortress, 1989), 441: "'Israel' refers to the totality of the cultic community assembled for worship."

expressing its belief that they, as the proper bearers of the name Israel, have experienced a deliverance by Yahweh, God of Israel. This interpretation is made possible by a tradition about Yahweh's disposition to deliver "Israel" from distress, as evidenced in other situations, now past. What was true in those past situations and events can become true in new ones, in new ways. There may indeed be a layered reception history behind the appearance of this expression of faith in this place in the Psalter, embracing a succession of reapplications. The psalm has, in any case, had the capacity to travel, to carry with it a history of connotations and to accrue new meanings on the way. It is a metaphorical process.

Both particularity and metaphor are deeply embedded in the Old Testament literature and its capacity for meaning. Historical memory, with its high points in the exodus from Egypt, the possession of land, and the rule of a powerful Israelite king in David, is inseparable from its conceptuality. But these historical kernels become the nub of imaginative reexpression. Thus, around the youngest son of Jesse, who became king against the run of convention (1 Sam. 16), a web of memory and expectation is woven. He becomes the "son" of Yahweh, enthroned on Zion (Ps. 2:6–9), his rule established over other nations, and a guarantee of the moral and natural order (Ps. 72). This then gives shape to future hope. In Isaiah 11, set against the broad context of the Assyrian threat to both Israel and Judah, the "shoot from the stump of Jesse" becomes the paradigm of just rule (Isa. 11:1–5), inaugurating a paradisiacal peace (vv. 6–9). At the same time, the memory of exodus is applied to an expectation of a regathering of the exiles of Israel and Judah from the four corners of the earth (vv. 10–12), with Assyria in the place of Egypt and the "River" (the Euphrates) the decisive body of water that they cross miraculously, dry-shod (vv. 15–16). What God has done for Israel in the past thus becomes a way of conceiving of all of history.

The book of Isaiah carries the point further, so that the reader's hold on original contexts becomes gradually less secure. In Isaiah 7 the prophet's confrontation with King Ahaz has a tangible context in the Syro-Ephraimite crisis of 734–733 BCE, and in chapters 36–39 he addresses King Hezekiah during the Assyrian siege of Jerusalem (701 BCE). It is in this Assyrian part of the book that Davidic-messianic hopes are expressed (Isa. 9:2–7[1–6]; 11:1–9). But in the striking hiatus between chapters 39 and 40, which passes over the fall of Judah and the exiling of many of its people to Babylon, there is a strong hint that historical context has become subordinate to an overarching theological purpose. The new background is the hope of deliverance from Babylonian captivity, now accompanied not by overt messianic expectations (it is the Medo-Persian King Cyrus who is *māšîaḥ* here; 45:1) but by a new concept of Israel as "Servant," into which hopes of a deliverer have somehow been rolled (42:1–7; 49:1–6; 50:4–9; 52:13–53:12) and which evidently involves suffering. The assignment of a historical identity to this figure, and an occasion for his suffering, is notoriously hazardous. And while Isaiah 56–66 is usually assigned to the postexilic Persian period in Palestine, the background historical issues are by now quite elusive, and the image of a deliverer figure has become a kind of composite of those that went before (as in Isa. 61:1–4).[5] For this reason, Brevard Childs thought that the canonical shaping of the book of Isaiah testifies to a kind of theological reflection that is not dependent on the original context of individual sayings; rather, its "various witnesses hold in common a concern to testify to the ways of God with Israel and the world, both in judgment and in redemption."[6]

This ability to turn the specific into paradigm is completely central to the Old Testament imagination. Parallels, or doubling, are not just effects in poetic expression,[7] but run through the Old Testament story. Israel crosses the Reed Sea out of Egypt (Exod. 14–15), then, in a clear echo of that event, crosses the River Jordan in spate, again by miraculous means and with heavily symbolic overtones (Josh. 3–4). By this means the connotations of the first miraculous deliverance are carried over into the second. Even the (double) narrative of the Reed Sea crossing is already a reimagining of divine battles with Chaos, extant in the broad background of the biblical literature.[8] By this means, through narrative and poetry, a fundamental view of the ordering of things in God's world is expressed and reexpressed, always in dialogue with changing scenes and new events.

As well as this feature of doubling, there is in the language a potential for extension beyond "literal" meanings. The language of sacrificial worship is a case in point. In a well-known prophetic argument, shared with a number of psalms, the true meaning of worship is distinguished from the practice of sacrifice as such (Isa. 1:10–17; Hosea 6:6; Pss. 40:6–8[7–9]; 50:7–15). The effectiveness of the rhetorical arguments made, however, depends to an extent on the ambiguity of the language. Does *tôdâ* mean "thanksgiving" or a "sacrifice of thanksgiving"? English translations of the superscription to Psalm

5. See H. G. M. Williamson, *Variations on a Theme: King, Messiah, and Servant in the Book of Isaiah* (Carlisle, UK: Paternoster, 1998), 167–202.

6. Brevard S. Childs, *Introduction to the Old Testament as Scripture* (London: SCM, 1979), 337–38.

7. This feature of Hebrew poetry is well known, but see especially James L. Kugel, *The Idea of Biblical Poetry* (New Haven: Yale University Press, 1981).

8. Frank Moore Cross thought that in Israel's literature the "battle with sea," with its mythic origins, "came to be identified with the historical battle in which Yahweh won salvation for Israel" (*Canaanite Myth and Hebrew Epic* [Cambridge, MA: Harvard University Press, 1973], 137–38).

100 (*mizmôr lětôdâ*) hesitate between the two (KJV, "A psalm of praise"; cf. ESV, "A Psalm for giving thanks"; RSV, "A Psalm for the thank offering"). Similarly, the terms *nēder* and *nědābâ* may mean, respectively, either vow or vow-offering, and either free will or free-will offering. Thus when the psalmist says: *zěbaḥ lē'lōhîm tôdâ wěšallēm lě'elyôn nědāreykā* ("sacrifice to God *tôdâ* and fulfill your vows to the Most High"; Ps. 50:14), it might mean either that one's sacrifices should be attended by thanksgiving and firm purpose, or that the attitudes themselves should replace the sacrifices. (Note that the verb *šallēm*, here rendered as "fulfill," is also a sacrificial term, as in the sacrifice of "peace-offerings," *šělāmîm*.) The NRSV offers the latter alternative in its margin. There is in this language both a rootedness in the external realities of Israel's worship and a sense that there is meaning that is not contained by them.

Something similar operates when the prophets call their hearers to "repent," or "return" (*šûb*). In Jeremiah 3, for example, there is a play on the idea of "turning" exhibiting the double meaning of a turning of the human spirit back to God and a physical return to the worship of God in Jerusalem (Jer. 3:6–14). Both Hosea and Jeremiah exploit rhetorically the concept of turning to express their hearers' tendency to "turn away," or "backslide" (Jer. 3:22–23; Hosea 14), a tendency that Yahweh promises to "heal." These passages air the complex theological relationship between the people's responsibility to "turn" themselves back to God and the action of God in enabling them to do so (as also in Deut. 30:3, 10). And closely connected with this, most clearly in Jeremiah 3:14–20, is the implication of the restoration of a repentant people to land and possession of city and temple.

The idea of turning and the interplay between historical and spiritual actualities occurs in a different but equally creative way in Deuteronomy 1–2. Moses, addressing the people of Israel on the plains of Moab, is recalling how, following the exodus from Egypt, they had failed to take possession immediately of the land that Yahweh was leading them to, and so a whole generation was condemned to linger in the wilderness. The scene is one of geographical progress and regression, mirroring the spiritual condition of the people. It is a comedy of errors. When they should go boldly into the land, they fail to do so because of fear (Deut. 1:26–33); when they do gather their courage (1:41–43), it is too late because Yahweh has already spoken the word that will keep them from it, and they are routed by the enemies whom he would have overcome for them (1:44–45). The motif of "turning" runs through this narrative (with two terms for "turn," *šûb* and *pānâ*). When Moses and the people decide to send spies into the land to "bring back word" (*wěyāsîbû*; 1:22), we read that "they turned (*wayyipnû*) and went up into the hill country . . . and brought back (*wayyāsîbû*) word to us" (1:24–25). When Yahweh closes the door of the promised land on them he says: "turn (*pĕnû lākem*), and journey back toward the wilderness and the Sea of Reeds" (1:40)! After the doomed attempt to go into the land anyway, they "returned (*wattāšubû*) and wept before Yahweh" (1:45). But bowing to the inevitable, in Moses' words, "we turned (*wannēpen*) and journeyed back toward the wilderness and the Sea of Reeds" (2:1). In a final twist, after a long time, Yahweh's command comes to turn again (*pĕnû lākem*) and head north, finally on their way to the land (2:3; see also 2:8; 3:1, 20 [*wĕšabtem*]). It is evident that the motif of "turning" plays a key part in the literary conception of this section of Deuteronomy. It seems too that the author has used the template of Israel's changes of direction in order to illustrate, at the outset of the book, its contention that blessing and fullness of life depend on the faithful hearing of the word of Yahweh. The regression toward the wilderness and the Reed Sea, in a kind of "anti-exodus," is the most striking example of the point. Deuteronomy 1–3 is not a simple narrative of possession, but a moral and spiritual reflection on it. It is relevant to recurring situations well beyond the setting of the first possession of land that is the subject of the book.

The entire Old Testament depiction is predicated on change and newness. Whole books illustrate the point, not least the book of Isaiah, where the contrast between "old" and "new," extending even to "new heavens and new earth," is fundamental to its evocation of God's promises of future salvation (Isa. 43:18–19; 62:2–5; 65:17). Deuteronomy, appropriately misnamed,[9] reinvents the Mosaic covenant and law for a new audience. Through this inexorable process of rethinking, the notion of Israel persists, but because of both the force of historical change and the need to account for this theologically, there is persistent reflection on what it truly means. It is this characteristic of Old Testament thought that enables the particularity of the life of Israel to become a story of *'ādām*, or humanity as such.

Language and the "Spiritual Sense"

This power of the language and forms of the Old Testament lies behind what might be called "spiritualizing" interpretations. The long history of this goes back to the early Christian adoption of several "senses" of Scripture, often

---

9. The name of the book goes back to the LXX and the Vulgate, where it is based on a misreading of Deut. 17:18. In that verse, the phrase *'et-mišnēh hattôrâ hazzō't*, "a copy of this law," is taken as "a second law." Deuteronomy is not strictly "a second law," yet in its form and content it does exhibit the need for reinterpretation and reapplication of what has previously been received.

counted as four,[10] in which the plain or literal sense was merely the foundation for deeper layers of meaning. The method, with its roots in Hellenistic Judaism and exemplified by Origen, was an important mechanism in the church's appropriation of the Old Testament as Christian Scripture. But while it sought a "spiritual" sense, it did not regard the "literal" sense as redundant or lacking in meaning.[11] Origen, indeed, claimed that the Bible as a whole "demanded a spiritual interpretation," on the basis of a passage such as Psalm 119:18 ("Open my eyes that I may behold wondrous things out of thy law").[12] A modern recovery of this as a proper feature of Christian interpretation of the Bible is attributed to the work of Henri de Lubac.[13]

There were indeed various factors behind the idea of "spiritual" senses, not least influences from contemporary philosophy, as well as the morality of some of its stories and characters. However, it was driven fundamentally by the belief that Scripture's meaning could not be identical with the literal meaning of its disparate texts. This remains the dominant factor in Christian interpretation.

The "spiritual sense," so understood, should be distinguished from certain kinds of "spiritualizing" interpretations. Readings of the Old Testament have sometimes been predicated on a kind of ascent from the old and "primitive" in religion to purer, enlightened forms, in which, for example, the exigencies of a sacrificial cult were superseded by the recognition that true religion was a matter of the "heart." Texts such as Jeremiah 31:31–34, with its "new covenant" in which the Torah will be written "on the heart," could easily be annexed to such a theory, as could those psalms and prophetic words (noted above) that criticize routinized sacrificial worship.[14] Spiritualizing of this sort is based on a particular understanding of the nature of religion, in

10. See Barnabas Lindars, "Part 3: The New Testament," in John Rogerson, Christopher Rowland, and Barnabas Lindars, eds., *The Study and Use of the Bible* (Basingstoke, UK: Pickering; Grand Rapids: Eerdmans, 1988), 275. He traces the idea to the desert fathers, such as Antony (251–356), "the founder of Christian monasticism" (259).

11. For Origen's view of this, see John Rogerson, "Part 1: The Old Testament," in Rogerson, Rowland, and Lindars, *Study and Use of the Bible*, 32–34; and on Jerome, 43–44. Both of these respected the literal sense of Scripture, but regarded the "spiritual" sense as more important.

12. Ibid., 33.

13. See Glenn W. Olsen, "The Spiritual Sense(s) Today," in *The Bible and the University*, ed. David Lyle Jeffrey and Stephen Evans (Grand Rapids: Zondervan; Carlisle, UK: Paternoster, 2007), 117–38. Olsen notes the influence of Henri de Lubac, *Exégèse médiévale: Les quatre sens de l'Écriture* (Paris: Aubier, 1959–64); in English, *Medieval Exegesis: The Four Senses of Scripture*, 3 vols., trans. M. Sebanc and E. M. Macierowski (Grand Rapids: Eerdmans, 1998–2009). See also John J. O'Keefe and Russell R. Reno, *Sanctified Vision: An Introduction to Early Christian Interpretation of the Bible* (Baltimore: Johns Hopkins University Press, 2005).

14. John Skinner's classic work on Jeremiah is a case in point: Skinner, *Prophecy and Religion* (Cambridge: Cambridge University Press, 1922).

which religion becomes confined to the "inward" part of a person and tends to be individualistic. The "spiritual sense," in contrast, is a hermeneutical concept in which Scripture becomes intelligible and applicable in new ways not determined by putative original, literal meanings. The "spiritual sense," therefore, may apply in principle to matters in any sphere of life, whether physical, emotional, psychological, social, political, gendered, or ecological.

The language of the Old Testament lends itself to the imagining of the world. This resides partly in its rootedness in the ordinary world and the basic constituents of life. The first creation account (Gen. 1:1–2:3) proceeds by making distinctions among the components of the world as experienced: between the heavens and the earth, between encompassing water and dry land, light and darkness, day and night, the greater and the lesser lights (sun and moon), between animal and vegetable, the "kinds" of creatures, nonhuman and human, male and female, six days and the Sabbath. The whole world of experience is grounded here. When Moses in Deuteronomy calls his hearers to "choose life" (Deut. 30:19), this life is given form in pictures of food and drink, family and household:

> He will love you, bless you, and multiply you; he will bless the fruit of your womb and the fruit of your ground, your grain and your wine and your oil, the increase of your cattle and the issue of your flock, in the land that he swore to your ancestors to give you. (Deut. 7:13 NRSV)

The love and blessing of God are thus made palpable in terms of the elements of life. The language expresses the giftedness of life itself and the means of life, well caught in the analogy between the "the fruit of your womb" and "the fruit of your ground," preserved in the NRSV. There are springs of water here too, and wheat and barley, vines, fig trees and olive trees, pomegranates and honey, as well as iron and copper (Deut. 8:7–10) and cisterns and cities (6:10–11).

The tropes of hunger and thirst loom large in the biblical writers' repertoire to express both longing and satisfaction (Pss. 42:1–2[2–3]; 63:1[2], 5[6]). Water can express danger and death too (18:4–5[5–6]). The torment of a human soul, between longing for God and the darkness of despair, resorts to powerful remembered impressions of land and water:

> My soul is cast down within me;
>   therefore I remember you
> from the land of Jordan and of Hermon,
>   from Mount Mizar.
> Deep calls to deep
>   at the thunder of your cataracts;

> all your waves and your billows
> have gone over me. (Ps. 42:6–7[7–8] NRSV)

The poet's mind ranges from the river valley of the Jordan to the snow-capped Hermon in the far north of the land he knew. What kind of connection exists in his mind between these dominant images of the land that cradled his life and his own present condition is hard to articulate. There may be a connection in water, as the Jordan has its source at the foot of Hermon, but it is no mundane connection. The word "Hermon" is actually a plural in the context, a form that suggests both majesty and the reality of a mountain range, so that with its smaller companion Mount Mizar, it evokes a grandeur that cannot be encompassed. The calling of "deep" (*tĕhôm*) to "deep" suggests unfathomable sources that lie beyond the roar of the waterfalls; the phrase is beyond analyzing for meaning, yet in it we seem to hear a sound that wells up from the primeval ocean itself, as in the "deep" of Genesis 1:2.[15]

Natural imagery is the stock-in-trade of the biblical poets. It is deployed to depict the ways and the power of God—in darkness, wind, cloud, hail, thunder (Ps. 18:7–15[8–16])—while the eagle can convey the renewal of a person's strength (Isa. 40:31). Yahweh roars like a lion (Amos 1:2), and his people are "the sheep of his pasture" (Ps. 100:3; cf. 23:1–3). Metaphors are drawn from a known and observed world that is pastoral and agrarian yet also untamed and dangerous. They tumble over each other in this depiction of human experience, with all the possibilities of life and good, danger, dearth, and death. A table is prepared in the presence of enemies (Ps. 23:5). Light and darkness are pervasive, coming from a world in which the contrast between them could be extreme, and where darkness was readily associated with peril and sinister intention, while light might readily be aligned with salvation (Isa. 9:1–2[8:23–9:1]; Pss. 23:4; 50:1–2). The trope of the journey is ubiquitous too. Journeys evoke all the associations of parting and arriving, of familiarity and unfamiliarity, so that the traveler must choose the way well; companionship and enmity; progress itself together with obstacles to progress and, again, danger to life. The specific world of journeying is that of the biblical writers, with its dark places, steep valleys, and unmade roads, starkly contrasting with well-trodden, fertile places, refreshed by streams.[16] By means of such imagery,

---

15. For the metaphor of water, and a reflection on Ps. 42, see William P. Brown, *Seeing the Psalms: Theology of Metaphor* (Louisville: Westminster John Knox, 2002), 105–34.

16. In this "going" there is a natural transfer to the "going" of the moral and religious life, as in the term "halakah." Jewish moral thought and teaching is traditionally depicted as either what is *spoken*, hence "haggadah" (based on Hebrew *higgîd*, "to say, speak"), or as *journeying*, "halakah" (based on Hebrew *hālak*, "to go"). For the metaphor of the "pathway," see further

the imagined world of the biblical writers touches the imagined worlds of readers far removed from it in time and place.[17]

The supreme example of this capacity of Old Testament language is the Song of Songs, with its echoes of Eden in its portrayal of the lovers in a garden setting. The language of the Song works evocatively with imagery from the natural world, both to convey human beauty and passion and to celebrate the richness of the garden and so the created world. Language itself enters into the sensuality of the subject, with its melding of erotic love and the sights, sounds, smells, and tastes of the natural world. There is a dark side here too, in the fear of danger and loss (Song 3:1–5; 5:1–8) and in the wary sense that "love is strong as death" (8:6). The specific world of the poet is always in focus here ("Come with me from Lebanon, my bride" [4:8]; "I adjure you, O daughters of Jerusalem" [5:8]). Yet the power of the Song is not contained within that world. This is the genius of the biblical writers' creativity. Their language is rooted in their worlds in such a way that this rooting is essential to its power to convey meaning; yet it also somehow floats free of it.

Characterizing Old Testament Language

How should we characterize the language of the Old Testament and its capacity to make meaning? We have seen that it is of its essence to transcend "original" situations and speak into new ones. In its merging of history and theology it comes close to what some call "myth," understood as the expression not of history for its own sake but of the way in which societies make meaning out of historical experience. Northrop Frye writes: "The universal in the history is what is conveyed by the *mythos*, the shape of the historical narrative. A myth is designed not to describe a specific situation but to contain it in a way that does not restrict its significance to that situation."[18] This is recognizably close to what I have described above in relation to the book of Isaiah.

Frye's observations about the relationship between words and meaning in the biblical text carry echoes of the "spiritual" sense of theological interpretation. Such interpretation drew on a variety of categories in order to

---

Brown, *Seeing the Psalms*, 31–53. Brown also deals with other metaphors, including "refuge" and "the transplanted tree."

17. See also Northrop Frye: "The Bible's structure of imagery, then, contains among other things, the imagery of sheep and pasture, the imagery of harvest and vintage, the imagery of cities and temples, all contained in and infused by the oasis imagery of trees and water that suggests a higher mode of life altogether" (*The Great Code: The Bible and Literature* [San Diego: Harcourt Brace Jovanovich, 1982], 139).

18. Ibid., 46.

explain meanings that could not be confined to the "literal," but were broadly speaking "figurative." In typology, for example, relationships are observed between characters or events across the biblical literature. Thus Joshua may be seen as a "type" of King Josiah, because in his characterization and actions he anticipates within the narrative the portrayal of that king. The same typological line can be extended to Jesus because, like Joshua, he is the bringer of "salvation" (Matt. 1:21).[19]

In theological interpretation, metaphor is close to typology. Metaphor is, of course, pervasive in the Old Testament, in its usual sense as a figure of speech, where Yahweh may be pictured as a shepherd (Ps. 23:1), or Israel as a vineyard (Isa. 5:1–7). But it can also be used in Christian interpretation of the Old Testament. Brevard Childs, describing "the figurative or metaphorical" interpretation of Theodoret of Cyrus, says: "Old Testament words are rendered metaphorically when they are heard to reverberate with the Christian message."[20] For example, Mount Zion in Isaiah 2:2–4 "becomes the image of the church to which the nations are drawn."[21] The example shows how close it may be to typological readings, but it is distinguished from these because metaphor "lacks the explicit appeal to a temporal sequence moving from type to antitype."[22]

In expressly theological readings of the Bible, pressure is exerted by the need to understand Scripture in terms of Christ. But it is noteworthy that this pressure falls on the capacity of language itself to convey meaning. Childs also writes of Thomas Aquinas's hermeneutical method: "He does not distinguish between literal and figurative senses according to the Alexandrian tradition, but passes through the words of the text to their theological substance, which inevitably transcends the verbal sense of the passage."[23] The affinities between theological methods of reading and the more literary concerns of Frye overlap at this point. Frye also uses "metaphor" in an extended sense when he writes of the biblical imagery as envisaging an "apocalyptic world," in which the Bible presents "the vision, the model, the blueprint that gives direction and purpose to man's energies."[24] In this biblical apocalyptic portrayal, it is ultimately "the body of Christ" that is the metaphor that holds together all of reality.[25]

19. The name Joshua in the Greek Old Testament is *Iēsous*; the names Joshua and Jesus derive from the idea of Yahweh's salvation.

20. Brevard S. Childs, *The Struggle to Understand Isaiah as Christian Scripture* (Grand Rapids: Eerdmans, 2004), 143.

21. Ibid.

22. Ibid.

23. Ibid., 159.

24. Frye, *Great Code*, 139–40.

25. Ibid., 166.

What we have been observing about biblical language chimes with our contention that the reader is engaged with the biblical writers in the active business of understanding through engagement with the texts. In fact it implies a whole array of hermeneutical gambits that have become the common coin of modern biblical scholarship. These include, besides indispensable historical inquiries, the various forms of literary and discourse analysis, where the emphasis is on the text as such and the ways in which it coheres and articulates, as well as methods that center on readers, with the endless interests and conditioning factors that they bring to the activity of reading. These trends lie close to the view I have already expressed, that an inquiry into the Bible's view of being human necessarily involves the reader's personal commitment and openness to being changed. Yet this professed commitment in advance does not identify a specific "interest," whether political, gendered, ecological, or other. Rather, it includes all such in principle, as part of the large canvas on which human beings seek to understand themselves through engagement with Scripture.

Conclusion

I have been suggesting that the biblical writers' use of metaphors belongs essentially to their method of depicting the human situation. By their rootedness in ordinary life and experience, and by their sheer imaginative power and vitality, they can appeal to readers for new receptions in their own times and places. They are inseparable from the character of the Bible to address human beings in ways that touch directly on their deepest concerns and that can lead to transformation. For this reason, an appreciation of the function of language in making meaning takes us beyond the notion of biblical "worldview," which might imply a certain fixed stance, to a recognition that biblical "seeing" is necessarily involved in transforming experience, which will always have a prophetic edge.

What we have observed here about biblical language touches on the metaphors that apply to human beings themselves in the Old Testament. As we have already observed, the trope of the human as "image of God" is far from the only metaphor used in the depiction of the human being in relation to God. Israel is in several contexts the "child" (or "son") of God. This is often tender, as when he is borne on the shoulders of his father God en route to the promised land (Deut. 1:31), or when the prophet Hosea movingly paints a picture of parental care (Hosea 11:1–4). The same metaphor occurs also in that special relationship with God that is described in the terms "holy" and "chosen" (Deut. 14:1–2). And sonship is predicated, in particular contexts, of the Davidic king (Ps. 2:7; Isa. 9:6[5]). God and humans can also be depicted in a marital relationship, as in Hosea 1–3, in a trope that for some is a primary expression of the intimacy between God and humans. Hosea in fact moves easily between the marital and the parental in his depiction of the divine-human relationship, in a poetic performance that presses metaphorical expression as far as it can go.[26] The erotic language in Hosea, and also Jeremiah (2:2–3), lends credibility to the interpretation of the Song of Songs in which human love is taken as a metaphor of the love of God.[27] Other important metaphors are "servant," applied to a number of Old Testament figures, including foreign kings (Nebuchadnezzar in Jer. 27:6), and "vassal," as implied in the extended metaphor of the vassal treaty, as applied to the covenant between Israel and Yahweh in Deuteronomy.[28] The list could be extended to include "artisan" or "artist," as in the case of Bezalel (Exod. 31:1–11), to which we shall return. The idea of friendship occurs in the relationship between God and Moses (Exod. 33:11) to express intimacy and mutuality. Humans are like God too in the function of speech. This accounts for the remarkable statement of God to Moses: "See, I have made you like God to Pharaoh, and your brother Aaron shall be your prophet" (Exod. 7:1 NRSV). The prophet as speaker on behalf of God is nowhere more evident than in Jeremiah, whose words are at times indistinguishable from God's (Jer. 9:1–3[8:23–9:2]). This last case brings us close to the notion of incarnation, because God is depicted as present among people through the presence of the prophet. In Jeremiah's case, this is evident not only in his words but in his sufferings on behalf of the people.

The metaphors we have noticed take their force from the specific contexts in which they arise. When we think of Israel as a "vassal" in treaty terms, for example, we have to understand all we can about the meaning of that status in ancient international politics in order to grasp more clearly what it might mean in new contexts. Moreover, the variety of metaphorical expressions for

26. See my "'I Am like a Luxuriant Juniper': Language about God in Hosea," in *Let Us Go Up to Zion: Essays in Honour of H. G. M. Williamson on His 65th Birthday*, ed. M. Boda and I. Provan, VTSup 153 (Leiden: Brill, 2012), 181–92.

27. The idea of human love as symbolic of the divine in the Song is found not only in traditional Christian allegorical readings of it but also in recent scholarship. See David F. Ford, *Christian Wisdom: Desiring God and Learning in Love* (Cambridge: Cambridge University Press, 2007), 384–87. It underlies, of course, the New Testament idea of the church as the bride of Christ (Eph. 5:31–32).

28. This was first observed by Meredith G. Kline, *The Treaty of the Great King: The Covenant Structure of Deuteronomy* (Grand Rapids: Eerdmans, 1963), and is widely acknowledged in Deuteronomy scholarship. See Dennis J. McCarthy, *Treaty and Covenant: A Study in Form in the Ancient Oriental Documents and in the Old Testament*, AnBib 21 (Rome: Biblical Institute Press, 1978).

the human requires that we read them in terms of each other. The "vassal" is also, somewhat contradictorily, a "son." Behind the specific instances of metaphorical portrayal lies an impetus to express what it means to be human in terms of an understanding of God. The inextricability of theology and anthropology is a hallmark of the Old Testament's discourse.

6

Embodiments: Place and Memory

Aspects of Human Embodiment

At this stage of our inquiry, we have dealt with certain foundational aspects of an inquiry into the meaning of being human in Old Testament perspective. In the remaining chapters we turn to a number of selected topics through which to continue to build a picture. The accent will continue to be on notions of formation and transformation.

In our review of the Old Testament's presentation of the human person, we have seen that we require some concept of embodiment applying to both the individual and the social contexts in which he or she is placed. This idea of embodiment is a fruitful point of entry for exploring aspects of the human in the Old Testament, and I plan now to investigate some of these. Topics include the importance of place in the Old Testament's vision, the social, economic, and political life of Israel, gender, and worship. These belong together in such a way that it is somewhat artificial to deal with them separately, but their coherence in a broad picture will emerge as the treatment progresses. We begin by taking further the fact of cultural specificity by considering the topics of place and memory.

Placedness

The importance of place has been increasingly recognized as a significant theological and anthropological topic in the Old Testament's portrayal of the human situation, as we have seen above (ch. 4). Craig Bartholomew sees it as "a major contender for the central theme of biblical faith."[1] The story of humanity and of Israel is rooted in geography and political history, and played out in the midst of events involving the powers that ebbed and flowed on the ancient Near Eastern stage. The moral and spiritual life of its characters is inseparable from the ways in which they are connected with environments, both local and international. Land in the Old Testament is not merely promised as a prize or reward; on the contrary, human existence is interwoven with the way in which it is inhabited, cultivated, shared, and held.

We have seen already that this is the case in Genesis 1–3, in which the being of the human, *'ādām*, is intrinsically connected to the earth, *'ădāmâ* (Gen. 2:7), and where the moral relationship of the man and the woman to the earth is enacted in the story that runs from harmonious interaction with the delightful garden to expulsion from that place into a life gained from the earth only with pain and great effort. These profound relationships continue in the story of Israel. The physical movement of Israel from Egypt to Canaan recounted in Exodus–Joshua is charged with moral significance. This is not just a migration but a movement from slavery to freedom. The language of enslavement is deeply entwined with this memory, not least in the play on the Hebrew root *'bd* ("slave, serve") in Exodus 1:13–14.[2] This recalls the created purpose of the human in Genesis 2:5 (to "work" [*'bd*] the earth), but now it has become bitter hardship. It also stands in contrast to Yahweh's demand of Pharaoh through Moses that he let his people go to "serve" him (Exod. 8:1). This rhetorical sequence portrays the movement of the people from one location to another as a transformation from the character of slaves to the character of free people. The manner of their relationship to land is an intrinsic part of this portrayal.

The story of Israel is inextricably associated with land, in a trajectory that begins with the promise to the patriarch Abraham (Gen. 12:1–3) and proceeds through a pentateuchal narrative that always has land before it as destination, in contrast both with enslavement on alien soil and the hardships of the Sinai desert.[3] Possession at last is recounted in the book of Joshua, but immedi-

---

1. Craig Bartholomew, *Where Mortals Dwell: A Christian View of Place Today* (Grand Rapids: Baker Academic, 2011), 31. For him, the biblical story of place continues into the New Testament, in Jesus Christ and the new Jerusalem.

2. It occurs five times in these verses, a point that usually does not appear in English translations. See also Deut. 4:20; 17:16; 28:68 for the memory of Egypt as the antithesis of the good life in the given land.

3. In classic pentateuchal analysis, the interest in land was found to be present in varying degrees across the different pentateuchal sources, becoming most prominent in D (Deuteronomy). The source J (Yahwist) appeared to lack a narrative of possession, which was supplied in due

ately becomes a chronicle of repeated loss (Judges–Kings), culminating in the respective exiles of the kingdoms of Israel and Judah (2 Kings 18–25). In one account of this, Genesis–Joshua is a salvation history (*Heilsgeschichte*), while Judges–Kings is the antithesis, an *un*-salvation history (*Unheilsgeschichte*).[4] In this formulation, a profound relationship exists between land and "salvation" (German *Heil*, Hebrew *yeša'*). The political, historical character of the Old Testament story has its rationale in this connection.

Israel's life story can be plotted around an arc that stretches from Babylonia to Egypt and back, via Palestine, somewhat mirroring the journeys of Abraham from Ur, through Haran (Gen. 11:27–32) and Canaan to Egypt (12:1–20), and back to Canaan (13:1). The Old Testament might be described as the record of Israel's long and tumultuous engagement with land. Their relationship with it takes many forms, from a loose tribal association (as in Judg. 5) to a quasi-imperial concept of Zion, in which a dynastic king rules over nations from his royal-sacral court. The reckoning with land continues through and beyond the rupture of the Babylonian exile. The "restoration"—that is, the partial return of exiled Judeans to Judah documented in Ezra and Nehemiah—is only part of the picture. The longing for true "landedness" is evident even within those books (Neh. 9:32–37), and Israel is regularly pictured in the Prophets as poised indefinitely between possession and nonpossession, with images of secure possession now the province of eschatological hope (e.g., Isa. 62).

Human attachment to land in the Old Testament is portrayed not just on large canvases but also more microscopically. The book of Joshua, with its well-known sweeping account of land possession, is marked also by its painstaking geographical description of a multiplicity of individual places. The lengthy account of the borders and cities of Judah in particular (Josh. 15) shows an intimate and comprehensive knowledge of the land.[5] The tireless

---

course by Joshua. P (the Priestly source) idealized Israel around a tabernacle that was located outside the land. In more recent integrated readings of the Pentateuch, the land functions as a running topic throughout, so that David J. A. Clines can state the "theme of the Pentateuch" to be: "the partial fulfilment—which implies also the partial non-fulfilment—of the promise to or blessing of the patriarchs" (Clines, *The Theme of the Pentateuch*, JSOTSup 10 [Sheffield, UK: JSOT Press, 1978], 29). Joseph Blenkinsopp also finds the land to be an essential component of the ancestral traditions (*The Pentateuch: An Introduction to the First Five Books of the Bible* [London: SCM, 1992], 110–11).

4. Konrad Schmid, *Erzväter und Exodus: Untersuchungen zur doppelten Begründung der Ursprünge Israels innerhalb der Geschichtsbücher des Alten Testaments*, WMANT 81 (Neukirchen-Vluyn: Neukirchener Verlag, 1999); published in English as *Genesis and the Moses Story: Israel's Dual Origins in the Hebrew Bible*, trans. James D. Nogalski, Siphrut: Literature and Theology of the Hebrew Scriptures 3 (Winona Lake, IN: Eisenbrauns, 2010).

5. The lists of borders and cities in Judah are generally found by commentators to derive from periods later than Joshua. See Richard D. Nelson, *Joshua: A Commentary*, OTL (Louisville:

accounts of land distribution amount to a patient unrolling of long stories of people in place, testifying that the specifics of this elemental relationship are enormously important in the biblical concept of a land inhabited by a people. The possession of a land by a nation comes down to the inhabiting of many localities, albeit connected by the larger commonality of memory and territory, by clans, families, and individuals, with all the shared familiarities of ordinary life in ordinary places. The great contrast between Egypt and promised land is lived out, as Michaela Geiger has shown, in the ordinary spaces occupied by families, the "house" within whose walls and courtyards the deepest wisdom is passed on from generation to generation (Deut. 6:6–9).[6] There is ultimately an intimacy in placedness that has rightly been called "sacramental."[7]

In a different way, the deep connection between a person and his "place" is poignantly expressed in an image in the book of Job that depicts the precarious and fleeting nature of life. For Job his life is a "breath" (*rûaḥ*), and he is vanishing, no longer to be seen by human eye, as he descends finally to Sheol (Job 7:7–9). The term *rûaḥ*, which stands often for the "spirit" or the most profound being of a person, here denotes rather the insubstantiality of life, drawing on its meaning as wind. The loss of life means no longer being connected with other humans, and then strikingly: "He will not return again to his house; nor will his place know him anymore" (Job 7:10 NASB).

The "place" is unspecified, but the context is the life of an individual, and so we imagine house, family, locality, and a circle of intimates, or "network," in modern idiom. The thought is echoed several times in Job (8:18; 20:9; 27:21).[8] Such texts imply, of course, that a strong connection with place is part of human flourishing. This is expressed positively in Job 36:16, where the "broad place" (*raḥab*) corresponds to a blessed life. "Place" language, with a

---

Westminster John Knox, 1997); and Jacobus Cornelis de Vos, *Das Los Judas: Über Entstehung und Ziele der Landbeschreibung in Josua 15*, VTSup 95 (Leiden: Brill, 2003).

6. Michaela Geiger, *Gottesräume: Die literarische und theologische Konzeption von Raum im Deuteronomium*, BWANT 183 (Stuttgart: Kohlhammer, 2010), 155–60.

7. The term "sacramental" is Marilynne Robinson's, whose novels *Housekeeping*, *Gilead*, and *Home* are explorations in this intimacy of placedness. Of homes and homemaking—with yet another allusion to Deuteronomy—she says: "We have colonized a hostile planet, and we must stanch every opening where cold and dark might pour through and destroy the false climates we make, the tiny simulations of forgotten seasons beside the Euphrates, or in Eden. . . . I think of the acts of comfort offered and received within a household as precisely sacramental. It is the sad tendency of domesticity—as of piety—to contract and of grace to decay into rigor and peace into tedium. Still it should be clear why I consider the Homestead Act all in all the most poetic piece of legislation since Deuteronomy, which it resembles" (Robinson, "When I Was a Child," in *When I Was a Child I Read Books* [London: Virago, 2012], 93).

8. Forms of the noun *māqôm* (place) occur in all these texts.

range of vocabulary, is also employed by the psalmists to depict well-being, as in Psalm 16:6, with its "pleasant places" (*ně'îmîm*) and "my inheritance" (*naḥălātî*),[9] echoing the Deuteronomic land theology that roots possession in ancient memory and the intimacy of family entitlement (cf. Pss. 18:19[20]; 31:8[9]; 118:5).[10] Also in the conception of Israel's social existence found in Leviticus, the possession of land is relational and familial, and an indispensable factor in the experience of freedom. This is evident in the Jubilee provision, where land expropriated due to poverty and debt is restored to the family in the fiftieth year (Lev. 25:8–12). In Deuteronomy too, release from debt slavery is release back to land, seen as an essential resource for a flourishing life and a function of the freedom whose archetype is Israel's release from slavery in Egypt (Deut. 15:12–18).

These soundings in a biblical view of place have their ultimate context in the Old Testament's view of creation. If Israel's life is predicated on land, this is a reflection of a more profound relationship between humanity and the created order. Terence E. Fretheim, among others, has elaborated the creation dimension of Old Testament theology, highlighting especially the factor of the relationship of people to land, and has traced the creational dimension of the various aspects of Israel's life as depicted in the Old Testament, in its laws, its prophetic traditions, its wisdom, and its worship.[11] Craig Bartholomew has rightly argued that the wide creation horizon of biblical depiction does not diminish the local and particular, but rather imparts a powerful intensity to it.[12]

The Bible therefore gives good reason to see placedness as an essential aspect of our being human. There are obvious echoes of this in experience, in our sense of identity with places, whether countries, cities, or other localities. Placedness is a consequence of embodiment, in the sense that our bodies limit us in time and space. Our whole experience as humans is conditioned by the fact of being "from" somewhere. This unchosen aspect of human existence has various implications, including the languages and cultures that individuals inhabit. Place tends also to determine one's citizenship, with both the benefits and inhibitions of this. There are certain impediments to free movement in the world, because individuals generally hold the passport of only one state. There can be economic and religious consequences too, because of prevailing norms and conditions. These are some of the hard realities of the close link

9. MT lacks the first-person suffix; reading here with LXX.
10. These latter texts all employ the term *merḥāb* (broad place). The meaning of the root *rḥb* sometimes borders on "freedom" (Ps. 119:45 NRSV, NIV).
11. Terence E. Fretheim, *God and World in the Old Testament: A Relational Theology of Creation* (Nashville: Abingdon, 2005).
12. Bartholomew, *Where Mortals Dwell*, 25–26, 31.

between *'ādām* and *'ădāmâ*. The constraints are not absolute, but they affect the vast majority of people greatly, and all people in some degree. The reality of placedness is most acutely revealed when people are *dis*placed by famine, disaster, or war; for millions of refugees, the rupture of rootedness in their native place results in the most tenuous hold on life.

There are, of course, aspects of this placedness that are benign and to be enjoyed. Probably every people group has ways of celebrating its individual identity, in music and poetry, and in solemn and festal occasions. There are levels of partisan competitiveness, such as international sporting events, in which a national identity can be expressed with a kind of joyful goodwill toward others. Bartholomew develops a vision of how humans can occupy place in positive ways. For him, the prominence of cities in the Old Testament story is significant. Rejecting the idea that the story moves in an arc from a garden to a city, and drawing on the analogy with ancient Near Eastern royal gardens, he argues that Eden in Genesis 2–3 should be imagined not as the primitive wilderness of Romantic imagination but rather as cultivated, planned, and landscaped, perhaps even including buildings.[13] In his reading, the concept of the earth as a dwelling place for humans implies an invitation to develop it in constructive ways. Because the Bible, as he sees it, affirms the development of cities, this should be seen as "the normative opening up of the cultural potentials built into the creation."[14] He goes on to consider scope for "placemaking" in other facets of life, such as the garden and the home, farming, universities, and the church.[15] Conversely, it can become pathological, expressed in forms of xenophobia that result in wars and ethnic cleansing. Cain's refusal to allow his brother to live on the same land as himself is writ large on the modern world.

It follows that human placedness, whether individual or corporate, is not an absolute given, but is constructed for good or ill as part of the making of human lives and histories.[16] It comes with a spiritual and ethical charge, which is felt throughout the Old Testament, notably in Deuteronomy and the Prophets.

The promises to Abraham in Genesis held out the hope of a numerous people occupying a land of their own (Gen. 12:1–3; 15:5). They both build on the creation blessing-command to "be fruitful and multiply" (Gen. 1:28) and

13. Ibid., 26–27, and n. 99.
14. Ibid., 249.
15. Ibid., 249–318.
16. The idea of place as "constructed" is now a commonplace of sociological analysis, as exemplified in the work of Henri Lefebvre, *The Production of Space*, trans. Donald Nicholson-Smith (Oxford: Blackwell, 1991).

are taken up in Deuteronomy, where promised blessing to Israel takes the form of "multiplying" livestock, produce, and the human population itself (Deut. 7:12–16). In the same ideal vision, even illness is banished (v. 15). In a modern world of large populations, to the point of overcrowding and stretched resources, this ancient vision seems to lack important caveats! The Old Testament is starkly out of kilter with modern fears and warnings about an unsustainable imbalance between needs and resources, going back at least to Robert Malthus.[17] The issue has a presence in theological interpretation, among those who wonder how the Old Testament's optimism can be justified in the modern world.[18] In a critical vein, some have seen the Old Testament's theology of election as giving impetus to destructive competition for scarce resources.[19]

The question whether the Old Testament has warrants for restricting population affords no direct answers. More promising are questions concerning the nature of human relatedness to the earth. Here we find that the placedness of people in land is inseparable from both worship and social policy. When we consider the biblical texts in the light of this, they will be found to have surprising relevance to modern ways of thinking.

Deuteronomy's portrayal of the occupation of a particular land at the expense of others has led many readers to align it on the side of violent competitiveness. Its monotheism has been taken to imply not only violence but also a sense of acquisitiveness because of a perceived scarcity of resources. But this does too little justice to its exploration of the nature of the relationship between a land and its human population as a microcosm of the relationship between humanity and the earth, or *'ādām* and *'ădāmâ*. Its premise, in its own terms, cannot be called "competitive." Its occupation at the expense of the Canaanite population is part of its conception of how a land should and should not be held, which is ultimately inseparable from worship. In the definition of the land of Israel, with borders marking it off from lands given by Yahweh to *other* nations (Deut. 2:1–15), it is a model for noncompetitive development within given limits.

17. Robert Malthus, *An Essay on the Principle of Population* (1798; repr., Oxford: Oxford Paperbacks, 2008).

18. In forms of the movement known as "natalism," the Genesis blessing-command (Gen. 1:28) is regarded as still having a force that tells against population controls. For a critical account, see John McKeown, *God's Babies: Natalism and Bible Interpretation in Modern America* (Cambridge, UK: Open Book, 2014).

19. See Regina Schwartz, *The Curse of Cain: The Violent Legacy of Monotheism* (Chicago: University of Chicago Press, 1997), 176. She thinks that her preferred alternative to monotheism, an open polytheism, "subverts the dominant vision of violence and scarcity with an ideal of plenitude and its corollary ethical ideal of generosity" (176; cf. 11, 58–62). See also n. 42 below for works by Jan Assmann on memory, in which he is critical of the legacy of monotheism.

The nature of the relationship between people and place has an obvious focus in the importance given in Deuteronomy to a central place, in the formula: "the place that Yahweh your God will choose, out of all your tribes, to put his name there, as its dwelling-place" (Deut. 12:5).[20] This typical Deuteronomic idea was at the heart of the critical reconstruction of Israel's religious history, according to which the "book of the law" discovered by King Josiah in the temple was a form of Deuteronomy and provided a warrant for his centralization of worship in Jerusalem.[21] But more important for our purpose is its theological relevance to the idea of placedness. Yahweh's choice of a special place of worship is part of the book's understanding of how the life of Israel is bound up with the place which they are to possess. Paradoxically, while it seems to mark out one place within the land from others, it actually underlines the significance of the entire land. The convergence of the chosen place and the whole land is illustrated by Deuteronomy 26:9, in which the worshiper, in bringing an offering, confesses that Yahweh "has brought us to this place and to this land." The two terms can be taken as being in parallel here, so that "place" conveys ambiguously both the place of worship and the land. In the "politics" of Deuteronomy, the land is a "structured space," and there is a complex conception of the relationship between the central worship place and the distributed locations of the nation's territory, in which the conduct of worship at the center has the effect of sanctifying the whole.[22]

Just as the "earth" is a key player in the drama of creation in Genesis 1–3, so is the land in Deuteronomy. With its life-giving images, as in Deuteronomy 6:10–11; 8:7–10; 11:8–12, this "good land" ('ereṣ ṭôbâ) echoes the notes of abundance and pleasure struck in Genesis 2:8–14, as well as God's repeated judgment of his work as "good" in Genesis 1. In Genesis, humans are of the same substance as the earth (Gen. 2:7); in Deuteronomy, there is a hint of consubstantiality between human and nonhuman creation in the picture of blessing in 7:13, in which "your offspring" (lit., "the fruit of your womb" [pĕrî-biṭnĕkā]) is in parallel with "the fruit of your land [pĕrî-'admātekā], your grain, wine, and oil, the young of your herds and the lambs of your

20. I follow my translation in McConville, *Deuteronomy*, ApOTC 5 (Leicester, UK: Apollos; Downers Grove, IL: InterVarsity, 2002), 209. The formula is repeated with variations numerous times in Deuteronomy, especially in the laws about sacrifices and offerings in chs. 12–17, 26.

21. I have discussed this critical reconstruction in a number of places, such as McConville, *Deuteronomy*, 21–33; J. G. McConville and J. G. Millar, *Time and Place in Deuteronomy*, JSOTSup 179 (Sheffield, UK: Sheffield Academic, 1994).

22. See further McConville, *God and Earthly Power: An Old Testament Political Theology, Genesis–Kings* (2006; repr., London: T&T Clark, 2008), 91–92. The idea of "structured space" is taken from Jean-Marie Carrière, *Théorie du politique dans le Deutéronome: Analyse des unités, des structures et des concepts de Dt 16,18–18,22*, ÖBS 18 (Frankfurt: Lang, 1997).

flocks, in the land he promised your forefathers on oath that he would give you." The ubiquitous promise of land comes down to these elements of the means of life, and shades into the physicality of humanity itself. This is the substance of blessing. If blessing is a conditional possibility in Deuteronomy (28:1–14), this is tantamount to the conditional possibility of life itself. It is not surprising, therefore, that portrayals of land should take on a certain intimacy of expression. As a place that God "cares for" (literally "seeks" in 11:12), it has become Israel's "inheritance" (12:9; 15:4; etc.), to be received and passed on to generations to come.[23]

It follows that Israel's possession of its land is integral to its life. That is, it is not a kind of bonus, whether a reward for good behavior (expressly ruled out in Deut. 9:4–6) or a mark of arbitrary partiality (like Jacob's gift of a special coat to Joseph in Gen. 37:3). Rather, it occurs within the matrix of covenant and Torah and is essential to the vision of flourishing humanity conveyed by Deuteronomy and the wider Old Testament. This can be illustrated in the nexus of worship, food, and memory.

Worship, Food, and Memory

It is well known that Deuteronomy's provisions for worship have a character of their own when compared with other laws of worship in the Old Testament. The first chapter of the law code, chapter 12, which lays down the basic principles for sacrificial offerings, is distinct from other codes in two ways: first, it contains the programmatic set of commands requiring worship to take place at the "place that Yahweh will choose," and second, it is remarkably preoccupied with food. Paying very little attention to the technicalities of sacrifice, apart from its limitation to the chosen place, it stresses the communal and festal side of worship life, highlighting especially the twin components of eating and rejoicing (Deut. 12:5–7, 10–12).[24] These topics recur throughout the lengthy chapter 12 in a series of elaborations of the main precept (vv. 15–18, 20–28). While sacrificial slaughter is limited to the sanctuary, meat may be slaughtered nonsacrificially in all the towns of Israel, as long as the animal's blood is carefully poured off (vv. 15–16, 23–25). This provision has often been regarded as simply a necessary concession in

23. This commonality between humans and the earth has been stressed by, among others, H. P. Santmire in *Brother Earth: Nature, God, and Ecology in Time of Crisis* (New York: Nelson, 1970). See also Bartholomew, *Where Mortals Dwell*, 233–39.

24. In the syntax of 12:5–7, the commands to "eat" and "rejoice" complete a series of imperatives, beginning with "you shall seek" (*tidrĕšû*) and continuing with three verbs in a *waw*-plus-perfect series. Eating and rejoicing are not an afterthought, but essential to the picture.

the wake of the centralization of worship, on the hypothesis that this put an end to sacrificial slaughter up and down the country and so deprived people of the chance to eat meat.[25] However, there is considerable emphasis on the freedom of the people to eat as much as they desire, even depicting a craving for meat, as something natural and not to be condemned (12:15, 20). The point has been highlighted recently by Peter Altmann, who demonstrates the political significance of meat and feasting in Deuteronomy. In the ancient Near East, meat consumption had great symbolic importance and was used by kings at feasts to display royal power.[26] Deuteronomy's conspicuous insistence on meat consumption at Israel's feasts, therefore, is part of its sustained critique of ancient Near Eastern royal ideology and its portrayal of Yahweh as the true king in Israel and author of all the bounty of the land.[27] It is for this reason too that it stresses the free availability of the wealth of the land to the totality of Israel, regardless of social status, in contrast to the tendency under ancient Near Eastern royal rule—and increasingly under the kings of Israel and Judah—to bestow such wealth on the elite and favored.[28]

The emphasis on food and rejoicing characterizes Deuteronomy's laws of worship in general (see Deut. 14:22–29; 15:19–23; 16:1–17). Most striking is the law of the tithe (14:22–29). Unlike other Old Testament laws of tithe (Lev. 27:30–33; Num. 18:21–24), the focus here is all on a festal meal, in which the whole people participate at the central sanctuary. Here, as in chapter 12, there is some emphasis on the satisfaction of appetite and the consumption of meat as well as vegetables. There is even a provision for worshipers who travel a distance to sell their goods locally and repurchase at the sanctuary "whatever you desire, whether beef or lamb, together with wine and strong drink—anything

---

25. See, for example, A. D. H. Mayes, *Deuteronomy*, NCB (London: Oliphants, 1979), 227–28.

26. Peter Altmann, *Festal Meals in Ancient Israel: Deuteronomy's Identity Politics in Their Ancient Near Eastern Context*, BZAW 424 (Berlin: de Gruyter, 2011). Altmann documents iconographic representations and other records of the use of meat in banquets and finds that it often glorifies the king in battle and hunt (78–98, esp. 93). Nathan MacDonald also draws attention to this, showing that feasting played an important part in the development of the Israelite monarchies, both as a means of gathering support and of displaying success (MacDonald, *Not Bread Alone: The Uses of Food in the Old Testament* [Oxford: Oxford University Press, 2008], 45, 134–65 [esp. 135]).

27. I have written on this in *God and Earthly Power*, 74–98, and on unity and egalitarianism in Israel according to Deuteronomy, in "Singular Address in the Deuteronomic Law and the Politics of Legal Administration," *JSOT* 97 (2002): 19–36. See also Walter J. Houston, "Rejoicing before the Lord: The Function of the Festal Gathering in Deuteronomy," in *Feasts and Festivals*, ed. C. Tuckett, CBET 53 (Leuven: Peeters, 2009), 1–14.

28. Altmann, *Festal Meals*, 72–75, 97–98. His evidence suggests that extravagant consumption was typically the province of temple and palace elites (95–96). However, kings could also use royal banquets for social inclusion, "perhaps to bring about the integration of subject peoples" (95). This too, however, served the purpose of the king's prestige.

you wish" (14:26)[29]—and to rejoice. Again as in chapter 12, the festal meal has a strong aspect of social inclusion, with a command to welcome the dependent Levite into the feast. And a separate regulation for the tithe in the third year provides for its produce to be stored up for the needy (14:28–29).

The motif of food and feasting at the central sanctuary continues through the law of firstlings (Deut. 15:19–23) and culminates in the laws concerning the annual pilgrimage feasts (16:1–17). These also emphasize the solidarity of the whole community around the enjoyment of the produce of the land, symbolized by the locale of the central sanctuary, extending even to Passover (16:1–8), which elsewhere is celebrated in homes.[30] The cameo portrayal of the Feast of Booths (vv. 13–15) captures the essence of Deuteronomy's moral and religious vision, with its feasting, its inclusion of both household and the marginalized, and its extraordinary notes of joy.

Deuteronomy, therefore, has a distinctive conception of the place of food and feasting in the communal life, which is intrinsically related to its social and political vision. It has indeed a polemical edge in regard to royal and elitist deployment of resources. This should not be reduced to mere resistance politics, however; rather, it belongs to the book's profound understanding of how relationships should properly operate among people and between people and land.

In maintaining these close relationships among the elements of the created order, human and otherwise, Deuteronomy is in line with what we have observed earlier about the integration of reality in Genesis 1–3. Other parts of the Old Testament also make their contribution to the subject. The language of the Prophets concerning both judgment and salvation weaves images from the natural world into its rhetoric. Hosea 2, for example, stages a controversy between the rival claims of Yahweh and Baal for the allegiance of Israel, in which the proper fruitfulness of the land is at stake. Yahweh complains:

> She did not know
>> that it was I who gave her
>> the grain, the wine, and the oil,
> and who lavished upon her silver
> and gold that they used for Baal. (Hosea 2:8[10] NRSV)

When he revokes these gifts, the balance between people and land is broken. The feasts of Israel and the productiveness of the land cease together

---

29. The translation follows McConville, *Deuteronomy*, 242–43.

30. However, there is a close relationship between central sanctuary and distributed places in the conception of this feast; see, however, ibid., 271–75.

(vv. 11–12[13–14]), in a picture of desolation (*hašimmōtî*, "I will lay waste"). What was cultivated and life-giving becomes a "forest," devoured by wild beasts. Conversely, when Yahweh and Israel are reconciled, he makes for them a "covenant with the wild beasts, the birds, and creatures that creep on the ground" (2:18[20]). And the passage ends with a remarkable affirmation of a nexus between Yahweh, Israel, and the fruitful earth:

> On that day I will answer, says the LORD,
>   I will answer the heavens
>   and they shall answer the earth;
> and the earth shall answer the grain, the wine, and the oil,
>   and they shall answer Jezreel;
>   and I will sow him for myself in the land. (Hosea 2:21–23aα[23–
>   25aα] NRSV)

This interdependence of God, people, and land runs through Hosea's highly metaphorical mode of depiction. Metaphors for God in Hosea draw heavily on the natural world: he is variously, and provocatively, depicted as ferocious animals that tear and devour (5:14; 13:7–8), a moth (or maggot) and rotten-ness (5:12), rain and dew (6:3; 14:5[6]), and most remarkably, in the book's culminating image of him, as a noble and fruitful tree (14:8[9]).[31] Israel too is depicted in images of desolation or fruitfulness, notably in wordplays on the name Ephraim (*'eprayim*). This name, frequent in Hosea, itself connotes fruitfulness (*pěrî*), albeit ironically in 9:16. The people in their rebelliousness are also depicted as a "wild ass" (*pere'*, 8:9) and a stubborn "heifer" (*pārâ*; 4:16). On the credit side, the name Ephraim is also echoed in metaphors for healing ("I healed them [*rĕpā'tîm*]"; 11:3) and flourishing (*wěyiprěhû*; 14:7[8]). The dense linguistic web in Hosea has the effect of displaying the pervasive interconnections between human existence, relationship with God, and the created world. The ever-present possibilities of flourishing and desolation are realized throughout these deep relationships.

A similar thought underlies Amos's pictures of a darkened earth, famine, and the end of feasting in Amos 8. And also in a time of famine, Jeremiah mingles images of the mourning of the people with that of the land itself: "Judah mourns" (Jer. 14:2) and "the earth [*hā'ădāmâ*] is shattered [*hattâ*]" (v. 4) or perhaps "is dismayed" (RSV), in an echo of the "shame" of the

---

31. This is the only place in the Old Testament where a tree image is used directly for God, perhaps because of the perceived religious danger posed by trees in worship. For this and more extensive treatment of the language of Hosea, see McConville, "'I Am like a Luxuriant Juniper': Language about God in Hosea," in *Let Us Go Up to Zion: Essays in Honour of H. G. M. William-son on His 65th Birthday*, ed. M. Boda and I. Provan, VTSup 153 (Leiden: Brill, 2012), 181–92.

desperate farmer (v. 4).[32] Finally, we recall too the purposeful coexistence of all things in creation, animate and inanimate, in the great psalm of creation, Psalm 104.

In an important contemporary application of this biblical theme, Ellen Davis has stressed the importance of harmonious relations between humans and the earth in terms of how they work it in order to live. Developing her "agrarian reading" of the Bible, she finds that Israel's early prophets, Amos and Hosea, "were probably the world's first agrarian writers."[33] She has in mind their protest against forms of political and economic life in which agricultural surpluses are drained away from producers for the benefit of wealthy and powerful elites.[34] The uses of land are invariably at the heart of political and economic life: "Misuse of the gift of land, including maltreatment of those who work the soil, will ultimately undo every political structure."[35]

Sandra Richter too has pursued the idea of right relationship with the fruitful earth in an essay on the Mosaic laws. For her, the laws in Deuteronomy elaborate in practice the Genesis command to keep and work the earth (Gen. 2:15).[36] The idea of God's gift of the land to Israel is not merely a political statement, but comes down to everything that the land produces and sustains. Israel's continued free possession of the land, dependent on covenant faithfulness, takes form in its enjoyment of the produce. But it is the manner of this enjoyment that is striking, for it runs counter to instincts that would try to maximize benefit. So while the vineyards and olives of ancient Canaan played a major role in the land's economy and were the basis of trade with other parts of the Mediterranean world, Deuteronomy enjoins a kind of harvesting that simply leaves valuable fruit on the trees for the benefit of the poor (Deut. 24:20–22).[37] Yet this is not naïve or negligent; rather, the biblical laws have a wisdom that knows where true productivity lies. Richter compares, for example, the Old Testament's laws requiring a "sabbatical" year's rest for the land (Exod. 23:10–11; Lev. 25:4–7) with the well-known benefits of crop rotation and modern awareness that the overuse of land, and especially artificial attempts to boost its yields, can exhaust it, often with devastating

32. For the poetic rhetoric of Hosea and Amos on the integration of covenant faithfulness and care for the land, see Ellen F. Davis, *Scripture, Culture, and Agriculture: An Agrarian Reading of the Bible* (Cambridge: Cambridge University Press, 2009), 21–41.

33. Ibid., 120.

34. Ibid., 121.

35. Ibid.

36. Sandra Richter, "Environmental Law in Deuteronomy: One Lens on a Biblical Theology of Creation Care," *BBR* 20, no. 3 (2010): 356–57.

37. Ibid., 362.

consequences for poor populations.[38] She protests against the destruction of fruit-bearing trees for short-term military purposes, when their natural longevity is a factor in the capacity of a land to sustain people over many generations—an instance where a biblical law has disturbing modern echoes (Deut. 20:19).[39] Her carefully researched documentation of contemporary abuses of land and people for purposes of maximum short-term gain is sobering.[40] As a method of reading the Old Testament laws for today it is also a model of biblical hermeneutics. For it draws attention to their deep wisdom concerning true relationships between people, land, and animals, including animals that are raised for food. This kind of concern for animals, notably in the case of livestock management, is not sentimental, nor merely about "animal rights"; rather, it shows that when there is loss of respect for the elements of the creation as what they are in themselves, something changes in the human relation to the world, and perhaps in humanity itself. And strategies for the kind of benefits imagined in the short-term exploitation of resources are both self-defeating and the opposite of what is meant by "blessing."

Embodiment and Memory

Readers of the Old Testament cannot miss for long the crucially important theme of memory, which has played a major part in works on the theology of the Old Testament.[41] The entire Old Testament might be considered a work of memory. At its core are the decisive formative events of creation, exodus, and Mosaic covenant, and much of the Old Testament can be understood as a layered testimony both to those events and to the ways in which they have been remembered. In one perspective, the Old Testament as a whole is the body of memories that has been received by both church and synagogue as the basis for the self-understandings as "Israel" that are found in both Judaism

38. Ibid., 363–65. Her remarks about the potential damage done by chemical fertilizers recalls Rachel Carson's early exposure of the dangers of pesticides to both people and land in *Silent Spring* (Boston: Houghton Mifflin, 1962; London: Penguin, 1965); see above, ch. 4.

39. Richter, "Environmental Law in Deuteronomy," 367.

40. Examples include the routine abuse of animals in some industrial meat processing (ibid., 372–74) and forms of mineral mining that necessarily destroy the capacity of land for fertility (ibid., 368n44).

41. Gerhard von Rad's classic *Old Testament Theology* was constructed around the idea of Israel's confessional memories and memorialization of its history with Yahweh (von Rad, *Old Testament Theology*, vol. 1, *The Theology of Israel's Historical Traditions*, trans. D. M. G. Stalker [London: Oliver & Boyd, 1962], esp. 105–28). For a recent treatment of memory in Deuteronomy, see Ryan O'Dowd, *The Wisdom of Torah: Epistemology in Deuteronomy and the Wisdom Literature*, FRLANT 225 (Göttingen: Vandenhoeck & Ruprecht, 2009).

and Christianity. But the Old Testament is also, within its own horizons, laden with memory, in such a way as both to preserve and to re-create it.

The Old Testament's character as a memory text works on at least two levels. On one level it witnesses to the substance of ancient Israel's worshiping life. From various texts we deduce that Israel's faith was carried by acts of worship, which were performed in particular places and involved actions, including song and sacrifice. Most importantly, it celebrated annual feasts involving pilgrimage to centers of worship (and in time a single center), the most important of these being the Passover. These worship events, according to the texts, had memory at their core, the Passover commemorating the miraculous escape from Egypt, in which God inflicted plagues on the Egyptians but spared the houses of the Israelites and so overcame the pharaoh's hostility to their release.

This picture is created from various texts. We read of the exodus not only in the book of Exodus but also in Deuteronomy (Deut. 11:1–5), in the "historical books" (1 Sam. 12:8), and frequently in the Prophets and Psalms (e.g., Hosea 11:1; Amos 2:9–10; Jer. 2:1–8; Ezek. 20; Pss. 78:11–16; 106). There are provisions for the Passover in pentateuchal laws (Exod. 12; 34:25; Lev. 23:4–8; Deut. 16:1–8) and various records of its observance in the "histories" (2 Kings 23:21–23; 2 Chron. 35:1–19). The way in which the texts relate to the history means that the actual practices of Israel have to be reconstructed, since we obviously have no independent access to the practices themselves. As an example of how this can work, Psalm 81 recalls the exodus in a text presumably used in worship, with allusions to new moon, full moon, and "feast day" (Ps. 81:1–5[2–6]). By cross-referring to Leviticus 23:23–36, the psalm seems to relate to the ceremonies of the seventh month, including the Day of Atonement and the Feast of Booths. Correlating different kinds of texts in this way can serve as evidence of how Israel's memories were both inscribed and carried by the activity of regular worship. There is variety in the textual witnesses, however. Thus, the earliest law code concerning Israel's feasts (Exod. 23:14–17) apparently has no reference to the Passover. Exodus 12, by contrast, the text that documents the origin of the feast, is a combination of instruction and narrative. The Deuteronomic law of Passover differs in some ways from the picture given in Exodus 12 and exhibits certain specifically Deuteronomic characteristics, notably the requirement to celebrate it at the central sanctuary (Deut. 16:2), by contrast with Exodus 12:1–13, where it is evidently held in households.

On another level, the texts not only witness to events but also are themselves part of Israel's preservation of identity through memory. The texts enshrine a commemorative structure. The Pentateuch as a whole both anticipates life in the promised land and expressly provides for the practice of remembering the events that it narrates. This is found across a range of pentateuchal texts, both Priestly and Deuteronomic—for example, in Leviticus 23:10 and Numbers 15:2. These two texts (both Priestly) are followed by instructions for sacrifice, which shall be "a perpetual statute throughout your generations" (Lev. 23:14; Num. 15:15). The structure is best exemplified in Deuteronomy 26:1–11, situated at the end of the law code (chs. 12–26), which provides for a ceremony of sacrificial gift, together with a confession of faith that consists of a spoken memory of the exodus deliverance.

The kind of memory exhibited by the Old Testament is thus perpetuated in and by the communities of Israel and Judah over many generations. It has been variously called "cultural," "collective," "corporate," or "social" memory.[42] That is, distinct from the particular memories that individuals are aware of having and can consciously call to mind, and also from the knowledge of the past that can be gained from historical research, it resides in communities as a matter of habit and practice, which form the self-understanding that is transmitted from generation to generation.[43]

We noted above that memories are carried by societies in both actions and texts. These function in different ways: actions tend to conserve memories and traditions by repetition, while texts allow for ongoing reflection on meanings.[44] The two aspects are hard to disentangle, since our evidence for practice is overwhelmingly textual. But it is highly significant that Israel did not merely record those events in writing, but performed them regularly, and

---

42. Key works are Jan Assmann, *Moses the Egyptian: The Memory of Egypt in Western Monotheism* (Cambridge, MA: Harvard University Press, 1997); Assmann, *Das kulturelle Gedächtnis: Schrift, Erinnerung und politische Identität in frühen Hochkulturen* (Munich: Beck, 1997); Assmann, *Religion und kulturelles Gedächtnis* (Munich: Beck, 2000) (English trans.: *Religion and Cultural Memory: Ten Studies*, trans. Rodney Livingstone, Cultural Memory in the Present [Stanford, CA: Stanford University Press, 2006]); Paul Connerton, *How Societies Remember* (Cambridge: Cambridge University Press, 1989); John W. Rogerson, *A Theology of the Old Testament: Cultural Memory, Communication, and Being Human* (London: SPCK, 2009), esp. 13–41; Rogerson, "Towards a Communicative Theology of the Old Testament," in *Reading the Law: Essays in Honour of Gordon J. Wenham*, ed. J. G. McConville and Karl Möller (London: T&T Clark, 2007), 93–96. Rogerson sees cultural memory as the only way in which the Old Testament's historical traditions can be used positively for theology (*Theology of the Old Testament*, 19). The concept of collective memory was first introduced in a series of works in French by Maurice Halbwachs; see Connerton, *How Societies Remember*, 108n49, for references, and Rogerson, *Theology of the Old Testament*, 19.

43. Connerton, *How Societies Remember*, 23–25.

44. Connerton distinguishes between "incorporating practice," in which memories are conveyed by physical actions, and "inscribing practice," that is, writing (ibid., 72–73). In the latter, "the content of communal memory is subject to systematic criticism" (ibid., 76). The distinction between these two types is not absolute, however.

that such performance was rigorously imposed by statute and custom.[45] In Israel, the most important occasions of worship involved pilgrimage to the worship center, with all the entailments of journeying. Psalm 84, for example, affords a vivid picture of pilgrimage, where the psalmist longs to be present at the "dwelling place" of God (miškěnôteykā; 84:1–2[2–3]) and conveys in the course of the psalm the long, hard way that has to be traveled to get there; the places that connect the points of departure and of destination are brought into focus, both in their challenging reality and as metaphors of spiritual life (vv. 5–7[6–8]). The experience is both physical and emotional, in ways that cannot be separated from each other. The psalmist is close to exhaustion ("my soul faints [kālětâ napšî]"), and his "heart and flesh [libbî ûběśārî] cry out [yěranněnû] to the living God" (v. 2[3]). The event is also communal, for it is a group that is pictured on the journey to the sanctuary (vv. 5–7[6–8]). Communal memory is operating powerfully here, for the longing to be present in the temple at Jerusalem arises from the deep-rooted memories that compose the worshipers' shared mental image of it. The pilgrims long for Zion[46] because Zion has meanings embedded in their sense of history and identity.

The aspect of corporate memory comes out explicitly in Psalm 42. Here also a psalmist gives voice to a deep longing for God, which takes form in a desire to "see the face of God" (vv. 1–2[2–3]), a metonym for going to the temple. There is intense emotional disturbance in this longing, in which the poet's memory of going with the crowd in procession to the "house of God" is inextricably involved with the "pouring out of [his] soul" (wě'ešpěkâ 'ālay napšî; v. 4[5]). In both these psalms we see that the individual's experience of God is enmeshed with places, with physical acts of displacement, with time, and with other people. They are imaginative evocations of what is humanly involved in the instructions about keeping the annual feasts in texts such as Deuteronomy 16:1–17.

Why is this kind of embodiment so apparently important in the Old Testament's imagination of the spiritual life? The answer to this question lies not in differences between ancient and modern kinds of society but rather in factors that belong more generally to the ways in which human beings behave and apprehend. Commemorative ceremonies can be seen as a convergence of profane and sacred time. As profane time, the day of a celebratory feast is one day among others, taking its place in a sequence of days, weeks, and years. As sacred time, it becomes identical with the

---

45. For Connerton, commemorative ceremonies are necessarily "performative" (ibid., 4–5).

46. The term "Zion" does not appear in Ps. 84:5[6], though it is sometimes supplied there, because it otherwise seems to end abruptly. It appears in v. 7[8], however. The point holds for all "Zion" psalms, such as Pss. 76; 132.

corresponding day in the celebrations in all the years past. There is a merging of past time with the present, which Paul Connerton has exemplified
from numerous contexts, and which he finds specifically in the Jewish Passover and the Christian Eucharist.[47] The Old Testament writers are keenly
aware of this capacity of festival to bring about the convergence of past
and present in its sacred time. This is why the foundation text of the Passover, Exodus 12, can be at once a narrative of the first Passover and a set
of instructions for keeping the feast perpetually. The point is contained in
the opening line of Yahweh's speech in that text: "This month [ostensibly
the actual time of the first Passover] is the first of months for you; it shall
be for you [in perpetuity] the beginning of the months of the year" (Exod.
12:2). The components of the feast that are then set out, including the eating of lamb with unleavened bread and bitter herbs (v. 8), are designed to
re-create before the mind and senses the actuality of the first occasion. The
theological structure of Deuteronomy too is based on a repetition in time
of the formative event of the giving of the Torah at Horeb (Sinai). Thus the
covenant made between Yahweh and Israel on the plains of Moab converges
with the covenant made forty years earlier at Horeb, in a historical moment
that is perpetuated by the ceremonial reading of the Mosaic commands
every seven years at the Feast of Booths, so that subsequent generations
might experience the covenant summons in the way that the Israelites of
Moses' time did (Deut. 31:9–13).[48]

Such ways of remembering are not incidental, nor are they simply replace-
able by written records. Rather, there is something in the embodied actions
themselves that brings about the remembering. For Connerton, not only commemorative ceremonies but also other kinds of social understanding, such

---

47. Connerton, *How Societies Remember*, 47. In an example from secular history, he shows
how Hitler's Third Reich created an elaborate system of memorializing events held to be of
major importance for the Nazi movement, using concepts and language that drew heavily on
Christian theology and practice (ibid., 41–43).

48. Michaela Geiger writes: "Die Toralesung am einen Ort führt somit zurück in die Got-
tespräsenz am HOREB" (*Gottesräume*, 300). See also McConville and Millar, *Time and Place*.
For Millar, "Moab is presented as the place where the past and future of Israel coalesce in a
single moment" (*Time and Place*, 47). Geiger finds a difference between the positions of Millar and McConville, whose model of successive "places" in Deuteronomy's theological history
calls into question the claims of any single place to absolute preeminence (Geiger, *Gottesräume*,
37–38, citing McConville in *Time and Place*, 136–38). Geiger herself regards the "one place" as
having the special significance of realizing both Horeb and Moab in the present (*Gottesräume*,
37–38). I think there are separate questions here, however—namely, the question about the
specific function of the "chosen place" in Deuteronomy, and the nature of commemoration in
regularly repeated rituals. On the relation of the "children" to Israel's identity in Deuteronomy,
see Karin Finsterbusch, "Die kollektive Identität und die Kinder: Bemerkungen zu einem Programm im Buch Deuteronomium," *JBTh* 17 (2002): 99–120.

as "good manners," are effective by virtue of habitual bodily performance.[49] Habit memory is not a substitute for cognitive memory; rather, it entails it.[50] But it is indispensable in keeping alive the central tenets of a society's self-understanding. The aspects of habit and performance are evident in the Old Testament's accounts of memory events. When the pilgrims make their arduous way through difficult terrain to reach Jerusalem at last, or when they consume the festal meal together, these habitual performances belong to and sustain the meaning of what they are doing.

I am suggesting that the kind of performative memory that we find in the Old Testament has abiding significance for how we understand human persons. It is important to pause on this, because ritual performance of any sort may be thought to be irrelevant in the modern world. This could be because of a general modern tendency to individualism or an equally modern suspicion of perpetuating tradition. Where there is a cult of the "new," there is little room for performative memory. Theologically too, the New Testament's warnings against "vain repetitions" together with its teaching, notably in the Letter to the Hebrews, imply that the sacrificial actions, place, and personnel of Old Testament worship have been rendered redundant by the new covenant in Jesus Christ (Heb. 8, and passim). The specific rituals of Old Testament religion have indeed undergone radical reinterpretation. In Judaism, the Passover remains centrally important, though for most Jews not in Jerusalem, and without the sacrificial component that is impossible in the absence of a functioning temple and priesthood there. Yet performative memory is alive and well in the practice of the Passover liturgy, or *seder*. The Sabbath too, with its own liturgy and performances, retains its tremendous bonding power in Judaism. In Christianity, elements of the Passover have been taken up in the Eucharist, or Holy Communion, which, having the force of dominical command (1 Cor. 11:23–32), is practiced in all the churches, including those less given to liturgical repetition. The abiding potency of performative memory in Christianity can have no clearer demonstration than in the words: "Do this in remembrance of me" (1 Cor. 11:24). It is, moreover, a "body" that is at the center of this ritual act ("This is my body"), while the act also evokes the mysterious relationship between that body and the body that is constituted by the assembled participants, the body of Christ that is the church (1 Cor. 12:12–13). This body continues to have a living presence in the world, such that, in another place, the church can be exhorted to "present your bodies as

---

49. Connerton, *How Societies Remember*, 3–5. He gives the example of what passes for good manners in society, including posture, table manners, and food consumption itself (ibid., 82–86).

50. Ibid., 87–88.

a living sacrifice" (Rom. 12:1). Performative memory, then, is as much alive and well in Christianity as it is in Judaism. Even the author of the Letter to the Hebrews warned against the neglect of regular assembly (Heb. 10:24–25).

The kind of habituation involved in the commemorative actions of both Judaism and Christianity has both moral and pedagogical aspects. We have already met the pedagogical dimension in the context of Deuteronomy's commands to teach the Torah to each new generation (Deut. 6:6–9). The practices that are urged there are both embodied and habitual: "when you sit in your house and when you walk by the way and when you lie down and when you rise up. You shall bind them as a sign on your hand and they shall be as frontals on your forehead" (6:7b–8 NASB). And these practices are, of course, entwined with the learning of Torah, with all its potential for the transformation of life. The learning and practice of habit, therefore, are paradoxically both received and chosen. The Old Testament's "cultural memory" has aspects of what Assmann calls "willed memory."[51] It is in this sense what James K. A. Smith and others have termed *habitus*, a visible way of being in the world.[52] It is acquired slowly, by a process of "incorporation," by which the individual becomes part of a "social body" and acquires "an entire social imaginary."[53] The individual is schooled into a way of being that represents a whole complex of beliefs and that has a visible presence in the world.

Finally, it should be stressed that the kind of habituation here in view is fully cognitive, moral, and spiritual. This point needs to be made because it has been rightly pointed out that the Old Testament testifies to the existence of several different versions of cultural memory in ancient Israel. John Rogerson points to the narrative of King Ahab and Naboth's vineyard (1 Kings 21) as evidence of this. Whereas Ahab, encouraged by his Phoenician wife Jezebel, apparently acts from a tradition in which kings have ultimate rights over property, Naboth has a version of reality in which land remains in families by inheritance (as reflected in the laws of Jubilee in Lev. 25:8–55). Both these views have strong customary force and presumably had currency in Israel among different groups.[54] However, this points us back to the ways in which the biblical texts relate to the memories and practices of Israel. For they not only have become part of the transmitted memories of those practices, they

51. Assmann, *Religion und kulturelles Gedächtnis*, 18–19; also cited in Rogerson, *Theology of the Old Testament*, 20.

52. Smith, attributing the term to Pierre Bourdieu, defines it as "the complex of inclinations and dispositions that make us lean into the world with a habituated momentum in certain directions" (James K. A. Smith, *Imagining the Kingdom: How Worship Works* [Grand Rapids: Baker Academic, 2013], 79).

53. Ibid., 92–94. On Charles Taylor's concept of the "social imaginary," see above, ch. 4, n. 3.

54. Rogerson, *Theology of the Old Testament*, 21–22.

also exhibit a kind of critical reflection on the tradition. In the case of Ahab and Naboth, the depiction is in line with the tendency in the books of Kings to judge the kings according to clear criteria. There is a kind of critical his-torical consciousness at work here. This may not, indeed, merely select one form of cultural memory over another; rather, it testifies to the way in which received memories are passed on via a theologically critical filter. The same phenomenon is evident in the variable ways in which the ancient worship cer-emonies are evoked and prescribed. To take just one example, Deuteronomy adds to its sources for the sacrifices, Passover, and other feasts of Israel both a heightened emphasis on inclusiveness in society and the keynote of "joy" (e.g., Deut. 12:7, 12; 14:28–29; 16:13–15). *Habitus* is not thoughtless; rather, it is the powerful presencing in the world of a way of life, chosen from among all possible ways of life.

Conclusion

In the present chapter we have explored aspects of human embodiment, one of the implications of a theology of humanity that we have traced from the concept of the "image of God," as well as from the Old Testament evidence about Israel's basic concepts of the human constitution. Embodiment applied not only to the individual but also to the "social body" and to the ways in which the one related to the other. In that context we have pursued here the topics of placedness and memory and found them to be important factors in the Old Testament's expression of the human condition and experience. We have also observed connections between the topics and the pervasive theme of transformation. Regarding place, humans do not simply occupy space but impart to it a certain character by virtue of the way in which they occupy it, a character that has much to do with the quality of human relating in it, and the ways in which humans relate to the earth itself. Similar factors emerge in the context of the ways in which identity is expressed through commemorative acts. The two topics converged in regard to matters of practical justice. Place and memory, therefore, are not simply static factors in human experience, but have aspects of both givenness ("God gave us this land") and the most profound challenge to responsible thought and action.

We turn next to a further topic under the rubric of "embodiment," namely, politics.

The Political Self

The Political Theme in the Old Testament

In its depiction of the human experience, the Old Testament is inescapably political. This is signaled on its opening pages, in Genesis 1–3, and we saw above (chs. 1 and 2) how the idea of the human as "image of God" is set within a world of ancient Near Eastern political concepts. Humanity as "image of God," therefore, has (among other things) strong political implications, and expresses both a status and a vocation. The vocational aspect of the "image" involves rule in the widest sense, not only the ruling of human society but also the exercising of responsibility over the earth, with a basic liberative orientation. The *challenge* of godlikeness, therefore, with its inherent dangers of idolatry, took one of its forms in the political sphere. The first chapters of Genesis set the stage for a portrayal of the condition of humanity as a political animal. And the developing narrative tells of the formation of a people, extricated from the tyranny of an empire in order to become a nation among others, only to find itself subject to a gamut of political experiences: a successful, unified kingdom under David and Solomon; kingdoms divided against each other, then reduced by enemies; finally, overcome again by empire and forced to find new ways of living in subjection to overwhelming alien power. The tragic parabola of Israel's life can thus be described in the form of a political history.

There is, however, no systematic thesis in the Old Testament concerning ideal forms of political life.[1] Rather, the political dimension is embedded within the persons and events in such a way as to show that it is inseparable from the story of humanity itself, with its stubborn tragic tendency. The memory of Cain as a city builder, and of his descendants as founders of culture (Gen. 4:17, 20–22), captures this dilemma at the beginning of the biblical account of humanity. Cities become emblems of organized human life, with Babylon and Zion towering over the story in a perpetual tension. Corresponding to the cities are their rulers. Nimrod the hunter, a descendant of Noah through Ham, is described as the first "mighty man" (*gibbōr*) on the earth, and indeed the first to have a "kingdom" (*mamlaktô*)[2] by virtue of founding Babylon and Nineveh (Gen. 10:8–12). As with Cain's founding of the antediluvian city of Enoch, there is no comment, adverse or otherwise, on Nimrod's achievement. Rather, the thread of the story of human rule is enmeshed with Genesis's account of the early history of humanity, which is portrayed with all its capacity for both blessing and curse.

The Old Testament texts exhibit various forms of engagement with the political practices of the ancient world, which forms the matrix of the life of Israel. It stages the interplay of nations and kingdoms, great and small, with their rise and fall, their treaties and wars, their laws and customs. Its discourse is permeated with political concepts. Justice and righteousness, as well as peace and security, fall within the sphere of political responsibility. The famous Hammurabi stele is an icon of the common ancient Near Eastern belief that kings were mandated by their gods with the duty of upholding good order, with its depiction of the god Shamash handing to the Babylonian king the laws that are inscribed on the stele, in what has become known as Hammurabi's Code (ca. 1800 BCE).[3] The Old Testament is no exception to this ubiquitous concern for governance. At the heart of the Sinai covenant are laws regarding civic life, as in Exodus 21–23 and Deuteronomy 12–26, laws that must be administered in duly appointed ways. And among its greatest heroes and antiheroes are conquerors, rulers, and lawgivers.

---

1. This point is made in different ways by two important recent works: Mira Morgenstern, *Conceiving a Nation: The Development of Political Discourse in the Hebrew Bible* (University Park: Pennsylvania State University Press, 2009); and Michael Walzer, *In God's Shadow: Politics in the Hebrew Bible* (New Haven: Yale University Press, 2012). E.g., see Walzer, *In God's Shadow*, xii.

2. Claus Westermann, *Genesis 1–11*, trans. John J. Scullion (London: SPCK; Minneapolis: Augsburg, 1984), 515–17; see also Richard Bauckham, *The Bible in Politics: How to Read the Bible Politically*, 2nd ed. (London: SPCK, 2010), 10–13.

3. See Victor H. Matthews and Don C. Benjamin, *Old Testament Parallels: Laws and Stories from the Ancient Near East*, 3rd ed. (New York: Paulist Press, 2006), 105–14. The Hammurabi stele is located in the Louvre Museum in Paris.

Yet the Old Testament does not put forward an overarching political theory. Rather, its depiction of political forms of life exhibits reflection on the political domain in various ways. Mira Morgenstern puts this point well:

> Unlike many of its cultural contemporaries, Israelite political discourse does not develop exclusively (or even mainly) in venues specifically or traditionally recognized as public: there is no institutionalized agora in which to situate a growing awareness of the public commonality. Instead, in the Biblical text, national awareness develops in settings that are both quotidian and domestic, such as Gideon's granary, Samson's parties, or Ruth's conversations in privately owned farms or walking along a dusty path.[4]

At times this engagement is somewhat conservative; in the book of Proverbs, for example, its invitation to wisdom accords with a concept of education as likely to bring advancement in the royal court. In the stories of Joseph (Gen. 37–50), Daniel, and Esther, sometimes called "diaspora novellas,"[5] pious Jews live under imperial kings who are depicted on a spectrum from relatively sympathetic to ruthlessly tyrannical. The pharaoh of Joseph highly values his Hebrew vizier and extends the hospitality of his land to Joseph's burgeoning family, while the pharaoh of the exodus seeks to enslave and ultimately eradicate a people that he considers a danger to Egyptian security and his own power. Portrayals of both Nebuchadnezzar and Darius in the book of Daniel show how non-Israelite kings can be both extremely hostile to modes of life that do not conform to their religio-political status quo, and also capable of generosity to the nonconformist "other," even on occasion honoring the God of Israel (Dan. 2:46–49; 3:29–30; 4:34–37). Pictures of empire as potentially benign include the memory of Cyrus of Persia, feted as Yahweh's "anointed one" (*měšîḥô*) in Isaiah 45:1 and as the agent of the restoration of the Babylonian captives to their land and proper spiritual heritage (Ezra 1:1–4). Yet they can also be satirized as mockeries of power, as in the ludicrous self-importance of the court of the Persian king Ahasuerus (Esther 1) or in the depiction of Nebuchadnezzar in Daniel 3. More somberly, the history of the world can be depicted as a succession of increasingly atrocious empires, denaturing the human image in the savagery of their rule, and finally meriting destruction to make way for a divine kingdom that would also be truly human, established by "one like a human being" (Dan. 7:13).

4. Morgenstern, *Conceiving a Nation*, 5.

5. For the idea of the diaspora novella, see A. Meinhold, "Theologische Erwägungen zum Buch Esther," *TZ* 34 (1978): 321.

As for the Old Testament's own political stance, its story of Israel weaves between accommodation to the dominant forms of Iron Age politics and various critical stances toward them. The "primeval history," Genesis 1–11, is well known for its characterization of Babylon as hostile to God, especially in the first creation narrative (Gen. 1:1–2:4a), with its implicit critique of Babylonian polytheism, and in the Tower of Babel lampoon (Gen. 11:1–9), in which human organization becomes a kind of end in itself. The Babylonian religio-politics as exhibited in its Epic of Creation,[6] establishing Babylon as the center of world order under the god Marduk and the Babylonian king, finds a counter-echo in the biblical trajectory from creation to Jerusalem-Zion and the Davidic king. In the David-Zion tradition, Zion is the place from which Yahweh exercises his rule over the earth, symbolized by the kingship of his royal "son" (Pss. 2; 72; 132:11–18). These echoes of the biblical story in the Babylonian (as well as Canaanite)[7] analogues lie deep, including imagery of the subjugation of forces of disorder, or Chaos, in the defeat of the "Sea" in Exodus 14–15, also celebrated variously in the Psalms and Prophets (e.g., Pss. 74:12–17; 89:9–10[10–11]; Isa. 51:9–11). The Babylon-Zion tension that runs through the Old Testament forms part of the framework in which a number of the prophetic books express eschatological hope in the context of overwhelming imperial power.[8] The typology of powerful empire in hostile opposition to the rule of God is by no means limited to Babylon. In the book of Daniel, the successive empires of the exilic and Second Temple periods are joined together in visions of hostility to God and Israel (Dan. 2; 7). In that case, Babylon, the ostensible setting of the Daniel stories, takes on a symbolic role, which it retains into the New Testament in the book of Revelation.

The counterpoint of Zion and Babylon does not unfold straightforwardly, however. Rather, the story of Israel's extrication from dominant ancient Near Eastern forms of power is evidently one of perpetual struggle. Jerusalem-Zion as symbol of Yahweh's purposeful presence with Israel emerges slowly in the biblical narrative. The origins of both Davidic kingship and the worship of Yahweh in a temple are depicted as borrowing, in measure, the dress of Canaan or of the ancient Near East more widely. The transitions are reflected in the books of Samuel, with Samuel's prophetic warnings about the adoption

6. For the Epic of Creation, or *Enuma Elish*, see Stephanie Dalley, *Myths from Mesopotamia* (Oxford: Oxford University Press, 1991), 233–77.

7. For Canaanite myths of creation, see John C. L. Gibson, ed., *Canaanite Myths and Legends*, 2nd ed. (Edinburgh: T&T Clark, 1978).

8. See, e.g., Isa. 13–14 (cf. 2:2–4); Jer. 50–51 (cf. 25:15–26); 31:31–40; 33; Ezek. 36–48; Joel 3:9–21[4:9–21]. The typology is not confined to Babylon, but some of the fiercest polemic is directed against it.

of dynastic kingship and the monarchy's inauspicious beginnings with Saul (1 Sam. 8–12). They also appear in the initial resistance, again expressed by a prophet, to the building of a temple for Yahweh by a newly victorious King David (2 Sam. 7:4–7). These struggles no doubt reflect a historical actuality in which ancient forms of decentralized authority yielded reluctantly to centralized ones.[9] In the books of Samuel they are theologized in terms of the overriding rights of Yahweh as Israel's "king" (1 Sam. 8:7; cf. Deut. 33:5) and in Yahweh's affirmation that he cannot be placebound (2 Sam. 7:6–7). These theological hesitations find some resolution in the David-Zion synthesis already noticed. Yet this faced challenges both from hard historical reality, in which the two kingdoms of Israel and Judah could not withstand the forces of change around them, and from theological scrutiny. Theological resolutions continued, therefore, not least in the great history of the kingdoms (1 and 2 Kings), which portrays them as largely overwhelmed by powerful tendencies to conform with the models of the ancient world, symbolized in characters such as Ahab and Jezebel, rather than as being in distinctive covenant with Yahweh. The latter, represented by Hezekiah and Josiah (2 Kings 18–23), is a "minority report" and has no decisive effect.

The Old Testament's portrayal of the possibilities of the political life is not limited to this account, which emerges essentially from Samuel–Kings, and can be broadly classified as Deuteronomistic. When the larger block of literature from Genesis to Kings, often called the "primary history," is taken as the base text, other strands can be discerned. It is not accidental that the foundational events of Israel's existence occur outside the land of Canaan, in an exodus from Egypt and in the divine gifts of covenant, law, and worship. The centrality of worship in the story and structure of the Pentateuch is highly significant. Joseph Blenkinsopp's analysis, in which Leviticus is the central panel of the five books,[10] is an important foil to the perception of them as the story of a progression toward land.[11] The worship theme that unfolds in Exodus 25–40 and continues in Leviticus has a tabernacle at its center, which is echoed in the rationale for Yahweh's declining to accept a temple at the hand of David (2 Sam 7:4–7). The completion of the work on

9. This is analyzed, for example, by Baruch Halpern, "Jerusalem and the Lineages in the Seventh Century BCE: Kinship and the Rise of Individual Moral Liability," in *Law and Ideology in Monarchic Israel*, ed. B. Halpern and D. Hobson, JSOTSup 124 (Sheffield, UK: Sheffield Academic, 1991), 11–107.

10. Joseph Blenkinsopp, *The Pentateuch: An Introduction to the First Five Books of the Bible* (London: SCM, 1992), 52.

11. This perception underlay much of the critical discussion about the formation of the Pentateuch. It was reinvigorated by David J. A. Clines's account of it in his *The Theme of the Pentateuch*, JSOTSup 10 (Sheffield, UK: JSOT Press, 1978).

the tabernacle recalls the completion of the divine work in creation (Exod. 40:33b; cf. Gen. 2:2).[12] And when the high priest stands once a year in the tabernacle's holy of holies, this is, if only provisionally, a restoration of the close presence of God to humanity that was lost in Eden. The memory of an ancient existence of Israel outside the land, yet fully constituted around a place of worship, forecloses any idea that it must have the form of landed nationhood with a centralized religio-political administration. This vision, widely seen as Priestly, lies close to the possibilities that presented themselves to what remained of Israel in the postexilic time.[13] For Michael Walzer, the postexilic "temple-state of the priests . . . was a kind of prefiguring of rabbinic statelessness," which was in turn, for him, a genuine descendant of the political discourse of the Hebrew Bible.[14]

Politics and the Person I: Moses and the Prophets

The Old Testament's political vision for human society is carried by its rendering of the life of the people of Israel, both in their inner relationships and in their engagement with the other peoples of their world. This rich account is formed by the full gamut of its literature—poetry, narrative, law, and wisdom. These constitute collectively the "discourse" of the Old Testament on politics, a discourse that "emphasizes process rather than final closure."[15] But always, humanity itself—individual, family, and nation—is in the center of the focus.

In the earlier chapters, we have begun to see some of the components of a political life, both in the Old Testament's view of the human constitution (ch. 3) and in its understanding of place and memory (ch. 6). In Deuteronomy the individual is at the heart of Moses' rhetorical strategy. The foundational exhortation in Deuteronomy 6:4–9, with its appeal to love Yahweh with "heart, soul, and strength" (Deut. 6:4–9), gives an intimate portrait of home and

---

12. Notice also the echo of the seven days of creation on the threshold of the tabernacle narrative and the chronology that places Yahweh's instructions to Moses for its construction on a seventh day (Exod. 24:15–18).

13. The Priestly vision does not stand alone, however, but is integrated into the Pentateuch in a way that preserves diverse views of the possibilities for Israel's existence. See further McConville, *God and Earthly Power: An Old Testament Political Theology, Genesis–Kings* (2006; repr., London: T&T Clark, 2008), 54–63, and works referred to there, especially Bernd Janowski, *Gottes Gegenwart in Israel*, BTAT 1 (Neukirchen-Vluyn: Neukirchener Verlag, 1993), and Norbert Lohfink, *Theology of the Pentateuch: Themes of the Priestly Narrative and Deuteronomy*, trans. Linda M. Maloney (Minneapolis: Fortress; Edinburgh: T&T Clark, 1994).

14. Walzer, *In God's Shadow*, 142, 211–12.

15. Morgenstern, *Conceiving a Nation*, 4. Both she and Walzer recognize the importance of the "discourse" of the Hebrew Bible in the articulation of its political ideas.

family. Yet this same rhetorical strategy places the individual and family firmly in the context of the body politic. By means of the alternation of singular and plural address, and also by the Deuteronomic device of merging the generations of Israel as sharing the memory of exodus and Horeb, the individual experience is melded into the collective. The individual is called to right action by virtue of his identity, as it were, with Israel. The exhortations to release debts and slaves are parade examples of this (Deut. 15:1–18). The acts of the individual are therefore by definition political. Deuteronomy is unique in the Old Testament in its developed vision of corporate responsibility, which has been called "citizenship."[16] For Jean-Marie Carrière, the *idea* of the political consists in the subordination of the natural bonds of locality and kin to a greater commonality. Deuteronomy may thus be said to have invented the notion of a political nation.[17] In doing so it provides a genuine challenge and alternative to the prevalent monarchical and imperial models, which pressed so hard upon Israel and which also proved irresistibly attractive.

Moses as "Center of Memory"

However, the individual is by no means lost in this political vision, but inescapably bound up with it. The point holds true in more than one way, as we shall see. But one aspect of it is unfolded in the part played by leaders in the political history of Israel. The gigantic figure of Moses is inseparable from the Old Testament's memories of Israel's origins. The conflict between Yahweh and Pharaoh in the prelude to the exodus is at the same time a clash between the human protagonists, Pharaoh and Moses. Moses is the archetypal reluctant prophet, a man for whom Egypt has become dangerous territory, but who is called back under divine compulsion from his new life in Midian to lead Yahweh's people out of Egypt.[18] The desperate conflict between him and Pharaoh turns on the nature of human organization, with Moses contending that humans should be free, not slaves. The freedom would consist in the service of Yahweh rather than Pharaoh (Exod. 5:1; 8:1). But Moses' agency in this battle between powerful forces is intriguingly indispensable. Why is it that Moses must be persuaded, or coerced, to carry the fight to the Egyptian king? The actual power in the events that are to follow lies, after all, with God, as the narrative makes abundantly plain. Yet Moses is called not

---

16. Jean-Marie Carrière, *Théorie du politique dans le Deutéronome: Analyse des unités, des structures et des concepts de Dt 16,18–18,22*, ÖBS 18 (Frankfurt: Lang, 1997), e.g., 248, 269–78.

17. For Morgenstern this idea is too narrow, as she finds the invention of the idea of a nation in the language of the Hebrew Bible more broadly. We will return to this below.

18. Aaron is also part of the picture, but is almost completely eclipsed by his younger brother.

merely to say things to Pharaoh, nor only to perform signs that the Egyptian magicians ultimately cannot emulate, but, in an extraordinary conceptualization of his role, to be "as God" to Pharaoh (Exod. 7:1). The statement apparently asserts that God chooses to be present in human affairs through human agency.[19] There is a connection between Yahweh's vision for a liberated Israel and his representation in this decisive moment of extrication by one who stands on behalf of Israel. Moses thus embodies in his person the character of the people of Israel, conceived as people of Yahweh and chosen to be the kind of thing that Pharaoh, in his own embodied politics, negates and rejects. Moses' embodied presence in this argument is therefore not incidental. It is no academic debate that he is conducting with Pharaoh, but a matter of life and death, the mission of a man who has killed in the cause of justice on Pharaoh's turf and who has had to flee for his own life (Exod. 2:11–22).

The interplay between the character of Moses and the character of Israel as people of Yahweh continues through the Exodus narrative. In the crisis of the golden calf episode, Yahweh threatens to make an end of his rebellious people and proposes to make a new start with Moses. The phrase "and of you I will make a great nation" (Exod. 32:10) is a precise echo of the promise to Abram in Genesis 12:2. It occurs once more in Numbers 14:12, in the further crisis between Yahweh and Israel provoked by their fearful refusal to go into the land following the reconnoitering mission of the spies (Num. 13). In both these cases, Moses adopts the prophetic role of intercessor in order to secure Yahweh's ongoing commitment to the people. But this intercessory work is not simply one role among others that Moses undertakes. Rather, it belongs to the conceptualization of Moses as one who in himself exhibits the true character of the people of Yahweh. In doing so, he also endures the hostility of the actual people in their hankering for Egypt, to the point of fearing for his life (Exod. 17:1–7; Num. 20:2–13). The burden of them is felt in the excessive strain of acting as their judge in disputes, as his Midianite father-in-law Jethro realizes (Exod. 18:17–18), counseling him to delegate. And it becomes intolerable when Moses is caught between the pressure of their resistance and his feeling that Yahweh has imposed this great weight upon him (Num. 11:10–15). He uses intimate familial language for the relationship he feels with the people, yet which at the same time is too much for him (v. 12), and he cries, "I cannot bear all this people entirely by myself" (v. 14; cf. Deut. 1:9). And he asks for death (v. 15).

Both representation of the people to God, and suffering in the performance of it, are traits that are associated with the prophetic vocation, not least in

19. See, for example, J. I. Durham, *Exodus*, WBC 3 (Nashville: Nelson, 1987), 86–87.

Jeremiah. Moses is indeed remembered as a prophet without parallel (Deut. 34:10–12) and as the giver of Yahweh's Torah. Before his death outside the land, he is allowed two parting shots, his song (Deut. 32:1–43) and his blessing (Deut. 33). In the song he adopts a prophetic voice, leaving with Israel a perpetual memory of their vocation to remain faithful to Yahweh, their persistent tendency to relapse, and the character of God to renew his favor to them. In the blessing he takes a quasi-paternal role, bequeathing blessings to the tribes in the manner of a dying father.

Moses as a political figure leaves a complex legacy. We have pursued so far his prophetic, representative role. In a sense this makes him "like" other figures, in an echo of his own declaration that Yahweh would in the future raise up "a prophet like me" (Deut. 18:15). This strand of the story, with its link between individual character and the true nature of Israel, continues into the books of Joshua to Kings. Joshua first appears alongside Moses as one who calls the people to act in faith (Num. 14:5–10), and he and Caleb are singled out—alone among the wilderness generation—as worthy to enter the land (Num. 14:24, 30). Joshua is developed as a political figure in the books of Deuteronomy and Joshua, marked by his courageous faith ("Be strong . . . Do not fear"; Deut. 31:6, 23; Josh 1:6) and his holding tenaciously to the Torah (Josh. 1:8). The resemblance between this requirement of Torah faithfulness and the Deuteronomic law about the king whom Yahweh may appoint at the people's request (Deut. 17:18–19) has been well observed. And in consequence Joshua has been seen as a foreshadowing of King Josiah, another model of political rectitude in the Deuteronomistic perspective.[20] A line may thus be traced from Moses through those who are seen to uphold the Torah, in a block of literature (Joshua–Kings) known to Jewish tradition as the Former Prophets.

Yet he is also unlike all other prophetic figures, in accordance with the contrary note struck by his epitaph: "never again did a prophet like Moses arise in Israel" (Deut. 34:10). In Moses' unique story, his destiny not to lead the people into the land is a decisive feature.[21] The tradition supplies explanations for this which imply fault on his part, albeit somewhat opaquely (Num. 20:12; 27:13–14; Deut. 1:37; 3:26; 32:51). It is part of a picture in which Moses, though he has in one respect represented what Israel is to become, is yet untypical. His entire life is lived outside the land that is "given" by Yahweh to Israel, and that is one of the people's defining characteristics. He occupies no role in Israel that becomes fully replicated in any other figure. He has no dynastic

20. Richard Nelson in particular has drawn attention to these affinities in "Josiah in the Book of Joshua," *JBL* 100 (1981): 531–40.

21. See Dennis T. Olson, *Deuteronomy and the Death of Moses: A Theological Reading*, OBT (Minneapolis: Fortress, 1994).

succession, and his protégé Joshua succeeds him only in a limited way, in his tasks of conquering and distributing land and of obeying the Torah.[22] In a sense he is succeeded by the Torah itself and by the mechanisms provided for in Deuteronomy for its administration (Deut. 16:18–18:22).[23] Moses' failure to enter the promised land is a symptom of his "strangeness," in Morgenstern's terms. For her, the depiction of Moses as a figure apart, an outsider who has been brought up in the Egyptian court and has lived and married in the land of Midian, belongs essentially to the Hebrew Bible's political conception: "The very presence of power represents an ethical difficulty. Thus the central question of the Israelite political order is . . . the minimization of power's estranging elements."[24] The picture of Moses as a political leader who represents what Israel can and should be is juxtaposed with one that knows how the exercise of power is necessarily entangled with the particularities of human experience and character.

The political legacy of the Moses narratives, therefore, points in two directions, each of which will now be pursued. We take up, first, the prophets as representative figures in line with Moses' memory. Then we shall go on to consider how the complications of power itself are manifest in the stories of certain of the Old Testament's leading characters.

The Prophets as "Centers of Memory"

In the portrayals of Moses as a political figure, one of the features is the function of memory in calling to mind the true character of Israel. In Moses' case, his articulation of the need to "remember" is imprinted not only on the Song of Moses but also on the rhetoric of the entire book of Deuteronomy. The pentateuchal portrayals of Moses, therefore, carry a consciousness of the nature of the true Israel. And this is not only intellectual but also moral and embodied, for his life is dedicated to the fulfillment in reality of the Israel that he conceives. We have previously noticed the close link between memory and identity, in connection with the "embodied memories" entailed in sacrifice and feast (ch. 6). Now we see that the prophet functions as a further embodied center of memory.

Certain moments in the confrontations between kings and prophets illustrate how prophets are shown to embody the true nature of Israel. The

---

22. On Joshua as successor to Moses, see Christa Schäfer-Lichtenberger, *Josua und Salomo: Eine Studie zu Autorität und Legitimität des Nachfolgers im Alten Testament*, VTSup 58 (Leiden: Brill, 1995).

23. See McConville, *God and Earthly Power*, 96–98.

24. Morgenstern, *Conceiving a Nation*, 49.

dramatic conflict between King Ahab and the prophet Elijah begins with king and prophet each accusing the other of "troubling" Israel (*'ōkēr yiśrā'ēl*; 1 Kings 18:17–18). The nature of Israel is plainly at stake: What is "Israel" and what would "trouble" it?[25] Elijah accuses Ahab of having "abandoned the commandments of Yahweh" (*ba'ăzobkem 'et miṣwōt yhwh*; v. 18). His pitch to the crowds on Mount Carmel is their need to choose between Yahweh and Baal, with the assumption that they should know the difference. In setting up twelve stones he memorializes the twelve historic tribes, with an allusion to the origin of "Israel" in the new name bestowed on the patriarch Jacob (v. 31; cf. Gen. 32:28). And in his prayer for Yahweh to demonstrate his superiority over Baal, he invokes Abraham, Isaac, and "Israel" (v. 36). Elijah has close affinities with Moses, not least in his return to Mount Horeb (Sinai) and his encounter there with Yahweh (1 Kings 19:11–18). And his prophetic vocation entails a path of suffering, in which, like Moses, he had a sense of threat to his life (v. 14).

Of the prophets, Jeremiah is perhaps the outstanding "center of memory."[26] The book that bears his name is situated on the brink of the first depredations of Judah and Jerusalem by the Babylonian king Nebuchadnezzar, and takes in the destruction of the temple, the exiling of many of the people of Judah to Babylon, and the descent of others, including the prophet, to Egypt. These shattering disruptions in the people's history pose starkly the notion of identity through the memory of formative events. In Jeremiah, though there is a notional sense that Israel properly encompasses the northern territories long since lost (Jer. 3:12), the destiny of Israel is contained, in effect, in Judah and in those who are exiled. Israel is thus being re-formed in practice, yet is still to be understood in terms of its origins. From the beginning, the book recalls its audience to the past, with images of exodus and wilderness and an evocation of that time as one of faithfulness to Yahweh (2:2–3). But it is now contrasted with a story of rebellion, expressed in terms of rejecting Yahweh's gifts of land and Torah, and his exclusive claims upon them, vested in that history. Whereas the pentateuchal traditions depict religious dangers as future possibility (as in Deut. 32), Jeremiah now looks back, its pages peopled with kings, officials, priests, and prophets who have perverted the practice and institutions of Yahwism (Jer. 2:26–28). Creation itself is undone here (4:23–26). Jeremiah pleads with his hearers to turn again to the "ancient paths" (6:16–17; cf. 18:15), though in the perspective of the text the

25. I have shown elsewhere how the story of the two kingdoms, each with a claim on Israelite identity, addresses this issue (McConville, *God and Earthly Power*, 156–65).

26. Jeremiah has much in common with Hosea in this respect, another prophet in whose thought history plays an enormous part.

message has already fallen on deaf ears. The result of this corruption of a true character is a monstrous and shameful thing, as recognized even by "all who pass by" (18:16).

In the midst of this picture of dissolution and crisis is the ever-present figure of Jeremiah. Jeremiah, the weeping prophet, surpasses all other prophets, and perhaps all other Old Testament characters, in the severity and the persistence of his sufferings. Some of his sayings betray extreme emotional or psychological disturbance (Jer. 4:19–22), and he apparently experienced the compulsion to speak the words of Yahweh as having a power destructive to himself (20:8–9). Opposition extended to plots against his life (11:21; 12:6; 18:18). He is suspected of treason and imprisoned (37:11–21), and on another occasion thrown into a muddy cistern (38:6). At the nadir, he curses the day on which he was born (20:14–18). Jeremiah's isolation is Elijah's sense of abandonment writ large.

Crucially for the conceptualization of the prophet in the book, these sufferings are by no means incidental, but come as part and parcel of his prophetic agency. In the prayers often known as his Confessions, he embodies the contention between Yahweh the judge and the people that is under judgment. As one of the people, he stands with them, feeling and expressing the dread of an approaching enemy (Jer. 4:19); as spokesman of God, he feels and expresses the divine anger against the corruption of the same people into the monstrous thing he deplores, so that at times it is not clear whether we are hearing the voice of the prophet or that of God (4:22; 9:1–3[8:23–9:2]). His inner conflictedness emerges vividly in Jeremiah 15:10–21, in which he both delights in the words of God and protests bitterly to him that he has "deceived" him, inflicting on him an incurable wound (15:16–18). There is a certain "incarnational" aspect to Jeremiah's portrayal, representing in his person the presence of Yahweh to the people, and of the people to Yahweh.

There are important political implications in this portrayal of Jeremiah. Like Moses, he recalls Israel to its true self not only by the words he says but also by the manifestation in his own life of what it is that Israel should be. His critical stance over against the kingdom of Judah is a political act, demanding that it take on a different character, consistent with its historic relationship with Yahweh. His opponents in Jerusalem are keenly aware of the political nature of his message, and hear his words as treasonous support for the enemy Babylon. To the reader, in contrast, it is presented as a form of judgment intended ultimately to renew the people to a character in keeping with its spiritual ancestry. Jeremiah embodies "alternative" Israel in his life, true Israel contracted to the span of a single individual. He shows forcefully what the political self may have to become in order to be present faithfully in public life.

The figure of Jeremiah is thus not far distant from that other icon of vicarious suffering, the Servant of Yahweh in the book of Isaiah. The identity of the Servant is impossible to identify certainly with any known historical person, despite many and various attempts to do so. In addition, Isaiah scholarship has more or less abandoned the old familiar idea that four Servant Songs, which seemed to be uttered by the Servant as an individual, could be isolated from the discourse of Isaiah 40–55.[27] Rather, the idea of servanthood runs through that section of Isaiah, in which the Servant is identified already in Isaiah 41:8–10 with historic Israel, the "seed of Abraham."[28] In places, however, the poetics of Isaiah appear to produce a sharply drawn portrait of an individual who has a role that can be distinguished from the group of which he is a member: he is a "teacher"[29] who encourages the weary and who suffers, offering his back to those who beat him and his cheek to those who pulled out his beard (Isa. 50:4–6). Yet the relationship between individual and community in the Servant passages is hard to resolve in a simple way, as Isaiah 49:3–6 testifies, where the Servant is addressed as "Israel" (v. 3) yet also has a mission to "bring back the tribes of Jacob" (v. 6).[30]

It is likely, therefore, that the passages formerly identified as the Servant Songs have behind them the known experience of an actual member of the exilic community. However, it may be no accident that the composition of the book has made it impossible to identify him, not even according to one of the familiar categories of king, priest, or prophet, though he has some marks of all of these.[31] It is a striking feature of Isaiah that the Davidic shape of the future hopes expressed early in the book (Isa. 7–11) retreats in this latter part,[32] in favor of a figure who is marked above all by the notion of service, which implies both a way of being in the world and a readiness for

27. These were, according to Bernhard Duhm, who originated the idea: Isa. 42:1–4; 49:1–6; 50:4–9; 52:13–53:12. See Brevard S. Childs, *Isaiah: A Commentary*, OTL (Louisville: Westminster John Knox, 2001), 323. Isaiah 42:5–9 was thought to be secondary to 42:1–4, and therefore not included in the original delimitation of the first song.

28. More fully, "the offspring of Abraham, my friend" (Isa. 41:8 NRSV). The Hebrew *'ōhăbî* is taken in LXX as *hon ēgapēsa* (whom I loved), echoing the theological tradition of the election of Israel.

29. The "tongue of a teacher" (Isa. 50:4 NRSV) is more precisely "the tongue of those who are taught" (*lĕšôn limmûdîm*); cf. NIV: "a well-instructed tongue."

30. It has been held that the qualifier "Israel" has come into this text under the influence of 41:8, though this view now seems less strong than it once did. See Childs, *Isaiah*, 383.

31. He brings justice, like kings (Isa. 42:4), and has some presence on an international stage (52:15); he has a mission to "raise up the tribes of Jacob and to restore the survivors of Israel" (49:6 NRSV) like a prophet; and in suffering on behalf of Israel, he combines prophetic and priestly roles (ch. 53).

32. Yahweh's covenant with David is remembered in 55:3, in a passage which seems to apply it in a new way to the redeemed people, without implying that they would actually have

sacrifice. The voice of the Servant continues to be heard after the profound evocation of chapter 53, in 61:1–3, where again his role cannot be confined to a single office in Israel.[33] And now, besides the Servant, we also have "the servants of Yahweh" (54:17), a group that presumably takes its example and character from the Servant and is identifiable among the returned community of Israel in chapters 56–66, equated with a kind of remnant (63:17; 65:8–16). In the Servant and the servants, a certain character of Israel is projected. In its commitment to costly service, it does not cease to be political, for this servant-Israel is the authentic exemplar of Jacob and Judah (65:8–10) and has its existence among the nations.

The Old Testament's political theme may be said to reach its high point here, in a vision that looks deeper than the tenure of offices, and beyond ways and means, and aspires to the most far-reaching kind of human transformation.

Politics and the Person II: Narrative Portraits

The trajectory traced above from Moses through the prophets is only one angle on the political theme in the Old Testament. From another angle, one can observe it in the warp and woof of the life of Israel as depicted in the literature. This searching focus on the texture of the literature has been well advocated by both Michael Walzer and Mira Morgenstern, not least in their interest in deliberation, discourse, and dialogue themselves as functions of political life. Walzer considers deliberation to be central to politics,[34] and finds in the biblical narrative of change and adaptation such "democratic" features as popular assent and the revisability of law.[35] Israel indeed, for this reason, is an "almost-democracy,"[36] one deposit of which he finds in the rabbinic value of practical deliberation. For Walzer, however, the writers of the Hebrew Bible take a low view of political life. It offers no political theory, and in its theology of one all-powerful God he finds that there is little room for meaningful decision making by humans. God's earthly rule is "apolitical," and the prophetic opposition to the policies of kings he sees as "anti-political."[37]

---

a king. The eternal validity of the Davidic covenant now undergirds the future of the "servants of Yahweh" (Childs, *Isaiah*, 434–35).

33. H. G. M. Williamson thinks that this passage unites features of the various characters who have carried Isaiah's expressions of hope up to this point. See Williamson, *Variations on a Theme: King, Messiah, and Servant in the Book of Isaiah* (Carlisle, UK: Paternoster, 1998), 167–202.

34. Walzer, *In God's Shadow*, 72–73.

35. Ibid., 201–4.

36. Ibid., 200.

37. Ibid., xii–xiii, 66–67.

In his view, "politics, secular, everyday politics, the management of our common affairs, is not recognized by the biblical writers as a centrally important or a humanly fulfilling activity."[38]

Morgenstern, in contrast, avoids this curious polarization between the practice of political virtues and politics itself, and looks to the narratives of the Hebrew Bible to portray in ordinary scenes, events, and characters, what actually constitutes political life. It is in the "quotidian and domestic"[39] that a political picture emerges. A number of her extended examples are taken from what the Hebrew Bible identifies as the time of the judges. This is suitable to her purpose, because it is a period of transition in Israel's political life, and also because it manifests a certain element of what she calls "strangeness" in its portrayals of human behavior and situations.

The book of Ruth is a prime example for her of the "quotidian and domestic." Here is a story of obscure people in an ordinary place in Israel. Its actions and conversations happen in the home, on the road, in the field. It has the additional quality of considering the life of Israel from the point of view of its margins. Its perspective is largely that of women, indeed of women bereft of their men. Naomi is displaced at the outset from the land of Israel because of famine, only to return years later accompanied by a Moabite daughter-in-law. There is a complex obverse here of the landed Israelite male, who is in center stage in, for example, the law codes. His place is taken in Ruth by Boaz, who in a certain sense normalizes Ruth's doubtful place in Israelite society by marrying her. Yet the story does not admit of an ending in normalization. This is partly because of the enormous subtlety of its depiction, leaving many of the questions it poses unanswered. Why, for example, is the son born to Boaz and Ruth portrayed as Naomi's child? Has Ruth in the end been conveniently sidelined (Ruth 4:13–17)?[40] How too does the closing genealogy, tracing a line from Perez through Boaz to King David, relate to the narrative? This seems to be a curious return to a patriarchal conception of legitimacy and identity after the overwhelmingly feminine depiction of the story. Yet the effect is probably the reverse—namely, that the narrative has a destabilizing function in relation to such a conception. The Moabite ancestress lies hidden within it, and behind her the reminder of Perez, "whom Tamar bore to Judah" (Ruth 4:12, cf. v. 18). Tamar is a leading example of irregularity and liminality in the memory of Israel, a Canaanite woman who is taken by Judah for his son and who assumes the guise of a prostitute to bear a child

---

38. Ibid., 186.
39. Morgenstern, *Conceiving a Nation*, 5.
40. See below, ch. 8, for a consideration of this point, in the context of the relationship between male and female characters in Ruth.

to Judah himself—namely, Perez (Gen. 38). Ruth and Tamar together preside over the finale of this story. In the process, they make a powerful bid for a radically inclusive view of what may be involved in being Israel. The idyllic tale turns out to be political dynamite. As such it has left its mark on the cultural memory. Jo Carruthers notes an example of this in Rider Haggard's novel *King Solomon's Mines*, in which allusions to Ruth function as a critical foil to a dominant voice opposing sexual relations between black and white, drawing on Ruth's status as the Moabite woman who became ancestress to King David.[41]

In what follows, however, we turn from stories of "ordinary folk" to two highly prominent figures in the Old Testament's story—namely, Joseph and David.

Joseph: "The Man" Exercises Power

Joseph is a prime example of the political theme in the context of individuals and familial relationships. Paradoxically, it is in the very motif of estrangement that this story enables a profound reflection on the true nature of Israel. In the foreign land of Egypt, one of twelve brothers is unrecognizably transformed, so that he is known by them only as "the man, the lord of the land [*hā'āreṣ*]" (Gen. 42:30). In this *hā'āreṣ* there is an unmistakable allusion to the human mandate to rule the earth (1:26, 28). Thus the narratively contrived estrangement between Joseph and the brothers becomes a way of refocusing on the ideal of human rule in the earth, and at the same time, on the possibility of harmony among brothers.

As is well known, the story begins in a depiction of seriously fractured family relationships (Gen. 37:2–4). The main fault line lies between Joseph himself and the rest of the brothers, and the breach is marked, crucially, by their inability to "speak peaceably" with him (*wĕlō' yākĕlû dabbĕrô lĕšālōm*, v. 4). As the issues are played out in the following narrative, in which the tables are turned and Joseph finds himself in a position of power over them, his behavior toward them seems puzzling and brutal. Why does he not reveal his identity to them at an earlier stage and so achieve his own ambition to see his father again? The likeliest explanation is that Joseph is pursuing a plan to bring about a well-founded reconciliation in the family. The series of deceptions that he employs serve the purpose of a kind of test on Joseph's

---

41. Jo Carruthers, "Literature," in *The Blackwell Companion to the Bible and Culture*, ed. John F. A. Sawyer (Oxford: Blackwell, 2006), 259: "The Book of Ruth disrupts the apparently anti-miscegenation text of *King Solomon's Mines*."

part to see if the brothers show signs of having changed since they sold him off as a slave into Egypt.[42]

The story throws into sharp relief the puzzlement of human character and the dilemmas of the participants as they seek to interpret each other, a dilemma that falls in turn upon the reader. It stages powerfully the tension between appearances and reality. The motif of dress plays a part in this when Joseph, flaunting his colorful coat as a symbol of his preeminence among the brothers, is cast ironically by them as a "master of dreams" (Gen. 37:19). The dreamer does not see that, in the reality portrayed in Genesis 37, the brothers have the power to consign him to an uncertain fate in Egypt, stripped of his finery, and effectively taken out of the family dynamics. He returns dramatically to their lives, even more finely arrayed as Pharaoh's vizier, now properly a "master of dreams," and having the power to conceal and disclose the new reality of the brothers' situation as he chooses. The discrepancy between appearance and reality is further expressed in the motif of Joseph's "face." The term "face" (*pānîm*) occurs twelve times between Genesis 43:3 and 45:3 and ironically underlines the brothers' inability to recognize him even though he is before their eyes.[43] The paradox of the face that both reveals and conceals belongs to the story's exploration of the relationship between the public and private spheres in human experience. Joseph the public figure uses his power to orchestrate events according to his intention to produce a better order of things, in his family as in Egypt. At the same time, Joseph experiences the hopes and the torments of a human being possessed by the natural affections of a son and brother. The moment of disclosure to his brothers (45:3) is also the moment at which he can no longer endure the tension entailed in the separation of these two parts of his being that his plan has required.

This awkward coexistence of the private and the political in an individual manifests an essential aspect of the political life. Morgenstern takes this story as one example of what she calls "conceiving a nation." Joseph's well-recognized desire to bring about reconciliation is thus given an extra quality— namely, the imagining of a nation founded on harmony and mutual respect. In this picture, discourse plays a crucial part. Just as the initial fracturing of relationships among Jacob's sons was marked by an inability to "speak peace," so the first effect of Joseph's disclosure of his identity to the brothers—after

42. I have dealt with the interpretation of Joseph in McConville, "Forgiveness as Private and Public Act: A Reading of the Biblical Joseph Narrative," *CBQ* 75 (2013): 635–48. On reconciliation as the theme of the narrative, see also Georg Fischer, "Die Josephsgeschichte als Modell für Versöhnung," in *Studies in the Book of Genesis: Literature, Redaction, and History*, ed. A. Wénin, BETL 155 (Leuven: Peeters, 2001), 243–71.

43. McConville, "Forgiveness as Private and Public Act," 640.

a short interval in which Joseph tells his story and they perhaps are silently astonished—is that they now speak with him (Gen. 45:15). For Morgenstern, Joseph's aim all along has been to "create the possibility of discourse among people . . . whose only shared memories are mutually destructive."[44] Past events cannot be changed, but they can be reinterpreted, differently remembered,[45] and so Joseph "enables discourse to be born."[46] The functions of speech and memory have been well recognized in the interpretation of the story, and it is no accident that it is a speech of Judah, subtly but convincingly reshaping memory, that finally breaks through the artificial barrier between appearance and reality (44:18–34; 45:1–3).[47] The restoration of authentic discourse between the brothers becomes the basis for the hope of a renewed kind of society. In contrast with the narrative's Egypt, with its overt and impressive power structures, Joseph knows that "the essence of nationhood consists primarily as a set of common tropes, or ways of thinking."[48]

In the sense that the narrative expresses an aspiration toward a kind of society based on shared values, it postulates a "transcendental moral (God-centered) standard" as a condition of success.[49] Joseph himself attributes the course of events to the hand of God, and in doing so he acknowledges that "God's role in politics emphasizes the consciousness of the Divine in the full realization of the human self."[50] This is in some contrast to the view of Walzer, noted above, that the Hebrew Bible's conception of God as all-powerful left little room for human decision making, and that politics was not considered a fulfilling human activity. Rather, political engagement is seen here to be a part of a realization of the human self, in which the relationship

44. Morgenstern, *Conceiving a Nation*, 27.
45. The factor of memory in creating new possibilities is epitomized in Joseph naming one of his sons Manasseh, based on the Hebrew meaning "to forget," and in his explanation that God had made him "forget all my hardship [*ʿāmālî*] and all my father's house" (41:51). This may mean that he has chosen to "forget" the conflicts that he knew when he was among his family, at a point when he was ready to make such a choice, not yet knowing that he would have an opportunity to try to put things right (cf. Morgenstern, *Conceiving a Nation*, 30).
46. Morgenstern, *Conceiving a Nation*, 29.
47. Treatments of memory in the Joseph story have been offered by Meir Sternberg, *The Poetics of Biblical Narrative* (Bloomington: Indiana University Press, 1985), whose section on it is entitled "Joseph and His Brothers: Making Sense of the Past" (285); and Barbara Green, *What Profit for Us? Remembering the Story of Joseph* (Lanham, MD: University Press of America, 1996). For an analysis of how Judah's speech proves itself authentic, see McConville, "Forgiveness as Private and Public Act," 643–45.
48. Morgenstern, *Conceiving a Nation*, 31. She thus sees Joseph as a kind of forerunner of Benedict Anderson's idea of "imagined communities." See Anderson, *Imagined Communities: Reflections on the Origins and Spread of Nationalism* (London: Verso, 2006).
49. Morgenstern, *Conceiving a Nation*, 38–39.
50. Ibid., 39.

between the human and the divine plays an essential part. The point lies close to our perception in the preceding section that the prophet embodied both the standard of the divine word and the right human response to it. There the political voice of the prophet was typically heard in stark opposition to the corruption of an ideal conception of Israel, often at serious personal cost to the prophet; here, the political vocation can also carry a personal cost, yet it devolves upon all members of the community as a kind of "body politic" and invests in individual and mutual integrity the real opportunity to change society for the better.

Neither Joseph's conception of the renewed nation, however, nor his apparently successful strategy to accomplish it, entirely shakes off the entanglements of political life. In one reading of the narrative, the brothers seem not to have finally accepted that Joseph has truly become reconciled to them, and this bodes ill for the future (Gen. 50:15–21). In my view this passage is better read as a confirmation of the trajectory up to Genesis 45. Yet there is a certain shadow over the scene in Joseph's very use of pharaonic plenipotentiary power to achieve his ends. This culminates in the unpromising enslavement of the people of Egypt as part of his solution to the crisis of food shortage in the land (47:13–26), which may be regarded as a foreboding of the enslavement of the Israelites themselves in due course, under a pharaoh who did not know Joseph (Exod. 1:8).[51] The conduct of political affairs apparently carries with it all the ambivalence of the human situation in the world, as portrayed in Genesis's own overture concerning the human as "image of God." Far from promulgating a political theory or program, the Old Testament depicts a political process, an activity, a function of humanity finding its way as the "image of God." Unsurprisingly, therefore, it does so through lives and situations that are peculiar to themselves, with all the eccentricities of ordinary human existence.

David: A Man Changed by Power

The Joseph story exemplifies that aspect of "strangeness," or alienation, that we have observed to belong to the political depiction of Old Testament characters. The same notes of alienation, otherness, and ultimately inclusion can be traced through many of the Old Testament's stories.

The theme is woven into the story of Israel's possession, and nonpossession, of the land. To the Deuteronomic vision of a people fully possessing the land

---

51. So Aaron Wildavsky, "What Is Permissible So That This People May Survive? Joseph the Administrator," *PS: Political Science and Politics* 22 (1989): 779–88 (cited in Morgenstern, *Conceiving a Nation*, 23).

given to them by Yahweh is counterposed virtually the entire narrative from Joshua to Kings, in which they are largely alienated from the land, either by deprivation of it in whole or in part, or by some corruption in the manner of its possession. The chronic tension between having and not having is signaled already in Joshua through its ironic juxtaposition of notices about complete conquest (such as Josh. 11:23) and indications that the land has not yet been fully taken (as in 13:1).[52] The dissonance continues into Judges, where the postulate of incomplete conquest is reaffirmed at the outset (Judg. 1) and is augmented by the Deuteronomistic framing of the book in which periods of peace and enjoyment of the land alternate with periods of loss at the hands of enemies, attributed to the Israelites' own unfaithfulness (2:11–23). Judges in fact unsparingly depicts a failure of Israel to be Israel, a decline into religious, social, and political chaos, producing in the end the felt need of a king (18:1; 19:1; 21:25). Yet the advent of King David, loudly heralded in 1 Samuel, will produce a kind of "rest" (2 Sam. 7:1) that will have its own dark side.

The transition from rule by judges to dynastic monarchy unfolds at length in rich narratives from Judges to Kings, suggesting that the transition itself is revealing for the topic of political Israel.[53] We have noticed above that this transition has left its mark on the texts. There are evident tensions in the narratives of the rise of Saul to become king, between his portrayal as the one chosen by God for the role (1 Sam. 9:1–10:16) and the voices that point to the dangers posed by a king to the life of Israel (8:10–18). Source critics resolve these tensions by supposing that the text combined originally promonarchical and antimonarchical sources.[54] More recent treatments find that the narratives subtly express tensions and ambiguities present in the human exercise of power.

The political mutation in which occasional charismatic judges are replaced in Israel by dynastic kingship produces a narrative effect, in which a single figure comes to dominate the story line. David takes center stage from 1 Samuel 16 to the end of 2 Samuel and into 1 Kings 1–2; indeed, he is heralded already at the beginning of 1 Samuel, albeit anonymously, when the closing words of Hannah's song proclaim: "[Yahweh] will give strength to his king, and exalt the power of his anointed [$mĕšîḥô$]" (1 Sam. 2:10). The narrative is the

---

52. This aspect of Joshua has been widely recognized. See, for example, Robert Polzin, *Moses and the Deuteronomist* (New York: Seabury, 1980). I have dealt with this elsewhere, most recently in McConville, *Joshua: Crossing Divides*, PGOT (Sheffield, UK: Sheffield Phoenix, 2013).

53. This point is noted by Morgenstern, *Conceiving a Nation*; and Joel Rosenberg, *King and Kin: Political Allegory in the Hebrew Bible* (Bloomington: Indiana University Press, 1986), 1.

54. A form of this view was offered by Frank Crüsemann, *Der Widerstand gegen das Königtum: Die antiköniglichen Texte des Alten Testaments und der Kampf um den frühen israelitischen Staat*, WMANT 49 (Neukirchen-Vluyn: Neukirchener Verlag, 1987). See also Tomoo Ishida, *The Royal Dynasties in Ancient Israel*, BZAW 142 (Berlin: de Gruyter, 1977).

most sinuous and developed political portrait in the Bible. If Joseph had a dream of an Israel founded securely on harmony among brothers, David had a chance to realize it.

In fact, David's reign evinces stark contrasts between aspiration and reality. The triumphant warrior decisively overcomes the Philistine threat, unites Israel, receives from Yahweh a promise of a perpetual dynasty (2 Sam. 7) that enters deep into the corporate memory of Israel (Ps. 89; Isa. 9:2–7[1–6]), and is said to have reigned justly (2 Sam. 8:15). In his own final testimony, as "the anointed [*mĕšîaḥ*] of the God of Jacob," he declares in prophetic vein that "the spirit of Yahweh" speaks through him, and professes to have reigned in righteousness as the one who bore Yahweh's promise and covenant (2 Sam. 23:1–7). In such light he emerges well enough as "the man after Yahweh's own heart," chosen in preference to the spiritually uncomprehending Saul (1 Sam. 13:14).[55]

Yet the narrative centerpiece of his reign is his infamous adultery with Bathsheba, supported by his premeditated murder of her husband Uriah (2 Sam. 11–12). These events are followed by a civil war in which David's much-loved son Absalom takes the field against him, only to die in the battle (2 Sam. 15–18). And the final scenes of his life find him condemning to death his loyal general Joab (1 Kings 2:5–6) and the Benjaminite Shimei, an enemy whom he had previously promised to spare (2:8–9). Perplexingly, the sentence on Joab follows immediately on David's charge to Solomon to trust courageously in Yahweh and keep his commandments so that the dynasty might be confirmed, so long as Solomon's heirs walked before Yahweh "in faithfulness, with all their heart and all their soul" (2:2–4), in terms drawn from Deuteronomy's primary command to Israel (Deut. 6:5). The charge is reminiscent also of Yahweh's commissioning words to Joshua (Josh. 1:6–9), itself an echo of the Deuteronomic law of the king (Deut. 17:14–20). The man chosen to be king shows a dark side as he strives to establish himself in the role.

Through this jarring narrative, the focus falls constantly on the humanity of David himself. We know him first as shepherd boy and musician, scourge of fierce predators and the giant Goliath (1 Sam. 17:31–51), and intimate friend of the heir apparent Jonathan (1 Sam. 20). As he draws near to power we find him pulled in different directions, possessed to the end by deep affection for both Saul and Jonathan (2 Sam. 1:19–27), yet displaying a ruthless streak in his dealings with the overbearing Nabal (1 Sam. 25:9–13) and in

---

55. I take this to mean an affinity between David and Yahweh, rather than simply referring to one whom Yahweh has chosen; thus with Mark K. George, "Yhwh's Own Heart," *CBQ* 64 (2002): 442–59. For the latter view, see P. Kyle McCarter, *1 Samuel*, AB 8 (New York: Doubleday, 1980), 229.

his duplicity and pragmatic violence while at the court of the Philistine king
Achish (27:8–12). The uneasy relationship between David in his natural affections and in his political persona comes to unbearably poignant expression
in his lament for his son Absalom (2 Sam. 18:33; 19:1–4). The father's grief
is in stark contrast to the expectations of the messenger who has brought
the news of victory (18:28), and especially to the sentiments of Joab, who
accuses David of bringing shame on his fighting men and prevails upon him
to come out of his private mourning to a public place and assure them of
his love for them (19:5–8). Joab's language is of shame and love and hatred.
In his view, David has misplaced his love. Absalom is to be ranked among
those who "hate" David, and David's right response should be to hate him
in return. Conversely, those who truly deserve David's love are those who
have fought on his side to preserve his kingdom. David's failure to perceive
this has brought shame on his supporters.[56] In an honor-shame culture, this
is a serious accusation, undermining their integrity and credibility. David's
officers and men have acted honorably according to a code of behavior they
have judged right. The confrontation between David and Joab goes to the
heart of what is involved in political commitment.

The Samuel narratives can be said to expose the effect of political power
upon a human being. Edwin M. Good, in his influential analysis of the story
of Saul, showed how a character who initially had no thought of power, and
was reluctant to accept the responsibility of it, gradually acquired the taste
for it, to the point of throwing off the condition of subjection to the prophetic
word by which he had been made king.[57] David's story can be read in a similar
way—namely, as one who is assumed by power rather than assuming it. This
is the nub of Joel Rosenberg's analysis.

For Rosenberg, the adoption of monarchy in Israel is a "going indoors."[58]
David's trajectory is a movement from outdoors to indoors, from the field of
action to sitting in his "house." This relocation of the leader corresponds to
the momentous political shift from a tribal, covenantal conception of Israel
(which Rosenberg terms "confederate") to a monarchical one, informed by
all the symbols and conventions of Canaanite and ancient Near Eastern royal
typology. As Rosenberg has it:

> Henceforth, [Israel's history] will be largely a chronicle of palace life, of the
> dynasty and its counterdynasties, of throne and bed. A history of ancestors

56. On honor and shame in the present narrative, see Philip Esler, *Sex, Wives, and Warriors:
Reading Biblical Narrative with the Ancient Audience* (Eugene, OR: Cascade, 2011), 302–21.
57. Edwin M. Good, *Irony in the Old Testament* (London: SPCK, 1965), 56–80.
58. Rosenberg, *King and Kin*, 124–32.

and tribes will become a history of kings and their prophetic adversaries, of
the dynastic chains and dynastic begettings, of decisions made within that
enclosed space, *the royal house.*[59]

In David's case, the marks of the transition include the defeat of all his enemies,
the bringing of the ark of the covenant to Jerusalem, the declared intention
to build a temple for Yahweh (2 Sam. 7:1–2), and the apparent designation
of a site for it (24:18–25).[60] The transition is uneasy in the Old Testament's
narratives of Israel (though less so in the Psalms),[61] as the prophetic hesitations of Samuel and Nathan about monarchy and temple testify. And these
hesitations lie deep within the narratives. The path to monarchy exposes not
only a "clash between cultural codes"[62] but also powerful tensions within the
person of David.

This perspective informs the reading of the Bathsheba-Uriah episode, which
can be understood as a conflict between cultural codes. The issue for interpretation is present at the outset in the notice that, when David mustered and
dispatched his troops for the campaign against Ammon, he himself "remained
in Jerusalem" (2 Sam. 11:1). On the surface, this looks like a dereliction of
duty. In most English translations of the text, it is the time of year "when
kings go out to war," and so the reader is surprised to learn, in the final line
of the notice, that David is not out among his troops, but sitting in his house.
It is the first recorded time that David does not go out with his armies; this
indeed was what had distinguished him from Saul during the decline of that
king.[63] The events that follow, in his house, seem to confirm the view that
David is culpable in his absence from the field of battle. Yet not all agree
that the text implies this. A case can be made that David as king is now seen
conforming to a new code, in which the king remains at home in his power
base, a master of strategy and a symbol of national unity. For Rosenberg, this
is a mark of the new way of war and statesmanship.[64] In support of it is the
fact that David's officers are portrayed as persuading him to act just in this
way (2 Sam. 18:2–4; 21:17).[65]

59. Ibid., 124 (emphasis original).
60. Rosenberg offers a rather longer list, including "the ecstatic dancing, the ritual nakedness of the king, the clash of bells and timbrels; ululating throngs and women's choruses of
tribute" (ibid., 124–25).
61. Ibid., 124.
62. Ibid., 132.
63. So Sternberg, *Poetics of Biblical Narrative*, 194, citing 2 Sam. 5:2.
64. Rosenberg, *King and Kin*, 126–27.
65. See Robert Polzin, *David and the Deuteronomist: A Literary Study of the Deuteronomic
History; Part Three: 2 Samuel* (Bloomington: Indiana University Press, 1993), 110.

The meaning of David staying at home has long been a puzzle in the interpretation of the narrative, as can be seen already in the Hebrew text of 2 Samuel 11:1. The phrase that is usually read as "when kings go out to war" actually has the word "messengers" in the Hebrew, not "kings." The words are similar in Hebrew, but the former has the letter *aleph* (') while the latter does not (*mal'ākîm*, not *mĕlākîm*).[66] However, the form of the word in the MT is anomalous,[67] suggesting a degree of uncertainty about it in the transmission of the text. The reading "messengers," therefore, looks like an attempt to exonerate David from the suspicion of dishonorable behavior, or in Robert P. Gordon's words, "a scribal attempt to shade off the irony and salvage something for David's reputation as a warlord."[68] While there have been defenses of "messengers,"[69] the dominant solution in both ancient and modern times has been to adopt the reading "kings."[70]

The ambiguity in 2 Samuel 11:1 stands as a kind of signpost to the thematic development of the story that follows.[71] Robert Polzin writes about it: "This verse, I would suggest, is too intricately ambiguous to be the result simply of textual or editorial misadventure, and, consequently, one does not have to choose between kings and messengers, because both meanings hover over the verse from the start."[72] The idea of "messengers" certainly plays a part in the imagining of the scene of David and the royal household. The king's isolated situation means that he depends on a retinue of unnamed messengers to carry out his commands and convey information. As Polzin points out, the term "messengers" occurs five times in 2 Samuel 11 (apart from v. 1).[73] There are

66. The words are given here in their lexical forms.

67. The noun is pointed in MT as for the word "messengers" (*mal'ākîm*), but with a line above the aleph, rather than the expected pointing (the vowel *qamets*) under it.

68. Robert P. Gordon, *I and II Samuel: A Commentary* (1986; repr., Carlisle, UK: Paternoster, 2004), 252.

69. One such is Henry P. Smith, *A Critical and Exegetical Commentary on the Books of Samuel*, ICC (Edinburgh: T&T Clark, 1899), 317–18.

70. The reading "kings" is attested by a number of Hebrew MSS, the LXX, Targums, and the Vulgate, as well as 1 Chron. 20:1. See P. Kyle McCarter, *II Samuel*, AB 9 (New York: Doubleday, 1984), 279. An alternative defense of David lies in accepting the reading "kings," but supposing that the text refers to the specific mobilization of kings against David in 2 Sam. 10:6 (McCarter, *II Samuel*, 285). This involves reading the text, not in the sense that the "turn of the year" (*litšûbat haššānâ*) means the springtime, when kings regularly went to war, but "the coming around again of the time of year at which the Aramean kings marched to the aid of the Ammonites" (ibid.). Henry P. Smith found this reading already in the medieval Jewish commentator Kimchi, but rejected it (*Samuel*, 318).

71. On the ambiguity of the passage, see Sternberg, *Poetics of Biblical Narrative*, 186–229. See also Keith Bodner, *David Observed: A King in the Eyes of His Court*, HBM 5 (Sheffield, UK: Sheffield Phoenix, 2008), 80–84; Polzin, *David and the Deuteronomist*, 109–30.

72. Polzin, *David and the Deuteronomist*, 111.

73. It occurs in vv. 4, 19, 22, 23, 25 (ibid.).

correspondingly twelve occurrences of the verb *šlḥ* (send): eight with David as sender or initiator,[74] three with Joab, and one with Bathsheba, who "sends" the crucial message that she is pregnant (v. 5). Three of them come clustered in verse 6, where David commands the reciprocal sending on which all the action depends. In addition to the sending of messengers, Uriah himself is "sent," fatally carrying his own sentence of death (vv. 14–15). The sending of messengers thus makes possible both David's affair with Bathsheba and the complicated communications with the troops in the field, including the sacrifice of Uriah.

The frequency of "messenger" language is not merely due to the circumstance that David is at home in Jerusalem while the troops are at war. Rather, it lays emphasis on his isolation and creates an atmosphere in which he is surrounded by an unspecified number of courtiers and familiars, who both facilitate and observe the king's actions.[75] How far they are privy also to his thoughts and intentions, and indeed his "private" actions, is an unknown factor in the narrative. But precisely this element of the unknown, or its "gaps" in Meir Sternberg's term, is part of its very fabric. It is present in all the interplay between David and Bathsheba, David and Uriah, David and Joab. Is Bathsheba a willing agent, or a victim? Does Uriah know what David is plotting against him, even while he allows himself to become part of its execution? Is Joab merely a loyal servant of the king, or does he have an agenda of his own?[76] These questions are unanswerable, but their very unanswerability shows how the narrative conveys an atmosphere of intrigue and suspicion and opens doors for ambitious and covert action. The court of King David brings dangers for those who inhabit it, not least David himself.

The point finds its sharpest focus in the actions that transpire between David and Uriah. David, having made his neighbor's wife pregnant, first looks for a way to cover up the deed. Summoning Uriah from the field, he indulges in pleasantries, then suggests to him that he go home and "wash [his] feet" (2 Sam. 11:7–8). Uriah pointedly does not do so, and when David repeats the suggestion (v. 10), Uriah exposes both the king's real intent—that he should sleep with his wife—and also the underlying issue at stake. Uriah declares that he will not enjoy the comforts of his home and bed while the ark of the covenant, his fellow soldiers, and "my lord Joab" are camping in the open

---

74. Seven are in the narrative tense; the eighth (in v. 6) is actually an imperative, in which David commands Joab to "send."

75. The idea of David being observed by his courtiers is the subject of Bodner, *David Observed*.

76. Such questions are addressed by Polzin, *David and the Deuteronomist*, 117–18. Cf. Sternberg, *Poetics of Biblical Narrative*, 186–229 (esp. 190–93).

field (v. 11). With this, Uriah appeals to the ancient traditions of Israel, according to which the armies of Israel, a muster of the tribes, go out with the ark in a sacred enterprise. In this setting, refraining from conjugal relations is taken for granted, as once enforced by David himself (1 Sam. 21:4–6[5–7]). In the present scene, David has apparently taken it as his royal right to override these ancient beliefs and practices. This clash of cultural codes lies between the version of monarchical privilege that David assumes here and the Israelite "confederate polity" espoused by, ironically, the Hittite Uriah.[77]

At the same time, Uriah delivers a sharp rebuke to the king, who presumably should have understood that the thing for which he had summoned Uriah home was unthinkable in those terms. We may wonder what Uriah actually suspects of David at this point. Why would the king bring him in particular back from the battle to cajole him into sleeping with his wife? If he suspects something, his defiance is the nobler for it. At any rate, if David now thinks his actions justified in terms of some new code, the tenor of the narrative leaves little room for the reader to agree. As a character, he appears here in an exceedingly poor light, not just because of the idleness, lust, and abuse of power entailed in the adulterous action, but because of the low calculation and disingenuousness with which he manages the fallout: feigning concern for the battle-worn soldier, unchastened by the other man's high principle, and dispatching him as the "messenger" of his own death. If there were signs of self-serving ambition in David's earlier career,[78] here in the hothouse of his own power it emerges fully grown.

David's murderous behavior, therefore, arises from a mix of his personality, with its disposition to ambition, and the possession of power. As suggested above, David is assumed by power as much as he assumes it. Rosenberg speaks of "the specifically political and institutional vertigo that afflicts the king and underlies his action toward Uriah."[79] His story looks like a proof of Morgenstern's dictum that "the very presence of power represents an ethical difficulty." The theme of human rule is manifested in his case within an ideological framework in which the good of the people, the blessings of peace, stability, and prosperity, are mediated through a king who has a special relationship with God (or the god). It finds expression in a number of Psalms, notably Psalms 72 and 89:1–37[2–38]. The burden of it, however, places a strain on David the man that comes close to overwhelming him. It does so not only in

77. Rosenberg, *King and Kin*, 132.

78. Even when David appears to be speaking as a loyal subject of Saul in 1 Sam. 24:9–14, he may actually be educating his followers and hearers in what Rosenberg calls "the art of obeisance," having in mind his own future elevation to the role of king (ibid., 136–37).

79. Ibid., 105.

his moral life but also in the crushing blow of Absalom's downfall, in which the maintenance of power has had the unintended consequence of the death of a beloved son; and worse, where the man's grief for his son must yield to a public display of hatred for him as his enemy.

The story makes a shocking contrast with Joseph's use of power to promote harmony among the contentious sons of Jacob. It has also come a long way from the discovery of David as the one who was fit to be king in preference to faithless Saul. Where now is the man "after God's heart"? David's potentially redeeming feature seems to be his willingness to hear rebuke and change. We see this first in his encounter with the wealthy Nabal, during his time as an adventuring refugee from Saul. When Nabal refuses to pay what amounts to protection money to David's men, David angrily resolves to take revenge by killing all the males in his household (1 Sam. 25:22) but is dissuaded by the eloquence and insight of Nabal's wife, Abigail. Abigail enables David to see a larger perspective on the episode, in which it is the prerogative of God to take vengeance on his enemies. He sees too that, even as God is preparing him to be "prince over Israel," it will be good to have avoided incurring bloodguilt for the murder of Nabal in the process (vv. 26–35). The truth of Abigail's words is vividly demonstrated when Nabal suddenly dies (vv. 36–38).

If David has heard the prophetic voice in this case, it does not prevent him, as we know, from falling again into the temptation to murder, nor from yielding to it in the most cold-blooded way. Once again a prophetic voice awakens his conscience in the matter of Uriah's death, this time that of Nathan, who had uttered the promise of an everlasting dynasty (2 Sam. 7:4–17). Nathan, like Abigail, enables David to see his own actions from another perspective, by means of the parable of the rich man who steals the poor man's lamb (12:1–6). As a result, he repents, worships, and fasts, signaling some change of heart, though the child born to the illicit liaison with Bathsheba dies.

David's misadventures as king have cast a searching light on human frailty in the exercise of power. They show too how the consequences of the individual's evil acts can spin irredeemably out of control. In spite of his penitence, his corrupt actions within his household lead to the civil war that now besets Israel, this too in accordance with Nathan's words (2 Sam. 12:10–12). Everything now lies under the shadow of Uriah. There follows a kind of normalizing of relationships, when he conceives another child by Bathsheba, now as his wife, and finally joins his troops at Rabbah and leads the final conquest of the city (12:24–31). Yet the last recorded scenes of his life find him counseling Solomon, his son by Bathsheba, to show no mercy in "establishing" his kingdom by executing both Joab and Shimei (1 Kings 2:5–9). Such action, indeed, will count as "wisdom" (v. 9). David has finally become an icon of the ideology of tyrannical power into which, prophetic countervoices notwithstanding, he has allowed himself to be initiated.

Conclusion

We have seen that the political theme is an inseparable part of the Old Testament's depiction of the human experience. Indeed, the political dimension of human life is rarely far from the surface across the whole range of the Old Testament literature. Whether we consider the great personalities of its depicted world, or look at that world "from below" in the interactions among its rich cast of major and minor figures, we are almost always being exposed to the manifold possibilities of human interrelating. The Old Testament provides for our political interest and inquiry not a theoretical argument but a montage of human stories. Its understanding of politics is neither more nor less than its understanding of human beings in their life together, considered on a broad canvas. And as politics is the story of the human, so the human story is political. That story is carried by the Old Testament literature, deploying the full panoply of its literary invention. We have seen the power of this invention in the stories we have analyzed, with their capacity to attract and repel, to engage sympathy and create perplexity, to appeal to readers' minds and hearts while allowing them room for the engagement of their own imagination and judgment.

Yet certain issues and questions run through this depiction of a world. The question of Israel itself is to the fore. Here is a people chosen by God to be a place of justice and righteousness in the world, yet which appears to be perpetually challenged in its capacity to conform to its vocation. How is it to understand itself? How can it exercise political responsibility in the world and yet retain integrity? Can it negotiate between categorical polarities such as principle and pragmatism, inclusion and exclusion? Is power itself ethically problematical?

Instead of adjudicating such questions, the Old Testament brings disparate voices into play. The fundamental tension lies between the pragmatism that almost inevitably devolves upon rulers and the prophetic voice that seeks to turn it back to first principles—both the origin of all things in God and the particularities of Israel's heritage: the call to remember that they were once slaves in Egypt and therefore need to take their place in the world as a, literally, extraordinary people; the receipt of the goods of life as gift; the cultivation of harmony among fellow humans; a repugnance at the accrual of wealth and power in centers of privilege.

The Old Testament's story of Israel is little different from the stories of nations at large, past and present. It does not finish in a resolution of the tensions that are apparently built into the human condition. Its power as a depiction of that condition, however, lies precisely in this unfinished state. The corporate memory of Israel in the Old Testament segues into eschatological visions of a renewed Zion, in which

> They shall not hurt or destroy
>   in all my holy mountain;
> for the earth shall be full of the knowledge of the LORD
>   as the waters cover the sea. (Isa. 11:9 RSV)

This gives shape to the hope of the resolution of the most intractable human problems, which the Old Testament locates nowhere else than in the human heart. Though the fulfillment of the vision lies always in the future, it has the capacity to shape more immediate aspirations, both principled and pragmatic.

8

Male and Female

In the preceding chapter, we considered one aspect of humanity as the "image of God," namely, the political dimension of the responsibility to "rule" in the earth. We now look more closely at the idea of the "image" as "male and female" (Gen. 1:27). For Phyllis Trible, this text is the hermeneutical "clue" to her topic of "God and the rhetoric of sexuality,"[1] signaling both unity and differentiation in humankind as intrinsic to the "image" and suggesting equality rather than hierarchy as the essence of the human relationship.[2] More importantly, the "image of God" as the human, male and female, is a unique scriptural clue to the transcendence of God: "To describe male and female, then, is to perceive the image of God; to perceive the image of God is to glimpse the transcendence of God."[3] For Trible, human sexuality is central to a theological inquiry about the nature of God.

Our concern here will be to think about how the diverse texts of the Old Testament conceive of humanity in its sexual aspect, and how they contribute to the wider picture we are constructing of an Old Testament understanding of "the life of Adam." As in the case of politics, however, it is not a textbook of correct thinking or behavior in this area. Rather, the texts testify both to a struggle to live out the male-female relationship in Israel and to a theological

1. Phyllis Trible, *God and the Rhetoric of Sexuality*, OBT (1978; repr., Philadelphia: Fortress, 1992), 12.
2. Ibid., 18.
3. Ibid., 21.

149

engagement with this. In our approach to the topic, we are obliged to find a way of allowing the texts to speak as, inevitably, we also bring our own modern questions to the topic.

Trible's hermeneutical approach still offers valuable pointers to this task. Having taken Genesis 1 as a clue, postulating a harmonious, cooperative relationship between the man and the woman as a function of the "image," she traces the topic through female imagery in the Old Testament's poetry, the complication of the male-female relationship in the story of Eden (Gen. 2–3), the rediscovery of intimacy in the Song of Songs, and finally, in the "human comedy" of the book of Ruth, an engagement with the possibilities of love in the context of the hard realities of the world. We also have taken a cue from the idea of humanity as "image of God," and in what follows we will build on what we have observed about that topic in Genesis 1–3 (above, chs. 1–2) to consider how the language and imagination of the Old Testament enable us to think about human sexuality.

The creation texts in Genesis 1–3, as we have seen, give the humans a unique place in the world, embodying God's presence in it. Their life together as a commission to work out what it means to be in the "image of God" applies not only to the "dominion" entrusted to them but also to their very nature as human beings, male and female. The aspects of being and acting are inseparable, and their sexual unity in diversity is essential to their being.[4] We noticed above (ch. 4) the argument of Sarah Coakley that all human desire is at root a desire for God. The sexual relationship is primary in this respect, but spills over into other kinds of human relating. The radical and "democratic" concept of the "image," in its ancient Near Eastern background, has the potential to liberate from all kinds of tyranny. This potential rightly applies to the sexual relationship, indeed perhaps primarily there.

The story that unfolds after Genesis 1, as we have seen, takes us immediately to the harsh realities that beset the humans' task of realizing their condition as "image of God," and this is true as much of the sexual relationship as of any other aspect of their being. That relationship is at the heart of the fateful issue of life and death that is at stake in that overture. Yet we shall see that the story of man and woman is not wholly defined in terms of conflict and hardship, or indeed abuse, but also in terms of their vocation to engage creatively in imagining and playing out what this relationship might be, in the pursuit of embodying their being in "the image of God."

4. We saw, notably, that Karl Barth considers the relationship between male and female as crucial to his understanding of the "image" as relational, in the sense that this human relationship corresponds to the human capacity to relate to God. See above, ch. 1, nn. 47–48.

The Problem of Cultural Difference

The attempt to articulate a biblical view of human sexuality poses particular challenges for the interpreter. Foremost, as with all the topics we have considered, is the setting of the literature in an Iron Age culture. How far do texts simply reflect the norms of that culture, and do they ever challenge them? In addition, the Old Testament frequently uses sexual imagery in its religious language. Here too there are difficult questions about how far such language assumes a hierarchical, or even oppressive, relationship between men and women, and whether it is ever liberating.

We have just considered, in the preceding chapter, the brilliant narrative of David and Bathsheba (2 Sam. 11–12) as part of the expression of the tensions between a person's private and public life. This story also illustrates how much human sexuality comes to us wrapped in the garments of the biblical period. Sexuality is at the heart of that highly charged episode, inseparable from the entailments of power. David's annexation of Bathsheba has a background in assumptions about marriage as a function of royal status and rule. At the height of Absalom's rebellion, when briefly in possession of Jerusalem, he makes a public display of taking his father's concubines, whom David had left in charge of the household (2 Sam. 15:16; 16:20–22). The shaming of the king in the area of his sexual rights is part of Absalom's bid for recognition as the unrivaled force in the kingdom. While the Bathsheba narrative strongly implies guilt on David's part for adultery and murder, it does so within the context of codes of behavior that do not directly challenge prevailing mores in themselves, such as polygamy and concubinage.

The Old Testament texts are in fact largely dominated by male perspectives and concerns. The story of Israel has largely been told as a story of men, and presumably by men. This corresponds to the reality that women were subject to men in a hierarchical social pattern embracing the family, through localized village or clan structures, up to the organization of the centralized state. Women were inhibited in terms of legal status and property, and thus in general dependent on men. The case of the daughters of Zelophehad, who pressed successfully for a right to inherit their father's estate in the absence of male heirs, merely proves the rule that property is regulated within a system of patriarchal ownership (Num. 27:1–11; 36).[5] Marriage appears to have

---

5. The right of daughters' inheritance granted by Moses remains exceptional, within a provision that is still overwhelmingly male and is always in the interest of preserving the name of the father (Num. 27:1–11). The concession to the daughters is further restricted by the requirement that they may not marry outside the tribe, since that would entail the loss of a part of the tribe's inheritance (Num. 36).

been a negotiation between a woman's father and her prospective husband (Deut. 22). Widowhood was a marginalized state, as numerous texts show. The practice of levirate marriage, for example, where a brother of the deceased took on the responsibility for the widow, somewhat alleviates the widow's situation. Revealingly, however, the purpose of the practice, according to the law in Deuteronomy 25:5–10, is to address the problem of a man who has died without having had a son. The levirate practice aimed to redress this by reckoning the first son of the new union to the dead man's line. The legal issue is thus one of male succession to property.

Because the Old Testament is steeped in the cultural norms of the biblical world, it cannot directly address modern issues such as same-sex marriage or other lifestyle choices available to men and women today. Since, for cultural reasons, women (and men) in the Bible do not marry each other, if (on the whole) they do not go to war or govern, or write the narratives and poetry (mostly, probably), the texts that presuppose such patterns cannot translate into general prescriptions for life, based on "essentialist" characteristics of the sexes.[6] They merely tell us something about expectations and possibilities in societies in the biblical world. There may, of course, be liberating notes embedded in those expectations and possibilities. And we can certainly rethink what we have thought we understood about the Old Testament's depiction of reality, as feminist readings have taught us to do. These have sought not only to expose the patriarchal nature of the biblical world and texts, and what this meant for the place of women in society, but also to provoke reflection on the ways in which the texts have also been read through patriarchal lenses. In approaching the Old Testament for a view of male-female relationships, therefore, we encounter one of the slippery areas of biblical interpretation. Yet there is rich material for reflection here, which provides both stimulus and challenge as we think about modern gender issues.

Life, Death, and Sex

As we have observed, the sexual relationship is at the heart of the issue of life and death itself in the Genesis creation narratives (Gen. 3). And this interpenetration of sex, life, and death permeates the biblical texts. I now want to consider the topic in terms of its possibilities for both death and life, by means of an examination of specific texts drawn from several types

---

6. On "essentialism" as a concept in relation to gender, see Mark W. Elliott, "Human Embodiment," in *The Dynamics of Human Life*, ed. Mark Elliott (Carlisle, UK: Paternoster, 2001), 99–107.

of Old Testament material. We begin with narratives, and take as a first case a story of death.

The Levite's Concubine

Among what Phyllis Trible memorably called the Old Testament's "texts of terror," the account of the appalling fate of the Levite's concubine (Judg. 19) is perhaps the most chilling.[7] An unnamed Levite from Ephraim "takes" a concubine, also unnamed, from Bethlehem in Judah. After a time she leaves him to return to her father's house, and he sets out to bring her back. On their journey home, they come under siege in a house in the city of Gibeah in Benjamin, when, in a scene reminiscent of one involving Lot in Sodom (Gen. 19), men of the city demand that their host send out the Levite, intending to abuse him sexually. His host refuses, being strongly constrained by the rules of hospitality. But the outcome is that the Levite pushes his concubine out to them (Judg. 19:25), and they rape and abuse her all night. It is not clear whether she dies of her injuries. But the Levite, having carried her to his home on his donkey, cuts her body in twelve pieces and sends the parts throughout the territory of Israel. In consequence, the other tribes undertake a bloody war against Benjamin (Judg. 20).

The episode is evidently portrayed by the narrative as a terrible crime, and serves a redactor's purpose to demonstrate the social chaos of the time, in which "there was no king in Israel. Everyone did what was right in their own eyes" (Judg. 21:25; cf. 19:1). The Levite's action in sending her body parts as a call to war, and the response of the tribes, exhibits outrage at the "disgrace"[8] brought upon Israel by what the men of Gibeah have done. It even seems to have become notorious in the corporate memory of Israel (Hosea 9:9; 10:9).[9]

Yet it is not entirely clear what the outrage of the men in the story is directed at. The Levite himself at no time shows compassion or concern for the woman. It was he who consigned her to her fate in an act of self-defense. The storytelling leaves open the possibility that she did not die directly of her injuries during the night, but that the Levite actually kills her before dismembering her. He himself blames her death on her rapists (Judg. 20:5), but

---

7. Phyllis Trible, *Texts of Terror: Literary Feminist Readings of Biblical Narratives*, OBT (Philadelphia: Fortress, 1984), 64–91.

8. Judg. 20:10. The word in Hebrew is *nĕbālâ*, which means "folly," but with an implication of moral baseness. In the context it also implies that shame has been brought on Israel, and this is what must be requited. See also the phrase "purge the evil from Israel" (Judg. 20:13). That phrase is frequent in Deuteronomy, for the obligation on Israel to root out sin from the people (Deut. 13:5; 17:7; 19:19; 21:21; 22:21; 24:7).

9. Trible, *Texts of Terror*, 86.

the narrator had left it unsaid (19:26–28). The discourse relentlessly focuses on male thoughts and actions. The woman is scarcely granted the status of a person. The offense, as perceived by both the Levite and the men of Israel, is apparently an offense done to the Levite in an abuse of the hospitality custom that has deprived him of his property, the concubine. In his own account of it to the men of Israel, the hostile actions of the Gibeahites were aimed at him, and he covers up his own part in her terrible fate (20:4–5). Here, the male-female relationship is corrupted into the ultimate abuse of the woman by men. The culture of hospitality turns out to be predicated entirely on male honor, and in this case has required a female sacrifice. The episode also has a terrible aftermath in the war against Benjamin, resulting in not only the deaths of huge numbers of warriors on both sides but also the slaughter of women, children, and men in Jabesh-Gilead and the forcible abduction of six hundred virgins from both that city and Shiloh (Judg. 21). As Trible points out, the single rape at Gibeah has led to hundreds more.[10]

The story is deeply disturbing because it is told according to criteria that are as alien to the modern reader as the events are repugnant. While the narrative condemns the actions at Gibeah, it is not quite clear why, and this casts a shadow over its own analysis of social chaos and the necessary remedy. Does the kind of order that it seeks have at heart the well-being of all Israelites, men and women? If so, the advent of the desired royal rule, as we have already seen, falls short of fulfilling that hope.

Regardless of the redactional purpose, the story has made its own impact on the imagination and sensibilities of its readers. What kind of relationship did the Levite and his concubine have, and what went wrong in it? Is there any trace of justice here, even if mercy is clearly absent? The textual tradition provides no ready answer to this. In the MT of Judges 19:2 the woman is said to have "been unfaithful" or "played the harlot" against him (*wattizneh 'ālāyw*), and so left him. Yet there is no sense in the ensuing narrative that the unfolding events have been due in any way to guilt on her part. The MT's use of *znh* may not mean that she was actually guilty of adultery or prostitution; it may amount simply to a judgment on the fact that she left him. (The prophets use *znh* metaphorically to characterize Israel's religious disloyalty to Yahweh, as in Hosea 1–3.) When the Levite goes after her to bring her home, there is no sign of censure. So the narrative does not encourage us to look for a reason for her fate in her own actions. The reluctance of the textual tradition to shed light on the original rift between the two is evident in Judges 19:2 (LXX), which has "she became angry with him" (*kai ōrgisthē autō*). This

10. Ibid., 83.

may be based on Hebrew *wattiznaḥ* (she despised [him]),[11] a reading adopted by the RSV and NRSV. Taking these indications together, it looks as if the primary fact is simply that the woman left him for her own reasons, and that the texts are under constraint to supply some explanation. Yet the refusal of clarity on the point, or any development of it in the narrative, points away from finding grounds against her in the story.

There is, therefore, nothing to mitigate the dreadful crime at Gibeah. It is thoroughly a text of death, and one that, for the reader, can hardly do more than mirror dreadful possibilities. The challenge for interpretation is to allow the text to reflect back upon the reader's own world and open up ways in which contemporary attitudes, including the reader's own, may also tend toward "death" in the area of sexual relations. The reception history of the story makes sobering reading, as David Gunn has richly documented.[12] Interpreters have not been slow to fill the gaps in their own ways, with many ready to condemn the concubine as an adulterer and whore, and even to censure her father for receiving her home without demur. Others realize that the text is unclear on the point, while for others again the chief point, and lesson, is the breakdown of good order, a concern that could deflect attention from the nature of the crime itself.[13]

Trible finds the possibilities vividly brought to life by the text to be alive and well in her own modern world, and concludes her treatment of the narrative simply with the repeated call, addressed to whoever has ears to hear: "Repent. Repent."[14]

Tamar and Ruth

Somewhat different possibilities are opened up by the related stories of the patriarch Judah's daughter-in-law Tamar and that of the Moabite woman Ruth. Tamar, the wife of Judah's eldest son, Er, is given on Er's death to Onan, who is ordered by Judah to play the part of *levir* (Gen. 38:1–10; cf. Deut. 25:5–10). When Onan too dies, Judah refuses to give Tamar to his surviving son, Shelah, and the story continues with Tamar's daring strategy

---

11. See Daniel I. Block, *Judges, Ruth*, NAC 6 (Nashville: Broadman & Holman, 1999), 523.

12. David M. Gunn, *Judges through the Centuries*, BBC (Oxford: Blackwell, 2005), 243–60, esp. 250–51.

13. Ibid., 249–51. Among the more lenient, the poet John Milton, citing rabbinic precedents, thought "fornication" must be meant metaphorically as something like showing contempt for her husband. He finds it impossible that the father would have received her if she had in fact been guilty of "whoredom." Laurence Sterne is cited as an object lesson in nonjudgmental compassion (ibid., 252–53).

14. Trible, *Texts of Terror*, 87.

to force Judah to fulfill his obligations to her by pretending to be a prostitute and tricking him into making her pregnant himself (Gen. 38:11–30). The narrative tells much about the dangers to a woman who has lost her place in society, both in presenting prostitution as a reality of Israelite life, a recourse presumably of women rejected by family, and in the peremptory and terrifying way in which Judah sentences Tamar to death for having become pregnant while in her own father's house (38:24).

The story is remarkable for the centrality given in it to Tamar, a woman and (probably) a Canaanite.[15] A key moment in it is when Judah is forced to admit that she is "more righteous" than he (*ṣādĕqâ mimmennî*, Gen. 38:26). He has shown fierce indignation about her alleged prostitution, an inexcusable offense according to his patriarchal code while she is still, in some sense, part of his extended family. Judah's admission that Tamar is "more righteous" might imply a kind of legal judgment, in the sense that, in the case between them, she is in the right and he in the wrong.[16] Yet there is a stronger, ironic sense too, in which the Canaanite woman has taught the Israelite patriarch what is "righteous," the virtue that, in Mosaic Torah, stands over all right practice and understanding (Deut. 16:20). The episode sheds bright light on the norms and expectations of the world in which it is set. In a sense those norms are undisturbed by the subversive angle of the narrative, for Tamar's hope and intention all the while is to be received back into Judah's house, which she presumably sees as her only permanent place of safety. For her, the levirate arrangement, for all its patriarchal assumptions, was her only means of security. Even so, it is striking that this levirate story comes with a definite countercultural bite. In a narrative that highlights a particular, highly charged male-female relationship, we find a surprising level of reflection on what may count as right and true in the context of a certain accepted code of behavior.

The story of Ruth is expressly linked with that of Tamar. Ruth, a Moabite woman, has returned to Bethlehem with her mother-in-law, Naomi, after Naomi, her husband, and two sons had taken refuge from famine in Moab, and tragically the three men had all died there. Ruth is accepted into Bethlehem society through marriage to Boaz, a relative of Naomi who adopts the role of "kinsman-redeemer" (*gō'ēl*). When Ruth gives birth to Boaz's son Obed, "the father of Jesse, the father of David" (Ruth 4:22), the event is celebrated by the women of Bethlehem with the prayer: "May your house be like the house of

15. Judah himself married a Canaanite woman, Shua (Gen. 38:2), the mother of Er, Onan, and Shelah. The story shows him consorting freely with Canaanites, and Tamar's Canaanite origins seem to be implied. See Kirsten Nielsen, *Ruth*, trans. Edward Broadbridge, OTL (London: SCM, 1997), 15.

16. Nielsen takes it in this sense (ibid., 13).

Perez, whom Tamar bore to Judah" (4:12). Ruth's marriage to Boaz has echoes of the levirate practice, though the correspondence is not exact, and Boaz's role is presented throughout as "kinsman-redeemer" (gō'ēl). Here, as in the case of Tamar, the events are played out in a framework of male authority and power. Prospects of life and security depend, for both Orpah (Naomi's other widowed daughter-in-law) and Ruth, on finding a husband (1:9–13), and Ruth's assimilation into Israel is secured by her marriage to Boaz. The largely female story finishes with a thoroughly male genealogy, suggesting that the characters and action are ultimately surrounded by masculine concerns.

Yet the female perspective on life in rural Judah that pervades the book of Ruth has a powerful effect on the reader, posing sharp questions to the domination of the male point of view.[17] We have already considered the book in the context of its contribution to the Old Testament's political discourse, in which the centrality of women, and especially a Moabite woman, argues for the acceptance of the "stranger" into Israelite society (above, ch. 7). But the story has a distinctively male-female dynamic, too. The precise nature of this dynamic is difficult to tease out, given the complexities of both character portrayal and the social world of the text.[18] In Trible's analysis, the conventionally male pattern of focus and action in the opening verses (Ruth 1:1–2) quickly gives way to one in which the males have been removed from the scene, and initiative and action are left entirely in female hands.[19] The bold and unconventional nature of Ruth's decision to go with her mother-in-law to the strange country of Israel is thrown into relief by the decision of Orpah to remain within conventional boundaries by staying among her own people.[20] Ruth displays a commitment to another woman of a sort that might more naturally be expected in a marital relationship.[21] The relationship between the two women forms a dynamic narrative thread, in which Naomi is at first disposed to seek solutions within conventional norms, and is only gradually won over by Ruth's more adventurous attitude.[22] Ruth paradoxically maintains

17. Nielsen thinks the significance of the explicit connection with the Tamar story is that Ruth latches on to the positive side of the former story—namely, in the sense that a woman overcomes infertility, a condition that affects several of the women in the story of Israel's ancestry (ibid., 15–17).

18. The reading I adopt here is close to Trible's essentially positive take on the relationship between Ruth and Naomi. A somewhat more suspicious reading of that relationship is offered by Danna Nolan Fewell and David M. Gunn, *Compromising Redemption: Relating Characters in the Book of Ruth* (Louisville: Westminster John Knox, 1990), 69–82.

19. Trible, *God and the Rhetoric of Sexuality*, 168–69.

20. Ibid., 172.

21. Ibid., 173.

22. Ibid., 179–80. For Fewell and Gunn, it remains unclear till the end whether Naomi is in fact won over. For them, Naomi maintains a "patriarchal" view of social norms, and her

a primary concern for Naomi, while Naomi looks for Ruth to be settled in the house of a husband. When Ruth agrees to her mother-in-law's plan to go to Boaz at night, she does so in a way that, as Trible points out, exceeds Naomi's instructions and is never reported back to the older woman.[23] The silence leaves room for the reader's imagination, as do other silences in the book.[24] But it is clear that the sexual freight of the narrative is more complicated than its male-female aspect. The unfolding of a female experience, in the context of negotiating basic issues of life and death, is at the heart of this. We might well consider what sort of author can portray such things convincingly; Trible pointedly refers regularly to the author as "she or he."

The female experience, however, is interwoven with a whole web of relationships that constitute the social pattern of Naomi's Bethlehem. When it comes to decisions about Ruth's destiny, these are played out among men at the city gate (Ruth 4). Yet the nuancing of this interplay of male and female is more delicate than a mere ironic contradiction between official male channels of authority and the informal or actual power of female initiative. There is within the strong cultural constraints a convergence between male and female in plans and actions that lead to life and good, as the outcome of events that began with scarcity and death. As Trible has it, Boaz's appearance in the story "begins to restore a balance between female and male as creatures of life."[25] This male-female mutuality is not narrowly defined in terms of sexual love or marriage, but embraces the whole gamut of male-female relationships in the context of a social network, which in this case operates benignly. Even so, Ruth and Boaz come to occupy center stage. The mutuality of male and female is expressed in the counterpoint of the virtues of these two: she is, in Boaz's words, a "woman of worth" (*'ēšet ḥayil*, 3:11), echoing the narrator's introduction of Boaz himself as "a powerful man of worth" (*'îš gibbôr ḥayil*,

---

relationship with Ruth is affected both by a suspicion of foreign women, and by echoes of the jealousy felt by a childless woman toward one who can bear children, as in the narratives of Sarah and Hagar, and Rachel and Leah. At the end of the story, Naomi is left holding the baby, while Ruth appears to have been sidelined (Fewell and Gunn, *Compromising Redemption*, 74–76, 80–82).

23. Trible, *God and the Rhetoric of Sexuality*, 182–84, 186.

24. For Fewell and Gunn, it suggests not only that Ruth is sensitive to what Naomi needs but also that she wishes Naomi to understand that Naomi's "future is in fact in her daughter-in-law's hands, that she is included in whatever 'redemption' Boaz has in store for Ruth" (*Compromising Redemption*, 79–80). The book's silences include that of Ruth in the end. Has she been finally included or excluded? With Trible on the side of her inclusion is Ellen van Wolde, *Ruth and Naomi*, trans. John Bowden (London: SCM, 1997), 110–11. See also James McKeown, *Ruth*, THOTC (Grand Rapids: Eerdmans, 2015), 67–70. McKeown reads the story as one of blessing, with echoes of the Abrahamic promise.

25. Trible, *God and the Rhetoric of Sexuality*, 175.

2:1).[26] The term *ḥayil* has a range of possible connotations, including wealth, standing, courage, and virtue. Applied to Boaz it denotes the high regard in which he is held in the community; in Ruth's case it evokes her active, self-effacing loyalty to Naomi. Each has shown great stature according to their respective circumstances and opportunities.

Together with this *ḥayil* is the other characteristic virtue of the narrative, the concept of "steadfast love" (*ḥesed*). As an attribute of Yahweh, Naomi twice invokes it, in her prayer for Ruth and Orpah (Ruth 1:8) and when she learns that Ruth has encountered Boaz in the field (2:20). Boaz then applies it to Ruth, meaning the "kindness" she has shown him by coming to him at the threshing floor (3:10). This *ḥesed*, implying a trust in an underlying mercifulness in things, thus expresses an ethical quality that informs and explains both the good outcomes of the events narrated and the nature of the characters' actions. There is no sentimentality in this picture. The book of Ruth has reckoned with the sharpest of realities in famine and death, and in the dangers posed to an unprotected woman in a foreign land. But it does portray and celebrate potential good. In the resolution of this plot that has hovered between weal and woe, Trible makes the connection with the first Genesis creation account: "The image of God male and female rejoices at last in the goodness of daily life."[27]

The Old Testament's narrative texts are suggestive, therefore, in ways peculiar to each, of possibilities inherent in male-female relationships. As with other spheres of human existence, they can appear under the banner of curse or blessing, death or life.

Poetic Texts

The depiction of humanity, male and female, is powerfully accomplished also in the Old Testament's poetic texts. Here too, the texts do not seek to legislate for the conduct of relationships. Rather, the factor of sexuality is woven into the discourse, so that the evocative power of the theme combines with the poetry's rich capacity for metaphor and creativity. The language of male and female, furthermore, is not confined within human relating, but is also deployed to evoke the character and actions of God. To the familiar challenge of understanding the discourse within its ancient context is now added

26. Ibid., 184. The composite phrase applied to Boaz is hard to translate satisfactorily. The term *ḥayil* can convey both standing and wealth, and even courage, while *gibbôr* also has connotations of prowess.

27. Ibid., 196.

the elusive nature of the poetic speech, and even the entailments of religious language itself. Can we discern here too depictions of male and female that point to life? The poetic texts include sections of the Prophets, parts of the book of Proverbs, and of course the Song of Songs. The prophet Hosea's characterization of the relationship of Yahweh and Israel as a marriage, in which Yahweh is the husband and Israel his wife, became influential in the prophetic tradition. What does the use of this imagery tell us about attitudes toward men and women in the book?

In Hosea the prophet is commanded by Yahweh to marry "a woman of prostitution" ('ēšet zĕnûnîm), and with her to have "children of prostitution" (wĕyaldê zĕnûnîm), as a sign of Israel's unfaithfulness to him (Hosea 1:2–3). Hosea obediently marries Gomer, daughter of Diblaim, and their children then bear names that speak symbolically of Yahweh's plans for both judgment and salvation (1:4–11). The trope of female sexual unfaithfulness continues in chapter 2 with strong images of sexual violation and shame (2:2–5[4–7], 10[12]). Prostitution and adultery are combined in the characterization, which serves the prophetic accusation that Israel has been unfaithful to Yahweh by worshiping Baal. Baal has in fact been a false "lover" to Israel, while Yahweh has loved her truly. As in chapter 1, there is a trajectory from judgment to salvation, where salvation is depicted as the restoration of a marital relationship based on the covenantal virtues of righteousness, justice, steadfast love, mercy, and faithfulness (2:16–20[18–22]). Chapter 3 returns to the theme of the prophet's marriage to a promiscuous woman, who is not named Gomer, though the concept of Hosea's marital story matching Yahweh's faithfulness would seem to require this identification.[28] Here a period of enforced sexual continence is imposed on her, as a metaphor of Israel's exile, before their repentance and return to Yahweh.

Sexual imagery recurs intermittently throughout the book, with references to "prostitution" (zānâ, zĕnûnîm, Hosea 4:10–14, 18; 5:3–4; 6:10; 9:1), adultery (nā'ap, 4:13), "cult prostitutes" (qĕdēšôt, 4:14), and "lovers" ('ăhābîm, 8:9). Possibly under the influence of Hosea, the same trope has a significant place in both Jeremiah and Ezekiel, with a similar fundamental application to the relationship between Yahweh and Israel. Jeremiah 2–3 has numerous echoes of Hosea. But the image is expanded especially in Ezekiel 16, where Yahweh's early love for Israel is evoked in an image of an abandoned female newborn child, whom he cares for till she becomes mature and beautiful (vv.

---

28. The point is well made by Richtsje Abma, *Bonds of Love: Methodic Studies of Prophetic Texts with Marriage Imagery (Isaiah 50:1–3 and 54:1–10, Hosea 1–3, and Jeremiah 2–3)*, SSN 40 (Assen, Neth.: Van Gorcum, 1999), 211n216.

1–14). Israel's defection from Yahweh is then once again portrayed in terms of sexual promiscuity (vv. 15–34), and the image is pressed consistently, so that the punishment that falls as a result is depicted in terms of violent sexual humiliation (vv. 35–43).

What effect do these portrayals of Israel as unfaithful wife of Yahweh, with all the marks of shame that are heaped upon her, have on the Old Testament's depiction of male and female? It might be argued that the image participates in the trajectory from judgment to salvation that typifies the prophetic books, where the grace of Yahweh is expressed by his suffering and enduring love for his wife, as when, in Hosea, he "allures" the bride of his youth back to the wilderness, the place of her early faithfulness in Hosea (Hosea 2:14–15[16–17]). Yet the marital metaphor tends to fall away in the prophetic portrayals of redemption. There is the merest hint in Jeremiah (Jer. 31:4), and in Ezekiel it is notably quiet. Julie Galambush thinks, indeed, that the female representation of Israel in that book lends itself to the conception of the people's religious infidelity as ritual defilement. In the image of female sexual promiscuity, the temple as the place of Yahweh's presence has been illicitly entered by idolatrous men and their gods, and consequently Yahweh, as "husband," has been shamed.[29] Then in the conception of renewed Israel as temple (Ezek. 40–48), while the purified city "performs a *symbolically feminine role*," virtually all vestiges of the feminine have been removed in an idealization of purity admitting the presence only of Yahweh and male priests.[30]

Apart from this rhetorical strategy, evident especially in Ezekiel, does the language and imagery of female infidelity and prostitution constitute an abuse of women in itself? One approach to answering this question, well represented in commentaries on Hosea, is to ask whether the imagery in any way reflects actual practices in the ancient world or in Israel. Francis Andersen and David Noel Freedman exemplify this view: "The language of [Hosea 4:14b] makes it clear that promiscuity and sacrifice were part of a full-scale cult."[31] However, Alice Keefe and others have shown that this idea lacks supportive evidence and seems to have arisen simply out of assumptions made in the reading of

29. Julie Galambush, *Jerusalem in the Book of Ezekiel: The City as Yahweh's Wife*, SBLDS 130 (Atlanta: Scholars Press, 1992), 87–88.

30. Ibid., 156–57 (emphasis original); see also 88, 163.

31. Francis I. Andersen and David N. Freedman, *Hosea: A New Translation with Introduction and Commentary*, AB 24 (Garden City, NY: Doubleday, 1980), 370; cf. 157–58. See also Hans Walter Wolff, *Hosea: A Commentary on the Book of Hosea*, trans. G. Stansell, Hermeneia (Philadelphia: Fortress, 1974), 85–86; and James Luther Mays, *Hosea*, OTL (London: SCM, 1969), 8–12.

Hosea[32] and from a deficient understanding of metaphor itself.[33] The use of sexual imagery broadly reflects cultural assumptions, which may in themselves imply female subordination, but it does not give specific evidence of officially sanctioned promiscuity or ritual abuse.[34] The prophetic trope, therefore, is largely the product of the imaginative use of metaphor or allegory.

The question whether these prophetic images represent abuse, then, is chiefly one of reader response. Galambush considers the portrayals of the woman in Ezekiel 16 and 23 as "pornographic," not only in the strict sense of the word as "a prostitute's biography" but also according to its contemporary meaning as "the graphic sexually explicit subordination of women through pictures and/ or words."[35] The mere depiction of male violence against women, backed up by an implication of merited punishment, may have the effect of inviting or encouraging such violence.[36] In this approach to reading the marital metaphors, the woman is characterized as radically "other" to the man, as an object to be contemplated judgmentally by a male gaze.[37] Strictly speaking, we cannot know whether the ancient authors were motivated by what we might call pornographic or misogynistic intentions. For Cheryl Exum, however, this is not the point, and she declares: "I am more interested in the effect on the reader, and I experience this material as defamatory, insulting, and, ultimately misogynistic."[38]

32. Alice A. Keefe, *Woman's Body and the Social Body in Hosea*, JSOTSup 338 (London: Sheffield Academic, 2001), 66–78; Abma, *Bonds of Love*, 137–39. Keefe argues that Hosea's prostitution image serves his critique of the structures of royal power and political practice (*Woman's Body*, 95–103).

33. Sharon Moughtin-Mumby, for example, opposes a "substitutionary" view of the marriage metaphor for this reason (Moughtin-Mumby, *Sexual and Marital Metaphors in Hosea, Jeremiah, Isaiah, and Ezekiel*, OTM [Oxford: Oxford University Press, 2008], 6).

34. The public humiliation of both men and women in times of war was no doubt all too real, however, as its recurrence in prophetic texts such as Ezek. 16:35–39 implies (cf. 2 Sam. 10:1–5; Jer. 13:22, 26; Lam. 1:8).

35. Galambush, *Jerusalem in the Book of Ezekiel*, 124–25, citing the definition of Mackinnon and Dworkin via Jill Dolan, "The Dynamics of Desire: Sexuality and Gender in Pornography and Performance," *Theatre Journal* 89 (1987): 157. See also T. Drorah Setel, "Prophets and Pornography: Female Sexual Imagery in Hosea," in *Feminist Interpretation of the Bible*, ed. Letty Russell (Philadelphia: Westminster, 1985), 86–95.

36. Keefe, *Woman's Body*, 151–52. Keefe finds Ezekiel's imagery to be both pornographic and misogynistic, and its lurid imagery to have had an effect on the way in which Hosea is read (152).

37. Galambush, *Jerusalem in the Book of Ezekiel*, 104–5. On such "otherness" of the woman, cf. Keefe, *Woman's Body*, 143, 154–55; and Yvonne Sherwood, *The Prostitute and the Prophet: Hosea's Marriage in Literary-Theoretical Perspective*, JSOTSup 212 (Sheffield, UK: Sheffield Academic, 1996), 255.

38. Cheryl Exum, "Prophetic Pornography," in *Plotted, Shot, and Painted: Cultural Representations of Biblical Women*, JSOTSup 215 (Sheffield, UK: Sheffield Academic, 1996), 103; cited in Keefe, *Woman's Body*, 151–52. Exum is responding precisely to a point made by Robert Carroll that the comparison of the biblical texts with modern pornography is anachronistic.

For other feminist writers, however, the analysis of Hosea in terms of sexual ritual is positive and liberating for women, corresponding as it does to a version of feminist thought in which the female symbolizes an immanent form of religion, affirming "the sacrality of the body, nature and the feminine."[39] Yvonne Sherwood, for her part, adopts a deconstructive strategy in her exploration of the force of the language, finding that Hosea, by depicting male Israel as a promiscuous woman, undermines the notion of the female as the "other" to the normative "male" view of reality.[40]

Sexuality and Life

We have been considering ways in which the power of sexual imagery has been applied to the Old Testament's realization of the human experience, and have seen how the topic is woven into matters of life and death. The writers of Judges do not flinch from showing how desire can become murderous, in ways that go beyond the corruption of an individual to the maddening of a whole society. Ezekiel provides images in which theological messages of grace and judgment are hard to extricate from sexual violence. Elements of lust are mingled with cultural control. There is more fear than joy in this sex. The ideal of male and female together as "image of God" lies deeply buried here.

Yet there are more hopeful notes, as when the book of Ruth shows ways of working constructively within a set of social constraints to challenge divisive prejudice in a story of men and women, ways that are characterized by mutuality and admiration, indeed delight. And in the modern reception of Hosea, some have found notes that could subvert patriarchal prejudice and control.

The lines linking sex and life do not end there. The Old Testament's love stories include the beautiful, self-contained tale of the meeting of Isaac and Rebekah (Gen. 24). It is thoroughly "patriarchal" in its assumptions (the courting of Rebekah is put in the hands of Abraham's oldest, male servant [24:2]), yet it opens up a space in which generosity, tenderness, and love come to expression. The emotive quality emerges in the final verse, in which "Isaac . . . took Rebekah, and she became his wife; and he loved her. So Isaac was comforted after his mother's death" (24:67 RSV). The moment is a vignette of the possibilities of human love, which is undiminished by the fact that

39. It is characterized in this way by Keefe, *Woman's Body*, 63. The position is represented by, among others, Fokkelien van Dijk-Hemmes, "The Imagination of Power and the Power of Imagination: An Intertextual Analysis of Two Biblical Love Songs: The Song of Songs and Hosea 2," *JSOT* 44 (1989): 75–88; and Setel, "Prophets and Pornography."

40. Sherwood, *Prostitute and the Prophet*, 255.

Isaac and Rebekah would later be at odds in their affections for their two sons (ch. 27), though not, apparently, so as to destroy their unity (27:46–28:1). Jacob and Rachel too furnish an example of love that is based in true affection and endures (chs. 29–31). These depictions of love avoid sentimentality, being all too aware of the hardships and compromises of life. When Rachel dies giving birth to Benjamin (35:16–21), Jacob's inconsolable love becomes morbid and a catalyst for his destructive preference for Joseph over the sons of Leah and the servants (ch. 37). Yet the love of Jacob for Rachel retains its power over the imagination.

The interweaving of sexuality and life can also be found in the Old Testament's poetry. The memory of Rachel recurs in Jeremiah, where, as Trible has shown, her grief over her children (a metaphor for Israel in the anguish of devastation by enemies) is part of what she calls the "journey of a metaphor"—namely, that of "compassion" (*raḥămîm*), based on the Hebrew term *reḥem* (womb). The context is Jeremiah's so-called Book of Consolation (Jer. 30–33), the literary crucible of the great turn from judgment to salvation in that prophecy. As in Hosea 11:8–9, grief and compassion come together in vehement emotional language. Yahweh responds to Rachel's grief with assurances of restoration (Jer. 31:17), and in 31:20 his own anguish over "Ephraim" is superimposed on Rachel's, and he declares, in a double use of the womb metaphor: "I will surely have compassion on him" (*raḥēm 'ăraḥămennû*). Here feminine imagery of the womb is used to depict Yahweh in the role of mother.[41] The same thought recurs in Isaiah 49:15, with its own double womb image (*mēraḥēm ben-biṭnāh*),[42] in which Yahweh's love for Israel exceeds the undying love of a mother for her child, yet it is the mother love that is invoked to express it.[43]

It is a bold gambit of the prophets to depict Yahweh's love with a sexual trope, considering the Old Testament's predominant monotheistic and aniconic theology. On both these counts (one God, not imaged), as especially evident in Genesis 1 and the Decalogue (Exod. 20:4–6; Deut. 5:8–10), it might be expected that the use of the sexual in the ancient Near Eastern religious imagination would be foreclosed to worshipers of Yahweh. Yahweh is neither (male) god nor goddess. But the prophets confound this expectation in their readiness for anthropomorphic metaphor. Hosea's

41. Trible translates Jer. 31:20c: "I will surely show motherly-compassion upon him," and says, pointing out parallels between Rachel and Yahweh, "Strophe four [v. 20] is the voice of Yahweh the mother" (*God and the Rhetoric of Sexuality*, 45).
42. The line reads: "Can a woman forget her nursing child, or fail to have compassion on the child of her womb?"
43. Trible, *God and the Rhetoric of Sexuality*, 51.

theological control of it is evident when he both deploys the metaphor of Yahweh as husband and also categorically denies that Yahweh is "a man" (Hosea 11:9b).[44] In this way Hosea preserves the uniqueness and otherness of God yet displays the necessity of anthropomorphism in language about him. The inescapability of human language for God is redolent of the theology of humanity as made in the divine "image." And in the full gamut of prophetic anthropomorphic representations of God, both male and female images are deployed. The female part in such representation is well expressed by Trible: "The uterine metaphor encompassed by the root *rhm* signifies the image of God female."[45]

The Old Testament's language for the unity of male and female reaches its apogee in the Song of Songs. For Trible, this poem is "Love's Lyrics Redeemed," because the Song tends to put together that which was put asunder in the story of the garden of Eden (Gen. 3).[46] Here the man and the woman delight in each other in a natural setting, like a garden, in language of desire, tenderness, and respect. It is love without self-regard: "This is the only place in the Bible where the love between man and woman is treated without concern for the childbearing or the social and political benefits of marriage."[47] The Song "redeems" the loss in the former garden with a powerful affirmation of the sexual relationship as "good." In its eroticism it belies the idea that the sin in the garden lay in sexual discovery or experience in itself. On the contrary, the Song evokes the goodness of human love in a lyric of profound beauty, rich in sensuality both of language and of theme, in which the joy of the lovers' embrace mingles harmoniously with the scents, sights, sounds, and smells of the garden that is their world. This is a devotion of the Bible's highest art to the topic of male and female union. Its poetry presses to its limits what is involved in the reciprocity of male and female in the "image of God."

God is absent in the Song only in the most literal sense. In Genesis 3 it is supposed that God might come and go, might look and look away (Gen. 3:8–9). In the Song one can imagine a divine presence that knows how to look and look away. Here, differently from the first garden, no danger threatens a ruin of everything. The lovers' world knows and reckons with danger, power and hostility, the possibility of loss, and of death itself. Yet its performance

---

44. "I am God and not a man" (*'ēl 'ānōkî wĕlō'-'îš*).

45. Trible, *God and the Rhetoric of Sexuality*, 50.

46. Ibid., 144–65; cf. 72–143 ("A Love Story Gone Awry"). See also Ellen F. Davis: "The Song is about repairing the damage done by the first disobedience in Eden, what Christian tradition calls the 'Fall'" (*Proverbs, Ecclesiastes, and the Song of Songs*, Westminster Bible Companion [Louisville: Westminster John Knox, 2000], 231).

47. Davis, *Proverbs*, 236.

of love, and its invitation to it, are not mitigated by these facts of life. Love, indeed, is as strong as death (Song 8:6–7), and may even prevail over it.[48]

It is well known that the love of the humans for each other has been taken to convey the deeper meaning of the love of God for his creatures, or in Christian idiom, for the church. The traditional fascination with a "spiritual" meaning of the Song is more than a decorous aversion of gaze from its literal field of play. Just as in biblical anthropology the body is inseparable from the intangible realities of mind, will, and spirit, so in biblical poetry the literal is inseparable from the spiritual or metaphorical. The mutual love of human beings is irreducibly embodied, but is never "merely" so. The preoccupation of the self with another bespeaks transcendence, the fulfillment of the self in an outward reach toward the Other.[49] We have met already the idea that all human desire is at heart a form of desire for God.[50] And recent scholarship on the Song has sought to reestablish the intimate relationship between these two desires. For Ellen Davis, "the lover's garden is subtly but consistently represented as the garden of delight that Eden was meant to be, the place where life may be lived fully in the presence of God."[51]

The extraordinary power of sexual mutuality as a figure for the human-divine relationship explains why it is so prominent in biblical poetry. The tendency of poetry toward indeterminacy and incompletion opens imaginative spaces to explore relationships between humans, and between humans and God. The fulfillment of the self in the Other is an indispensable part of a biblical anthropology.

Sexual and Nonsexual Relationships

The symbolism of otherness in the sexual relationship can also act as a pointer to various kinds of relating among human beings as a function of being human. When human beings, male and female, are said to be in "the image of God" (Gen. 1:26), the primary reference is to men and women in marriage, as the sequel in Genesis 2 shows, but this form of relationship need

---

48. Trible notes an echo between 4:15, where the woman is "living waters" (*mayîm ḥayyîm*), and the "many waters" (*mayîm rabbîm*) of 8:7, with their hint of primeval chaos (*God and the Rhetoric of Sexuality*, 161).

49. Cf. Mark W. Elliott, *The Song of Songs and Christology in the Early Church 381–451* (Tübingen: Mohr Siebeck, 2000), 1–3; and Davis, *Proverbs*, 232.

50. See above, ch. 1, nn. 59–60; and ch. 4, n. 67, on Sarah Coakley, *God, Sexuality, and the Self: An Essay 'On the Trinity'* (Cambridge: Cambridge University Press, 2013); cf. Davis, *Proverbs*, 233.

51. Davis, *Proverbs*, 232.

not be exclusive of others. Genesis 1–2 sets up several relationships—human to human, human to God, human to the garden, or natural world—and these are developed in the biblical story on a broad canvas of social and political relationships, as we have been seeing. (The book of Ruth displays one instance of the expansion of the theme.) The Song of Songs too may be read in such a way that its unfolding of sexual love can also bespeak other kinds of love. David Ford draws on Paul Ricoeur to make this point. Ricoeur finds a metaphorical quality in the structure of the Song, in which erotic love is decontextualized, with the result that the sexual relationship is freed to become "the analogon for other configurations of love than that of erotic love."[52] Ford cites the work of Jean Vanier and the L'Arche communities as an example of how this has been applied, observing that Vanier weaves the Song of Songs into his reading of John's Gospel as he seeks words to characterize a community of self-sacrificing love.[53] As in Hosea, we are once again in the territory of metaphor, as an ever-present capacity of poetic expression. The Song is metaphorical in the sense that it cannot be understood in referential terms; we never know who the lovers are or place them in a social setting. It is therefore available for extension into other realms under the broad banner of love. Not only the sexual relationship between men and women is rewarding and challenging. So also, we may infer, are familial love and friendship, and even collegiality in creative enterprises or the workplace. The Bible affords examples of all of these.[54]

The friendship of David and Jonathan is a case in point. In the context of hostility between David and Saul, and our awareness that David is chosen and Saul rejected, the story of David and Jonathan is unexpected and even strange. On ordinary accounts, David poses a threat to Jonathan, Saul's son and natural successor, and we might expect suspicion and hostility on his part. But the story transcends the natural bonds that can exclude as well as include. Instead of hostility, we have a moving story of deep affection, con-secrated in a "covenant of Yahweh" (*bibrît yhwh*) marked by "faithful love"

52. Paul Ricoeur, "The Nuptial Metaphor," in *Thinking Biblically: Exegetical and Herme-neutical Studies*, ed. André Lacocque and Paul Ricoeur (Chicago: University of Chicago Press, 1988), 274, cited in David F. Ford, *Christian Wisdom: Desiring God and Learning in Love* (Cambridge: Cambridge University Press, 2007), 385–86. Ricoeur distinguishes between the "matrimonial" and the "nuptial" in his analogy between the sexual and other kinds of relating, a distinction that he thinks is suggested by the indeterminacy and metaphorical character of the Song's language ("Nuptial Metaphor," 274).

53. Ford, *Christian Wisdom*, 382, citing Jean Vanier, *Drawn into the Mystery of Jesus through the Gospel of John* (London: Darton, Longman & Todd, 2004), 299–300.

54. For the last named, one thinks of Bezalel and his colleagues in their fellowship of artisan-ship in constructing the tabernacle (Exod. 31). For more on this, see the next chapter.

(*ḥesed*; 1 Sam. 20:8). This is the very quality evinced by Yahweh himself in covenant, and which in Hosea is metaphorized in the love of husband and wife. David and Jonathan realize a possibility of loving, reconciled human relationship, which on a plain reading goes beyond strategy or calculation.[55] The language is deeply emotive. Jonathan loved David "as he loved his own soul [*napšô*]" (1 Sam. 20:17), or more plainly, "as himself" (cf. Luke 10:27). And in David's poignant lament for both the father and the son after their deaths in battle, he speaks as to Jonathan:

> I am grieved for you, my brother Jonathan;
> you were delightful to me.
> Your love was wonderful to me,
> more than the love of women. (2 Sam. 1:26)

The story of David and Jonathan is best taken to illustrate an affinity between sexual and nonsexual love, rather than as an instance of the former. Almost certainly, the narrative is not suggesting that the two men had a homosexual relationship. Apart from the cultural taboo in the biblical world, there is an unguardedness about the depiction that makes an intent to convey this unlikely. Even so, it is a remarkable picture of same-sex friendship that matches the intensity of most biblical depictions of male-female love. The Bible uses its language of emotion and mutual faithfulness here for a kind of relationship that is not heterosexual love.

This is the point that makes it extraordinarily difficult to appeal to biblical texts to adjudicate specifically modern issues of sexual identity and expression. The Old Testament only marginally engages with issues of sexual identity. The exclusion of the sexually maimed and the *mamzēr* from the Israelite assembly (Deut. 23:1–2[2–3]), and the later prophetic incorporation of the "eunuchs" (*sārîsîm*, Isa. 56:4), may be the closest it comes to reflection on this. In modern debate, in contrast, the cultural components of gender identity have come to feature prominently in discussions of sexuality,[56] and sexual orientation has become an issue in human rights. In theological conversation, the pressures on both sides of the debate—both appealing to Scripture—are strong. On the one hand, there is a proper concern for inclusivity, and, on the other, a belief that certain distinctions are built into the created order. The point that we have just considered, about the extension of language for heterosexual love into other kinds of relationship, plays into this conversation. If, as some argue,

---

55. There is even a hint of the reversal of the enmity of Cain toward Abel, when Jonathan says to David: "Come, let us go out to the field" (2 Sam. 20:11), in an echo of Gen. 4:8 LXX.

56. See Elliott, "Human Embodiment," 99–107, for discussion.

the essential characteristic of heterosexual marriage is covenantal faithful-ness, rather than procreation, then a logical extension to covenantally faithful homosexual relationships becomes possible.[57]

The issue turns on the inevitable hermeneutical question of which biblical theme or tendency to consider decisive. The Old Testament cannot resolve the question of same-sex relationships in isolation from the whole Christian theological tradition and ethical reflection on it. It can be said, however, that it takes the heterosexual marriage relationship as paradigmatic for the embrace of the other in the human call to be like God (especially but not only in Gen. 1–3).[58] Other kinds of "other-relating" fan out from it, nota-bly the parental (even in-law parental, in the case of Ruth and Naomi) and the sibling, as well as friendship. The language of such relating penetrates deep into the Old Testament's speech about the ways of God with people. Marriage offers a ready metaphor for the mutuality and faithfulness that also characterize God's way with humans. Parenthood affords imaginative avenues into the emotional quality of divine relating. The sibling relationship expands beyond the family to express the life-together of a whole society (as in the Deuteronomic concept of "brotherhood" in Israel, and the New Testament's reapplication of it to the church). These have in common with that other biblical construct of covenant their power to suggest that mutuality and loyalty are indispensable to human flourishing. The quality of "faithful-ness" (ḥesed) runs through all these.

Conclusion

Sexuality is the sphere above all others in which human being is shown to have an outward reference, uncontainable within the frame of an individual life. Humans are made for transcendence at least in this sense. Self-centeredness is therefore a negation of human destiny and vocation. On the contrary, the self is discovered precisely in the other. This is both the greatest gift and the greatest challenge to human living. In this respect, being "in the image of God" is evidently not a static given, but a matter of discovery, exploration, delight—like Adam's delight at his first sight of Eve—a recognizable but

---

57. This line has been taken by Robert Song, *Covenant Calling: Towards a Theology of Same-Sex Relationships* (London: SCM, 2014); see also Alan Wilson, *More Perfect Union? Understanding Same-Sex Marriage* (London: Darton, Longman & Todd, 2014). See now also Loveday Alexander, "Good Sex, Bad Sex: Reflections on Sexuality and the Bible," in *Conception, Reception, and the Spirit: Essays in Honor of Andrew T. Lincoln*, ed. J. G. McConville and Lloyd K. Pietersen (Eugene, OR: Wipf & Stock, 2015), 253–73.

58. But see above, n. 52, on Ricoeur's distinction between "matrimonial" and "nuptial."

entirely new possibility in the experience of the human condition. It is also an indispensable part of the responsibility to "image" God in the world.

Otherness, however, is a dangerous country, bordering on isolation and rejection. For the other is truly, unexpectedly, uncontrollably other. For this reason, male-female otherness can take destructive shape in miscommunication: "Blockages in communication occur because men and women use the same words in different ways."[59] The capacity of human relating for joy and shared flourishing has its obverse in mistrust, offense, danger, and fear. At worst, otherness can be experienced as objectification and rejection, even issuing in violence, as a number of writers have noticed.[60] The point applies not only in the sexual sphere but also in regard to differences of culture, color, creed, and sexual orientation. The embedding of difference in the human constitution is a powerful sign of the need for inclusion. The constructive embrace of our otherness as human beings is part of the unceasing challenge of spiritual and moral growth.

59. Elliott, "Human Embodiment," 105.
60. For example, Galambush, *Jerusalem in the Book of Ezekiel*, 104–5; and Keefe, *Woman's Body*, 143, 154–55; see above, n. 37.

9

Work and Creativity

On Human Possibilities

We have been observing that important aspects of the human experience can be said to unfold from the premise of the creation of human beings in the "image of God." In the light of it, we have considered the constituent parts of the human being, the topics of place and land, culture and memory, of organized living together, and sexuality. In each of these, we have tried to think what it means for humans to symbolize the presence of God in the world, to relate to him, and to manifest his ways. I want now to press our inquiry further by asking a basic question about the nature and limits of human potentiality in Old Testament perspective. In terms of genre, the question lies broadly in the realm of wisdom.

The creation narratives of Genesis 1–3 confront us starkly with the conundrum of human potentiality. In the first account, the humans, as "image and likeness of God," are assigned a place in a highly ordered representation of God's reality; in the second, their sphere of productive existence is placed under a specific restriction, which is quickly strained to breaking point when the serpent ironically tempts the human pair to be "like God." The human refusal of constraint leads to death and disorder, yet is not the end of the matter. There is a given godlikeness that continues to exert its power as mandate for human living, as well as the self-assertive godlikeness that bespeaks overweening human pride. We have seen abundant evidence that, under the banner of the former, the primary command to "rule" over the earth—to enable it to be fully itself—has a rich life after the garden of Eden. Obligations to justice, righteousness, goodness, and wisdom are undiminished by the serpent's cynicism and human fallibility, and the biblical story affords examples of human nobility alongside the cautionary tales of self-deceiving corruption.

Our question, then, is about the possibilities and limitations that apply to human beings as they seek to discover and live out what it means to be "in the image of God." Still in Genesis 1, a cue may be taken from God's repeated judgment on his works that they are "good." As we observed in our treatment of that chapter, the Hebrew *ṭôb* can connote "beautiful" as well as "good" in a moral sense, and in this beginning of all things the divine assessment is essentially aesthetic. The world in its ordered profusion is beautiful. Since it is beautiful in the eyes of its maker, it reflects the thoughts of its maker, and so the maker himself. The language of worship in the Old Testament often expresses the glory and holiness of God in terms of beauty: "Out of Zion, the perfection of beauty [*miklal-yōpî*], God shines forth" (Ps. 50:2 ESV). Beauty, or pleasantness (*nōʿam*), is predicated of Yahweh in Psalm 27:4.[1] Stephen Williams puts it thus: "As the aesthetically beautiful may attract us just on account of its beauty, so the God of Scripture is attractive just on account of his. He is glorious in his being, and this glory can quite properly be conceptualized as a form of beauty."[2] Indeed, he goes on, the loss of a sense of divine beauty is a function of idolatry.[3] Thus when the humans, who are themselves part of the beautiful creation, are created in the "image and likeness of God," they are presumably entrusted with a sense for the beauty of God, the world, and themselves. Beauty, however, as the story reveals all too soon, cannot be abstracted from the ethical and religious entailments of right thought and action. There is no abstract beauty of form here, nor an idealization of certain conceptions of perfection.[4] The Old Testament's wariness of idealizing either the divine or the creaturely form is well known

1. Cf. Ps. 96:6: "strength and beauty [*tipʾeret*] are in his sanctuary" (ESV); see also Isa. 52:1; 64:11; Ps. 48:2[3]: Zion is "beautiful in elevation" (*yĕpēh nôp*). Terms in the field of "honor" and "splendor," applied to God and his holiness, have also traditionally been rendered as "beauty" or "beautiful": "Worship the Lord in the beauty of holiness" (1 Chron. 16:29 KJV; see also 2 Chron. 20:21; Pss. 29:2; 96:9).

2. Williams in J. G. McConville and S. N. Williams, *Joshua*, THOTC (Grand Rapids: Eerdmans, 2010), 138.

3. Ibid., 137. See Williams's section "Touching on Beauty," 137–40, and note his allusion there to a dictum of Friedrich Nietzsche: "What decides against Christianity now is our taste, not our reasons" (139), cited from Nietzsche, *The Gay Science*, trans. Josefine Nauckhoff (Cambridge: Cambridge University Press, 2001), 123.

4. At the time of writing, an exhibition of classical Greek depictions of the human form in the British Museum in London is entitled "Defining Beauty" (March 26–July 5, 2015). It

from its prohibition of making images of God or creatures in the context of worship (Exod. 20:4–6; Deut. 5:8–10). Beauty, in biblical conception, is realized in the fullness of human living together in God's world.

If human living as "image of God" includes exercising a sense for the beautiful, this must affect our understanding of the notion of humans as "ruling" over the earth, and indeed of their function as "procreators." The notion of creation, applied secondarily to humans, pushes beyond an understanding of human vocation merely in terms of performing certain delegated tasks and points toward the imaginative exploration of the mind of God. As we explore the meaning of the "image," we now find ourselves asking, what is human beings' scope for godlike thought and action that may be called "creative"? In the words of Oliver O'Donovan, "If God in creation grants being and sense to a world that would be nothing without them, human creativity is an exercise of sympathetic intelligence, exploring and revealing the good things already latent in the order of nature."[5]

In fact we have begun to address the role of the imagination in the discovery of God's world (above, ch. 4), when we considered the part played in it by language, and the lead given in this by the language of Scripture itself. In the openness and suggestive power of language (also noted in ch. 8) there was a correspondence with both the spiritual sense of Scripture, and the spiritual nature of embodied human existence. The human in the "image of God" is invited into the knowledge of God, which is inexhaustible. Therefore, there is something endless about this human "imaging/imagining," that is both an accomplished given and a call into realizing new possibilities.

The Old Testament's exploration of human possibilities is attended, as might be expected, by its view of human existence as suspended between glory and corruption. As a starting point for reflection on this we can do no better than turn again to Psalm 8 and the psalmist's question:

> What is the human being [*ĕnôš*], that you should call him to mind [*tizkĕrennû*];
> or the son of man [*ben-'ādām*] that you should pay attention to him [*tipqĕdennû*]? (Ps. 8:4[5])

The question is born in an act of praise to God, whose "glory," or "honor" (*hôd*), is "above the heavens" (v. 1[2]). The human's place in the order of

---

demonstrates the Greek fascination with physical beauty yet also suggests, in the exhibition's title, that defining what deserves to be called beautiful is problematic.

5. Oliver O'Donovan, "Reflections on Work," in *On Rock or Sand? Firm Foundations for Britain's Future*, ed. John Sentamu (London: SPCK, 2015), 112.

things is thus laid alongside the incomparability of God. So the continuation is unexpected and astonishing in its extraordinarily lofty vision of the human. Though the psalm is throughout a hymn of praise to God, its thought moves back and forth between the glory of God and the glory (*kābôd*) and honor (*hādār*) of the human (v. 5[6]). This ascription of "glory" to the human is especially remarkable when one bears in mind the Old Testament's strong critique of human pretensions to the glory that belongs properly to God, notably in the book of Isaiah, where such aspirations are shown to be self-deceiving and doomed (e.g., Isa. 2; 10:12–19; 37–38). For the psalmist, however, the human is "little less than God" (Ps. 8:5[6]). Their call to exercise royal rule over the creation, reminiscent of Genesis 1, is further embellished here with the language of royal dignity ("you crowned them . . . made them rule over the works of your hands," vv. 5–6[6–7]).

Yet this assertion of the lofty capacity of humanity is couched in the form of a question, a question as much in wonder as inquiry. Though in one sense it receives an answer in the psalm, it also remains open, inviting exploration of what the extraordinary condition of humanity in God's world might come to mean. The pursuit of the question in the Old Testament is never far from tragedy. This noblest of God's creatures is heir to greatness, yet apparently unable to grasp it. Much of the rendering of human experience is painfully aware of the dissonance between what ought to be and what is; a longing to realize human glory, matched by a strong sense of chastened hubris. The point is illustrated by the fact that the psalmist's question recurs in two other places, in ways that show that its implicit assertions about human grandeur could not simply be taken for granted. Psalm 144:3 mirrors closely the formula in Psalm 8:4[5]: "What is the human ['*ādām*] that you should know him [*wattēdā'ēhû*], or the son of man [*ben-'ĕnôš*] that you should think of him [*wattĕḥaššĕbēhû*]?" The question turns here immediately to the fleeting nature of human life (Ps. 144:4) and so touches on a "vanity" theme. Yet the psalm is essentially one of petition and praise, in which human mortality is made a ground for marveling at the power of God both to rescue and to bless. In its sense of the great distance between human and creator it echoes something of the wonder of Psalm 8.

More radical is Job's version of the question (Job 7:17): "What is a human being, that you should make much of him [lit., "make him great" (*tĕgaddĕlennû*)], or pay attention to him [*tāšît 'ēlāyw libbekā*]?" This "paying attention" on the part of God, far from attributing glory to the human, is in Job's view an undue interest that takes the form of tormenting him. Job thus represents an ironic and skeptical take on what it is for God to "pay attention" to humanity (cf. *tipqĕdennû* in Ps. 8:4[5]). The "making great" seems particularly geared to querying the glory postulated in Psalm 8:5–9[6–10].

Job's question is in line with that book's tendency to stress the limits of human potential. The theme finds one of its chief expressions in Job 28, a speech in which Job celebrates human ingenuity and achievement, chiefly through the case of mining (vv. 1–11). He then contrasts this with wisdom, which human beings cannot discover—only God knows the way to it. And the poem finishes with the counsel: "It is the fear of the LORD that is wisdom, and to depart from evil is understanding" (28:28). The poem thus anticipates the book's finale in the speeches of Yahweh and Job's submission.[6] In Job 38:4, Yahweh asks Job, "Where were you when I established the foundation of the earth? Tell me, if you have understanding [*bînâ*]." Job, of course, was not there, and the fact that, consequently, he does not have access to the meaning of the creation is reinforced in the ironic rhetoric of verse 5: "Who determined its measurements—surely you know!" (NRSV). In these verses Job seems to be excluded from the divine joy in creation (38:7) as well as from the divine wisdom. There are echoes of Proverbs 8 in this passage, to which we shall return in a moment, and which seem to set Job at odds with the strains we shall find there (cf. Job 38:8–11 with Prov. 8:29). The tendency of this challenge to Job, however, and the speeches that follow, in which Yahweh unfolds his weird and wonderful (superfluous, gratuitous, useless) creation, is to put an end to Job's weary quest, as if wisdom in the end is not for him. Job's skeptical notes lie close to Ecclesiastes, as when the Preacher says: "He [God] has given them a sense of eternity [*hā'ōlām*], yet in such a way that they cannot plumb [find out (*yimṣā'*)] the work of God that he has accomplished, from beginning to end" (Eccles. 3:11).

It follows that the Old Testament offers no systematic answer to the question asked by the psalmist. It occurs in contexts of worship, with notes ranging from wonder and confidence to the gravest doubt about the divine goodwill to humanity. The Wisdom literature gives voice to the deepest questions about the purposefulness of existence, questions that have exercised human beings in every time and place.[7] As such, it is an invitation to discover boundaries and possibilities in actual experience.

---

6. The speech in Job 28 is sometimes thought to be wrongly attributed to Job on the grounds that its tone of acceptance seems premature in the structure of the book. For a defense of the speech and an exposition of its function in its present position, see Alison Lo, *Job 28 as Rhetoric: An Analysis of Job 28 in the Context of Job 22–31*, VTSup 97 (Leiden: Brill, 2003).

7. Hamlet clearly has Psalm 8 in mind when he says: "What a piece of work is a man, how noble in reason, how infinite in faculties, in form and moving, how express and admirable in action, how like an angel, in apprehension, how like a god: the beauty of the world, the paragon of animals!" (Shakespeare, *Hamlet*, ed. Cyrus Hoy, Norton Critical Editions, 2nd ed. [New

"The Glory of God Is the Human Fully Alive"[8]

The well-known formula of Irenaeus (ca. 115–202) expresses the high view of humanity that we have encountered also in Psalm 8, in which God and humans not only have a relationship, but God actually attaches his glory somehow to them. The Wisdom writers were well aware of the complications in the divine-human relationship. But in its dialogical character it has strands within it that express the potentiality of the human in strikingly positive ways.

In Proverbs 8:22–31 we find an extraordinary picture of *God's delight* in his creation, and especially in human beings. We are here in quite different territory from Job 28 (which has, in fact, been thought deliberately to oppose Prov. 8).[9] In our text, Wisdom is personified and stands in public places inviting all who wish to come and learn from her (Prov. 8:1–3, 17), somewhat in contrast to the book of Job, where humans cannot find the way to wisdom (Job 28:13).

The invitation to come and learn from personified Wisdom is crowned in the chapter with a poem about her creation. Here, with an echo of Genesis 1:1, Yahweh creates Wisdom "at the beginning [*rē'šît*] of his work" (Prov. 8:22 NRSV), or "*as* the first of his work [lit., "way" (*darkô*)]," and Wisdom then attends the creation of everything else.[10] What does this remarkable picture mean? Just that God exercised divine wisdom in creating the world? Was God obliged to create Wisdom first so that he could go on and create the world? Such a thought is too prosaic in this poetic context. (We recall that, in another context, God needs no "counselor" [Isa. 40:13].) Wisdom is not *in reality* a person other than God. Rather, Wisdom is personified here in order to express

York: Norton, 1992], 36 [act 2, scene 2, lines 288–91]). Hamlet speaks, no doubt, with mental reservations; indeed, he is feigning madness at the time! Also relevant is the chorus's "Ode to Humanity" in Sophocles's *Antigone*, lines 332–75—on the glittering human achievements, yet humanity's "terrible urge to dominate and to push beyond accepted limits" (Sophocles, *Antigone*, ed. Mark Griffith, CGLC [Cambridge: Cambridge University Press, 1999], 181). The notion of licit and illicit human aspiration is also exemplified in the figure of Prometheus, who stole fire from the gods. See J. W. von Goethe's contrasting poems, "Prometheus," celebrating the ancient hero's challenge to the gods, and "Grenzen der Menschheit," which has a skeptical tone: "Ein kleiner Ring begrenzt unser Leben." Hamlet is if anything more disturbing: "I could be bounded in a nutshell and count myself a king in infinite space, were it not that I have bad dreams" (*Hamlet*, act 2 scene 2, lines 245–46).

8. The phrase in the original Latin is: "Gloria Dei est vivens homo" (Irenaeus, *Against Heresies* 4.20. 5–7 [SC 100:640–42, 644–48]). Various translations are possible, but this common rendering introduces the next part of the argument well.

9. See S. Weeks, *Instruction and Wisdom in Proverbs 1–9* (New York: Oxford University Press, 2007), 156n1.

10. Note "when there was not yet" (8:24–26) as a motif in creation language, and compare and contrast Gen. 2:4b–7. It is remarkable that the line of thought that leads to "humanity" in Gen. 2 leads here to Wisdom!

the joy of God in the conceiving and unfolding of the creation. The closeness of the relationship between God and Wisdom is evident in this vision, so that what is predicated of Wisdom is also true of God.[11] There is even a hint of the "divinity" of Wisdom in the twice-repeated *wā'ehyeh* in Proverbs 8:30: "And I was beside him" (*wā'ehyeh 'eṣlô*), "and I was rejoicing daily" (*wā'ehyeh ša'ašu'îm yôm yôm*)—reminiscent of Yahweh's self-introduction to Moses in Exodus 3:14: "I am who I am" (*'ehyeh 'ǎšer 'ehyeh*).[12] The precise *imaging* of the relationship depends on how we read Wisdom's further self-designation as an *'āmôn* in Proverbs 8:30 (taken variously as "like a master-workman" or— with some repointing—"faithfully," or "like a child/one growing up").[13] But setting that provisionally aside, this Wisdom is strangely "on both sides"—as the Wisdom that comes from God yet belongs within the creation.

The picture is suffused with joy and delight and with a kind of resistance to being parsed. One can almost hear the animatedness of the anomalous plural in "I was daily delights" (*wā'ehyeh ša'ašu'îm* [*ša'ašu'āyw?*] *yôm yôm*) (Prov. 8:30). Does Wisdom experience this delight? Or is she the object of God's delight? This kind of uncertainty in the language bespeaks mutuality and playfulness. Delight and joy are indeed close to playfulness here. As Wisdom continues (in v. 30): "I was playing [or "laughing"] before him" (*měśaheqet lěpānāyw*). The whole picture is one of superfluity, gratuitousness, the op- posite of obligation. As Ellen Davis has it, "It was not necessary for God to create the world."[14] Finally, the playful delight of God (and Wisdom) finds its object in the human being (v. 31b), so that once again the passage echoes Genesis 1. With Wisdom's invitation to human beings to come and learn from her, the human is drawn into this sharing of delight.[15]

11. Tremper Longman writes: "Woman Wisdom is a poetic personification of Yahweh's wisdom"; and "Wisdom ultimately represents Yahweh himself" (*Proverbs*, BCOTWP [Grand Rapids: Baker Academic, 2006], 196).

12. So also John Goldingay, *Old Testament Theology*, vol. 1, *Israel's Gospel* (Downers Grove, IL: IVP Academic, 2003), 48.

13. Michael Fox takes *'āmôn* as "one growing up," on an analogy with Esther 2:20b. See Fox, *Proverbs 1–9*, AB 18a (New Haven: Yale University Press, 2000), 285–87. For Longman, the *'āmôn* is "master-worker," but the term refers primarily to Yahweh, and only by extension to Woman Wisdom "as a poetic personification of Yahweh's wisdom" (Longman, *Proverbs*, 196).

14. Davis, *Proverbs, Ecclesiastes, and the Song of Songs*, Westminster Bible Companion (Louisville: Westminster John Knox, 2000), 68. I question Fox's reading of the delight of God in Wisdom as simply a trope whereby Wisdom frolics before God as he creates (Fox, *Proverbs*, 287–89); I prefer to see play embedded in the act and concept of creating. Yet Fox's conception of *'āmôn* as a "child growing up" allows for an element of discovery built into the creation.

15. On this see also Zeph. 3:17–18, where again Yahweh rejoices over human beings (here Israel) with a pileup of terms for joy (*yāśîś 'ālayik běśimhâ . . . yāgîl 'ālayik běrinnâ*). And per- haps Job 38–42 comes in here as well, with its pictures of God's apparently playful invention in the nonhuman world.

These texts suggest that God's delight in God's creation has aspects of exploration, discovery, and enjoyment. In this connection we might refer to the now commonly accepted idea that God's creation is ongoing; creation is inseparable from the notion of God's continuing involvement in the world and the people in it.[16] I think that the ideas of divine delight and joy can be helpfully added to this. Tim Gorringe has even written of God's exploration of his creation through the created senses of the human being.[17] John Macquarrie speaks of the human capacity for the sublime—as in exquisite music and literature; the capacity for understanding the world and universe we inhabit, reflected in scientific inquiry; in short, the aspiration to "transcendence." Macquarrie's use of the term conveys the sense that the meaning of human life is not contained within the mundane, but is characterized by ever-new realization and possibility.[18] It is not precisely the same as the "self-transcendence" that is a belief in the possibility of transforming circumstances and a sense that resources for doing so lie beyond the self.[19] Yet the apprehension of the sublime may find a theological explanation in the perception that God has made human creatures to share his own delight in the creation and in themselves. God's joy in the beauty and superfluity of the world, therefore, may have corollaries in all manner of creativity, including art and even humor.[20] And the pursuit of these may in turn be a part of a person's path of transformation in the face of God.[21]

For the sages of the Old Testament, the human being in the world is inseparable from the divine creation-Wisdom. Wisdom is deep, and for the human, inexhaustible. If there is an invitation to explore it, it involves an orientation, a setting out on a path of discovery. Wisdom cannot be mastered by the human, but only sought with humility and awe.

16. On this see Terence E. Fretheim, *God and World in the Old Testament: A Relational Theology of Creation* (Nashville: Abingdon, 2005), 5–9.

17. Tim Gorringe, *The Education of Desire* (London: SCM, 2001), 4.

18. John Macquarrie, *In Search of Humanity: A Theological and Philosophical Approach* (London: SCM, 1982), 25–26.

19. See the definition of Sandra Schneiders above (introduction, n. 17).

20. John Macquarrie, *In Search of Humanity*, 187–98. See also Mark W. Elliott, "Human Embodiment," in *The Dynamics of Human Life*, ed. Mark Elliott (Carlisle, UK: Paternoster, 2001), 89: "Art is playful as well as serious; it combines the religious, the intellectual, the emotional and the physical. When it provokes 'the sublime' it reminds us of the 'connectedness of all things.' Is it then a pseudo-religion, to be avoided? It is better to take the sublime and the beautiful as a faint echo of what is fleshed out in Christ and in the dwelling of God with humans in the saints."

21. I am grateful to Richard Middleton, who made perceptive points about the various possible senses of "transcendence" in a response to an earlier form of the present chapter, given as the Institute of Biblical Research Annual Lecture in Baltimore, in November 2012.

The Glory of God in Human Work and Art

In this picture of God's delight in the world—and the human beings—that he created, there is a strong sense that the humans too are drawn into the delighting, simply by virtue of their being human. This is suggested by the writers just quoted and is implied in Proverbs 8, where Wisdom at once belongs closely with God, as in 8:30–31, and calls upon human beings to come and learn from her (8:4, 17).

This leads on to the question as to what such human delight and discovery might look like. It is clear from the foregoing, from both Genesis 1 and Proverbs 8, that the human mandate to act in the world is rooted firmly in the creation and belongs to its character and fabric. That is, the divine conception of the creation includes human activity and inquiry. The concepts of procreation and cooperation with God in the ongoing creation seem to me to be well-founded in these texts. In principle, therefore, our discovery of what it is to be human embraces the whole of human endeavor. This naturally includes the work we do, but extends also to the more obviously creative occupations such as art. Work and art have in common their sense of making real, or discovering, what is implicit or possible within God's creation.

The combination of work and art as God-given, purposeful, and creative activity is strikingly illustrated in the remarkable figure of Bezalel, who with his colleague Oholiab applied skills of workmanship to the construction and adornment of the tabernacle in the wilderness (Exod. 31:1–11). Their skills covered work in gold, silver, bronze, wood, and precious stone, and were applied to purposes both utilitarian and aesthetic. The abilities God gives in this connection extended not only to Bezalel and Oholiab, but to "all who had practical intelligence" (lit., "all who were wise of heart/mind" [kol-ḥăkam-lēb]) (v. 6). Crucial to this conception of God-given labor is the conjunction of "wisdom," "work," and the "spirit of God" (v. 3). The importance of wisdom is accentuated by the use of three terms: ḥokmâ (wisdom), tĕbûnâ (insight), and da'at (knowledge). These together suggest both God-given talent and the disciplines of learning and application, with their outcome in the experience that produces good judgment. There are echoes here of that human "mastery" that was acknowledged in Job 28, yet here the emphasis is more on possibility than on limitation. Nor is there any reason to suppose that this gifting of Bezalel and his colleagues was something exceptional, a special concession because of the "religious" need to have a well-constructed and decorated tabernacle. This I think would make the attribution of his work to "wisdom" meaningless.

The case of Bezalel seems to me to imply at least two parts of a theology of human endeavor—namely, creativity (related to wisdom) and individuality (related to the spirit). First, the creativity in Bezalel's art is entailed in a process of discovery at the boundaries of what is possible within the givenness of the world as it is. In his case, as with artists, engineers, and skilled artisans, it concerns materials. Here is creativity after the creativity of God. It corresponds to the human desire to know something of the divine desire to watch something new appear. Such desire is, I suggest, an act of faith, an acknowledgment of meaningfulness and beauty. Beauty, as we have seen, has its origin in God and is imprinted on his "good" creation. It is akin to God's glory and furnishes the language of worship. The beauty of holiness is signaled in the present context in relation to the attire of Aaron and the priests (Exod. 28:2, 40). It is a small step from the beauty of God to the appreciation and invention of the beautiful in God's world.[22] As a concept, beauty is akin to the created orderliness that underlies meaningful life. The worship of God, therefore, has an inalienable aesthetic aspect.

And second, Bezalel's particular gifts and skills were his specifically. His individual endowments are functions of wisdom, yet wisdom was imparted to him and his colleagues in ways that were not common among Israelites. The gifting of Bezalel may be regarded (with Miroslav Volf) as a charisma.[23] This corresponds to his being "filled with the spirit of God" for the purpose of learning and applying these particular skills. Remarkably, Bezalel is the only figure in the Old Testament who is precisely said to have been filled with the spirit of God (Exod. 31:3; 35:31).[24] What is interesting in the present context is the combination of empowerment by the spirit and the kind of wisdom that manifests itself in abilities that may be both natural and learned. Spiritual gifting (or charisma) here comes into the sphere of the everyday.[25]

Bezalel's labors have the rather special setting of the sphere of God's holiness—since he was building the tabernacle, the place where God would be present in his glory. Yet it seems to me that because of the adoption here of wisdom language, his case has implications for other kinds of human endeavor. Bezalel's work has aspects of both personal commitment and "wise" discovery. The idea of commitment seems to me to lie helpfully alongside that of charisma as a way of thinking about specific forms of human endeavor. Both suggest the dimension of self-transcendence. This is a commitment to

22. See Williams in McConville and Williams, *Joshua*, 137–38.
23. Miroslav Volf, *Work in the Spirit: Toward a Theology of Work* (New York: Oxford University Press, 1991), 111–12.
24. The spirit is said to motivate people in a variety of locutions in the Old Testament. Typically, the spirit "comes upon" them as a special empowering for specific purposes (e.g., Judg. 3:10; 6:34). The spirit may also be said to be "upon" a person, as in the case of the Servant of Yahweh (Isa. 42:1), or, in the case of Ezekiel, to have "entered into" him (Ezek. 2:2); but see Mic. 3:8.
25. Volf, *Work in the Spirit*, 111–12.

ends that, in Macquarrie's phrase, "lie beyond the self"[26] and manifests that delighting in God that is human beings' reciprocation of his delight in them. Part of the glory of it is the amazing variety of human experience, which is potentially enriching for all. A superbly executed concerto brings delight, no doubt, to the performer as well as to the audience—as it probably did for the composer. Uniting this diversity of commitments, when seen as expressions of the God-given capacity for creativity and discovery, is a belief in purpose and meaning.

The Bible as Cultural Mandate

In Bezalel a reader may find a model of a godly human being committed to his particular work. Here work is distinguished not by the relative prestige of various occupations but only by its orientation to the glory of God.[27] The artist may also find a resonance here with the cultivated understanding of materials and the challenge to discover the limits of their plasticity in the production of something beautiful.[28] We have in Bezalel, therefore, not only a narrative but also an invitation to see human action upon the world, in work or art, as both fulfilling and full of significance.

This point leads to the question how far the Bible may be said to model or mandate cultural activity more widely. The origins of such activity—city building, agriculture, metalwork, and music—are attributed in Genesis,

---

26. Macquarrie, *In Search of Humanity*, 143.

27. George Eliot's Adam Bede invokes Bezalel as the biblical model for his own commitment to his carpenter's craft, for him a function of godliness and integrity. Set in the context of early English Methodism, Adam has a discussion with his Methodist brother Seth about the religious life, and says:

> But what does the Bible say? Why, it says as God put his sperrit into the workman as built the tabernacle, to make him do all the carved work and things as wanted a nice hand; there's the sperrit o' God in all things and all times—week day as well as Sunday—and i' the great works and inventions, and i' the figuring and the mechanics. And God helps us with our headpieces and our hands as well as with our souls; and if a man does bits o' jobs out o' working hours—builds an oven for 's wife to save her from going to the bakehouse, or scrats at his bit o' garden and makes two potatoes grow instead o' one, he's doing more good, and he's just as near to God, as if he was running after some preacher, and a-praying and a-groaning. (George Eliot, *Adam Bede* [1859; London: Collins, 1965], 23)

28. On the artist's mastery of materials, see Nicholas Wolterstorff, *Art in Action* (Grand Rapids: Eerdmans, 1980), 91–93. He cites the great east window of Gloucester Cathedral as a tour de force in pressing the stone to the limit of its capacity to bear the weight of the glass, in an astonishing act of artistic creation. In contrast, for Wolterstorff, the accomplished craftsman stays comfortably within the proven capabilities of the material, as exemplified in the cathedral of Chartres (ibid., 93). Yet both craftsman and artist, whether cautious or daring, are balancing experience and discovery in their pursuit of beauty.

disconcertingly, to the antediluvian line of Cain (Gen. 4:17–22). Yet in the biblical narrative more broadly, it can scarcely be confined under the banner of the "curse," since all these activities plainly feature as aspects of blessing and in the life of Israel's worship.

The Bible as cultural mandate may be considered in a further way, namely, in its own literary forms. For Jo Carruthers, the Bible is "the archetypal literary text," and as such the ultimate source of much art in the parts of the world that have been influenced by it. She argues that the Bible is the source of the notions of literature and the book: "The very institution of Western 'Litera-ture'—the creation and reverential study of great books—owes its existence to the Bible." Indeed, the Bible as canon creates a notion of canon in secular literature, in the sense of a body of literature that is felt to exert the greatest claim on our attention.[29] Literature in English is profoundly influenced by the Bible in ways that are beyond computation.[30] They include a rich resource of topics and motifs that have become part and parcel of the common culture, as well as a shaping of the English language itself.[31]

In historical actuality, then, the Bible has had a powerful effect on liter-ary creativity. Much of this creativity, of course, does not acknowledge such a debt. And indeed, it can be openly at odds with the Bible's reality claims. For some, the very form of the novel poses a challenge to biblical authority because, in adopting an omniscient narratorial voice, it usurps the omniscient narratorial authority of the Bible.[32] Even so, the Bible's affinities with literary forms have been recognized and subjected to intense study over the last three or four decades.[33] Moreover, as an exemplar of literary virtuosity, the Bible discloses a human capacity to express and explore that readily becomes an invitation to pursue this experimentally. This raises a question about what

29. See Jo Carruthers, "Literature," in *The Blackwell Companion to the Bible and Culture*, ed. John F. A. Sawyer (Oxford: Blackwell, 2006), 253.

30. It is not possible to offer any kind of account of this here; but see David Lyle Jeffrey, ed., *Dictionary of Biblical Tradition in English Literature* (Grand Rapids: Eerdmans, 1992).

31. On this see Melvyn Bragg, *The Book of Books: The Radical Impact of the King James Bible 1611–2011* (London: Sceptre, 2011).

32. Carruthers, "Literature," 256. She cites Jeanette Winterson's novel *Oranges Are Not the Only Fruit* (London: Pandora Press, 1985) as a self-conscious attempt to do this, "over-writing" Genesis.

33. The seminal works of Robert Alter, *The Art of Biblical Narrative* (New York: Basic Books, 1981) and *The Art of Biblical Poetry* (New York: Basic Books, 1985), and of Meir Sternberg, *The Poetics of Biblical Narrative* (Bloomington: Indiana University Press, 1985), are the tip of a massive iceberg. Their titles alone suggest that the Bible exhibits features that belong within the category of literature, as it is conceived in nonbiblical disciplines in the humanities. Many practitioners of literary study of the Bible have had their training in departments of literature study and consciously employ methods of reading learned there. Alter is a case in point, as are Yvonne Sherwood and Robert Polzin.

kind of relationship there may be between biblical literary forms and nonbiblical ones. To answer this, we may consider the example of Song of Songs 4, a particularly beautiful lyric in that book of love's delight.

The opening lines set the tone: "How you are beautiful, my love, how you are beautiful!" (*hinnāk yāpâ ra'yātî hinnāk yāpâ*) (Song 4:1). In the exclamation and the repetition, there is rapture, recalling Adam's exclamation on his first sight of Eve in Genesis 2:23. What follows is a virtuoso act of admiration, depending chiefly on similes drawn from nature (apart from the unexpected military imagery of Song 4:4, a reminder, if one were needed, of the cultural specificity of all metaphorical language). The flock of shorn ewes (v. 2), all bearing twins and none "bereaved," nicely conjures up a full set of shining teeth. Yet the mind also turns to the fertile ewes themselves and the bounty of this picture. What is its language really doing? The thought (the beauty of the beloved) seems to defy expression. (Note the repeated "behind your veil"—the lover is at once present to the view and hidden.) There is a certain admission of this when the poem does a kind of circle from the opening exclamation (v. 1) to its echo in verse 7 ("You are entirely lovely, my love, and there is no flaw in you"). Its effect seems to lie precisely on the boundaries between sublime speech and speechlessness, a kind of consciousness bending. There is profound and nameless longing here. Verse 6 is an instance: "Until the day breathes and the shadows flee" (*'ad šeyyāpûaḥ hayyôm*), where the sounds of *šeyyāpûaḥ* both resonate with *yāpâ* (beautiful) and onomatopoeically evoke the breath-like vanishing of the day. In the next line (v. 6b), the lover says: "I will hie me to the mountain of myrrh and the hill of frankincense" (with RSV, capturing the reflexive, self-involving *'ēlek lî*). What is this mountain and this hill? They may perhaps be suggested by the lover's breasts (v. 5), yet the allusion is also exotic and replete with nostalgia and desire. There is a movement toward what is not yet possessed, what perhaps cannot be possessed, a movement in which both time and place play a part. The day (time) fades away in a breath, and the poet's eyes turn outward to far places—to Lebanon and Hermon with their high, inaccessible peaks, and to dens of lions and leopards. We have noticed before how the lovers' love interweaves with a wider-ranging delight in the created world, and Song of Songs 4 is no exception. The flocks and herds, the pomegranates, the fawns and the lilies, the myrrh and the frankincense, have more than walk-on parts, but are also themselves celebrated in this overflowing sensual feast.

How does this compare with other love poetry, or indeed any poetry that explores the sound of words to express something about the world? What marks out the Song from its many counterparts in the ancient and modern worlds? And is there any sense in which it may serve as a model for other creative writing? It may be that the Song is simply the best love poetry ever written, yet this is a matter of aesthetic judgment, and opinions are bound to vary. So the answer does not lie there.

I suggested a moment ago that the language of Song of Songs 4 verges on speechlessness, as if it had reached and must reach the limits of its power to say true things about the world. This brings us into familiar territory in modern thinking about language, with its philosophical question about the relationship between language and reality. The pioneer of structuralism, Ferdinand de Saussure, took the radical step of proposing a disjunction between linguistic systems, or structures, and the external world. After him, post-structuralists like Jacques Derrida have gone further, denying that structures themselves, including linguistic ones, are fixed or static. Rather, "post-structuralism, or deconstruction—a method of reading texts, philosophical as well as literary, indeed any texts whatsoever—dissolves any set structure into a play of structurings, a play of interpretation where truth is never finally arrived at; truth is always involved in a play of differences that keep deferring its full presence."[34] There are no fixed readings of texts; rather, "the reading of a past text becomes the writing of a new text in the present."[35]

Readers of modern biblical scholarship will recognize the influence of this sort of thinking on the plethora of rereadings, feminist for example, which often challenge familiar, well-established interpretations. Such rereading is not by definition skeptical; rather, modern readers often claim simply to expose the bias of vested interests that have dominated the previous reception of texts, and to find possible meanings that have hitherto been overlooked or neglected but that speak to pressing issues in the modern world. And this insight corresponds well with the character of many of the biblical writings, which, as we have seen, can be elusive in meaning. We have already noticed that the Bible exemplifies and invites the imaginative rereading of its texts (above, ch. 5); such rereading is one form of the creativity to which the Bible gives a prompt, and is even a condition of the Bible's enduring intelligibility.

The point can be extended, I think, to take in new literary and artistic work. In a sense, the great mass of such work that has taken a cue from the Bible throughout the Christian centuries may be seen as a rereading of the Bible. Figures like Michelangelo and Raphael stand in a long line of practitioners who have sought to communicate the Christian story in new forms of

---

34. Ann Curthoys and John Docker, *Is History Fiction?* (Sydney: University of New South Wales Press, 2006), 146. They refer to Derrida's *Writing and Difference* and *Of Grammatology*.
35. Curthoys and Docker, *Is History Fiction?*, 149.

expression. The cathedrals of Europe tell the same story in stone and glass. The poetry of George Herbert, John Donne, and Gerard Manley Hopkins is high literary art devoted to the praise of God. The best such work engages not only with the biblical and Christian tradition but also with its own age. Graham Sutherland's depictions of the *Crucifixion* were influenced by a book of photographic images he saw from the camps at Belsen, Auschwitz, and Buchenwald:

> In them, many of the tortured bodies looked like figures deposed from crosses. The whole idea of the depiction of Christ crucified became much more real to me after seeing this book, and it seemed to be possible to do this subject again. In my case, the continuing beastliness and cruelty of mankind, amounting at times to madness, seems eternal and classic.[36]

Here is a conscious reflection on the meaning of the biblical tradition in the light of profound experience and expressed in artistic creation. In similar vein, Barbara Hepworth compares her sculpture to prayer at moments of unhappiness:

> When there has been a threat to life—like the atomic bomb dropped on Hiroshima, or now the menace of pollution—my reaction has been to swallow despair, to make something that rises up, something that will win. In another age . . . I would simply have carved cathedrals.[37]

With Sutherland and Hepworth, the art is self-consciously "religious." Yet in its dedication to the praise of God there is a certain claim that the true vocation of art and the artist is to give glory to God. Hepworth, having been early troubled by the specter of the "graven image," "decided that it was sin only when the image sought to elevate the pretensions of man instead of man praising God and his universe. Every work of sculpture is, and must be, an act of praise and an awareness of man in his landscape."[38] Her rubric for sculpture may be applied to all creative activity, whether in literature, art, music, or architecture. This can include work that is not self-consciously religious, where the creative act, and the appreciation of it, may nevertheless express

36. From a letter to the *Daily Telegraph Magazine*, September 10, 1971, no. 359, cited in Lyrica Taylor, ed., *Still Small Voice: British Biblical Art in a Secular Age (1850–2014) from the Ahmanson Collection* (Irvine, CA: Pinatubo Press, 2015), 134.

37. From a letter to Herbert Read, December 30, 1946, in the Sir Herbert Read Archive, University of Victoria BC, cited in Taylor, *Still Small Voice*, 121.

38. Barbara Hepworth, *Drawings from a Sculptor's Landscape* (New York: Praeger, 1967), 10; cited in Taylor, *Still Small Voice*, 121.

true insights about God's world and lead to praise, or indeed to repentance and a quest for justice.

Artistic creativity therefore participates in the whole world of human possibilities, ranging from faith to skepticism, and beyond skepticism to hostility to God. The point brings us back to the biblical foundations for a theology of work, where work is understood broadly to include imaginative creativity.

I have already suggested that the human vocation to work may be seen as a kind of cooperation with God. This means that work should not be seen as merely the maintenance of the order of things, apart from God's deeper purposes, but, with Miroslav Volf, in the sense that human purposeful activity participates in the eschatological transformation of all things.[39] The activity God gives to humans in the world belongs to the nature and purpose of the human intrinsically, as part of God's creative imagination. In similar vein, Oliver O'Donovan finds three essential aspects of human work: the material, the social, and the spiritual. First, work is directed to the material world and makes a difference to it, in a way that is attuned to the character that God has imparted to it. Adam's naming of the animals is "a work of recognition and classification that unlocks the order within the variety of the animal kingdom (Gen. 2.19)."[40] Second, it entails communication with others in common purposes.[41] And third, in its proper alternation with rest it echoes the work and rest of the creator, and therefore implies a fellowship with him, "so that work and worship together become constitutive of ourselves."[42]

That these find biblical grounding may be illustrated by recalling Deuteronomy's view of work as gift, community, and worship. In its vision of the people of Israel enjoying the fruits of the "good land" (with its Edenic connotations), Deuteronomy may indeed be understood to place human endeavor, following the loss of Eden, within the story of the redemptive restoration of all things. In the liberation of Israel from slavery in Pharaoh's Egypt, the issue is whom Israel shall serve (ʿābad, Exod. 1:11–14), where "service" has a connotation of worship (Exod. 8:1; cf. 5:1, "hold a feast"); and in the Deuteronomic prospect of God-given life in a bountiful land, the labors of God's people are restored to their proper place within the purpose of worship and service, symbolized

---

39. This view of work is expressed by Miroslav Volf in his *Work in the Spirit*. It is strongest when it forms part of an approach to eschatology in which the "new heavens and new earth" are seen as a transformation of the present world, rather than one in which the present world is destroyed to make way for a radically new one (ibid., 102–22, esp. 104). Volf believes, however, that his understanding of work would not be wholly incompatible even with the latter kind of eschatology.

40. O'Donovan, "Reflections on Work," 112.

41. Ibid., 112–13.

42. Ibid., 113–14.

in the gifts they bring as they come together to the central sanctuary, or "the place that Yahweh your God will choose, out of all your tribes, to put his name there" (Deut. 12:5). The gifts that the Israelites bring to God are "the work of [their] hands" (16:15), and in this return of gift for gift there is "good" (Deut. 6:24–25), echoing the "goodness" of the original creation.

Moreover, the keynote of such labor-worship is *joy*. At the Feast of Booths the people are to "rejoice in [their] feast" (Deut. 16:14); they are to do so because Yahweh has blessed them "in all your produce and in all the work of your hands" (*bĕkōl ma'ăśēh yādeykā*) (16:15). The passage closes with: "so you shall be altogether joyful" (*wĕhāyîtā 'ak śāmēaḥ*). In Deuteronomy, the *feast* encapsulates the purpose of all living, an enactment of how the human heart finds joy and fulfillment in an orientation of all of life to God.

This conjunction of work, service of God, and joyful feasting suggests that our delight in God and his creation is to be realized in the business of daily living. The Torah is *lived*. Keeping Torah, the practice of righteousness (*ṣĕdāqâ*), is both an act of faith and a discovery of God's goodness in the warp and woof of life. The Deuteronomic vision knows that work is not accidental or instrumental, but belongs essentially to human beings in their own interrelationships and in their relations with both God and the world.

Conclusion

I have suggested that human creativity, far from being optional recreation for enthusiasts, has roots in the nature of the human person as made in the "image of God." As God created an orderly and beautiful world and delighted in it, so humans are invited to participate in the divine delight by also thinking and acting in ways that are creative. This invitation to human beings is extended not only through the theology of the "image" in Genesis 1, but variously, as in the nuances of the Wisdom literature, both cautionary and exhilarating, in the convergence of work and worship in Deuteronomy, in the exalted spiritual status of a Bezalel, and in the literary and poetic artistry of the Bible's own modes of expression. This creativity is not by definition exclusive or rarefied; rather, it takes in the full range of constructive purposefulness. People are creative according to ability, opportunity, interest, desire, and commitment. In biblical perspective, the overriding characteristic of such endeavor is its dedication to the glory of God. In that perspective, it has the character of adventurous discovery of God's world.

It needs no demonstration that creativity itself can take cunning and vicious forms. The comment of Genesis on the energy and inventiveness of human evil still rings true in the modern world (Gen. 6:5). Yet the capacity of humans for affirming the goodness of God's creation in ways that are full of imagination and integrity seems unbounded. We have noticed just a few examples here, out of an immense treasury of such commitment. We have seen too how faith in the meaningfulness of God's world can often be expressed through the depiction of great horror. Real engagement with the world cannot be misty-eyed about its evils. Yet in creative endeavor, God's human creatures are fundamentally thinking, working, and acting in hope, convinced of a glory still to be revealed, and committing themselves to a path of personal growth and transformation as they do so.

10

The Old Testament and Human Formation: The Psalms

Our question from the outset has been that of the psalmist: "What is the human being, that you [God] should pay attention to them?" (Ps. 8:4[5]). Yet as we have seen, there is no merely descriptive answer to this question. It is asked twice in situations of worship, and in Job's case, in existential anguish. The question about humanity is pursued, therefore, in and through the profoundest experiences of human being, experiences that are unfolded in the pages of the Old Testament. We find there a depiction of humanity as unfinished, not yet perfectly realized, but conditioned by eschatological hope. Such hope, however, is not otherworldly, but rather imparts to human existence its essential character. It is because of the Old Testament's ever-renewing orientation toward the imminent and future action of God that day-to-day human life in its many aspects is meaningful.

Our study of the Old Testament's portrayal of humanity, therefore, has focused on lived experience, both within the world of the Old Testament and on the part of its readers. We introduced at the outset the notions of transformation and transcendence, as used by some who have read the Old Testament as an engagement with Scripture and thus as an activity in biblical spirituality. And our own reading has tried to keep this dimension firmly in view as an exercise itself in spirituality.

189

The spirituality of the Old Testament, we have seen, resists the dualisms that are sometimes associated with that concept, as between body and "soul," mind and heart, or individual and corporate. The embodied character of human existence according to the Old Testament has a number of dimensions, not only in the individual's constitution but also in the interrelationship of persons, in the social and political spheres, in sexuality, and in the creativity of all manner of endeavor that enriches human life. People are embodied too in their historicity, that is, in their specific "placedness," within which their flourishing takes shape. Cultural expression, located in corporate memories, symbols, and rituals, therefore becomes an indispensable part of the human experience.

The theological foundation for this conception of a multifaceted human life could be found in Genesis's idea of humanity as "the image of God." This idea is unfolded in Genesis 1–3, where we saw that it does not consist in static inherent qualities of the human person, but rather applies to human persons in their wholeness and in their life together. It functions as a call to realize the defining human purpose of representing the presence of God in the world, and serving the divine intention to develop the created relationships among God, humans, and the world. This created purpose is charged with all the dangers inherent in godlikeness itself, as Genesis 3 makes plain. Yet, as we have argued, the challenge to embody the "image" remains inalienable from human existence.

The Old Testament is both a story of the human struggle to meet this challenge and an invitation to engage in it. The vastness of its range and its variety of form correspond to the endless possibilities entailed in human living: in its dramatizations of relationships, traumas, and joys; in its passionate demands for justice, truth, and peace; in its explorations of the outer limits of human understanding; in its poetic reach toward things too deep for words; in its command of linguistic and rhetorical possibilities in the service of sustaining memory and hope; in its expression of the human situation in the language of worship. The story is always attended by the dual possibilities of joy and flourishing (or salvation) and of tragedy and despair. These are enshrined formally in a number of ways: in the covenantal trope of the blessing and the curse (Deut. 28); in the psalmic dialectic between lamentation and praise; in the overarching narrative of Israel as a perpetual balance between possession and loss; and in the prophetic model of history as a conflict between the lust for power and the realization of the rule of God.

These tensions do not find definitive resolution in the Old Testament, although there are certain pointers toward it. One such is what may be called moments of theological crisis, brought about by the tensions themselves. These subject the divine-human relationship to the most intense scrutiny and strain and intimate the possibility of redemptive change. The book of Hosea offers a leading example, where the idea of God-as-human, and so the relationship between God and humans, is taken to an extreme stress point. God in Hosea presents himself both as human-like, in the image of Yahweh as husband to Israel (Hosea 1–3), yet decisively not human-like, at the moment when his anger and his compassion are brought into conflict. But crucially, his compassion predominates (11:8–9). In the figure of the Servant of Yahweh, the book of Isaiah takes the idea of servanthood to a point of ultimate endurance and death (Isa. 52:13–53:12), in a trajectory that stamps future hope with the mark of service.

A further pointer toward resolution of the tension between salvation and dereliction consists in the canonical forms of major books or literary blocks of the Old Testament. The major prophetic books broadly follow a pattern of the proclamation of judgment for sin, followed by a crisis, then restoration and salvation. The well-known turn in the book of Isaiah at 40:1–2, with its announcement of "comfort" to Israel because it has suffered enough for its sins, exemplifies the point. So too does Jeremiah's "Book of Consolation" (Jer. 30–33), with the famous "new covenant" at its heart (31:31–34). A similar structure can be discerned in Ezekiel and in some of the shorter prophetic books (e.g., Hosea, Joel, Micah, and Zephaniah). The point can be argued also for the "primary history" (Genesis–Kings) because of the tendency toward redemption that is expressed at key points (Deut. 30–34; 2 Kings 8; 25:27–30).

These two hints of ultimate salvation belong together, since the theological crises function within the structure of the books. Both, however, are tempered by the return to ambivalence in the same books. After the vivid pictures of restoration in Isaiah 40–55, new notes of judgment return in chapters 56–66, corresponding to suggestions of division within the restored community. And the twin possibilities of judgment and salvation remain right to the final terrible verse of the book. Jeremiah descends from the lofty heights of the new covenant to narratives of the end of the kingdom of Judah, the Babylonian exile, and the unpromising retreat of a dissident group to the apparent security of Egypt and the blandishments of polytheistic worship (Jer. 41–44; 44:15–19). The Old Testament's refusal to deliver finality to the human story may also be reflected in its disparate canonical forms, notably the MT and LXX, which suggest that its legacy to believing communities is such as to leave open the question of how God may continue to go with them into the future.

In consequence, the dual possibilities that are the Old Testament's persistent theme are held in perpetual tension, albeit under the banner of hope. It follows that the goal of humanity as "image of God" is given its specific quality by its involvement in the perpetual tension between flourishing and degradation. The human vocation to represent God in the world is inseparable from the imperative of what may be called "formation," or indeed "transformation." And this imperative operates in all the spheres of human life that we have examined.

The Psalms and Spiritual Formation

In our study so far, we have seen that, as in the issue of "Christ and culture" which we considered at the outset, a theology of humanity has to reckon with the perpetual tension that we have just mentioned. The present essay has been offered not as a theory but as a preamble to a practice, and in part as a practice itself. We have pursued along the way the concepts of growth and transformation. And these are inseparable, in biblical thought and practice, from worship. That is, we do not find formulas for steady progress in the spiritual life, but rather an invitation to a practice of living centered on worship, as a response to the paradoxical, dangerous condition of being human.

Of all the Old Testament's testimony to and resources for spiritual transformation and growth, primacy belongs to the book of Psalms. The Psalms are unique in the Old Testament because they gather up the full range of Israel's past, present, and future with God in the context of worship. While all parts of the Old Testament may be said to stage the relationship between God and Israel, it is only in the Psalms that Israel appears in a concentrated way as a first-person voice, the human addressing the divine. In their totality they are a massive testimony to human spiritual experience, with its dimensions of praise and perplexity, lamentation and thanksgiving, profound misgiving and exultant hope. In the Psalms, the quest for transformation and transcendence is examined microscopically and entwined irreversibly with the hardest edges of the human condition.

I have said that the voice encountered in the Psalms is that of Israel. And the voice is indeed often a plural, as in Psalm 44, which in form-critical terms belongs to a class known as a "lament of the people."[1] The communal character of the Psalms is clear in cases of this sort, and form criticism has distinguished systematically between such communal expressions and individual ones. The preoccupation of the Psalms with Israel as a community is apparent in other ways too, as the utterances of individuals are often bound into the life of the whole people. In some cases, for example, the singular and plural

---

1. See Claus Westermann, *Praise and Lament in the Psalms*, trans. Keith R. Crim and Richard N. Soulen (Edinburgh: T&T Clark, 1981), 52–64.

can interchange (Ps. 20:5–9[6–10]). And the speaker's relationship with the community is sometimes expressed as exhortation, or testimony, or simply in the fact that his or her memory is shaped by what the Old Testament tells us about the history of Israel with God. The human experience displayed in the Psalms, therefore, conforms in principle to all the dimensions of the human experience that we have been investigating.

It is remarkable, then, that at their center is the ubiquitous personality who speaks as "I." The pervasive utterance of this pronoun is both elusive and powerfully involving. It is elusive because it resists being contained within an identification with a particular historical figure or figures. The attribution of many psalms to David in superscriptions, together with explicit connections to his life (Pss.18:[1]; 51:[1–2]), is of course ancient. And the identification of the speaker with him is also invited by some of the Psalms' specific content, as in Psalm 2, where Yahweh says, "I have set my king on Zion, my holy hill," and a first-person voice continues, "He said to me, 'You are my son, today I have begotten you'" (2:6–7). The echoes of Yahweh's covenant with David (2 Sam. 7:14; 23:5) are unmistakable, and therefore the persona of David is never far from view in a reading of the Psalms. However, as has long been recognized, the pervasive "I" does not map easily onto the historical David. There is, in the first place, an evident extension from that David to the concept of the Davidic king as embodiment of the nation's right response to Yahweh and bearer of its future hopes.[2] Thus Psalm 72, with its prayer for the king as agent of justice and blessing in Israel, is headed, "Of Solomon." Correspondingly, the king in the Psalms has been seen as a construction of the "ideal Israelite," characterized by his piety and disposition to praise Yahweh.[3] Nor is David the only figure encountered in this legacy of memory and worship; others include Moses (Ps. 90), the more shadowy musical heroes such as Asaph (Pss. 73–83), Ethan the Ezrahite (89), and Korah (84–85, 87–88), not to mention the even more shadowy "choirmaster" (*měnaṣṣēaḥ*).[4] In Psalm 88:[1] it is close to "all of the above"! The question of attribution, therefore, leads only

2. For this reason the "I" is construed by a number of commentators as a royal voice, representative of the nation. John Eaton, for example, takes a large number of the Psalms to be "royal" (John Eaton, *Kingship and the Psalms* [London: SCM, 1976]). See also John Day, *Psalms*, OTG (Sheffield, UK: JSOT Press, 1990), 88–108, for a review of the interpretation of royal psalms.

3. Patrick D. Miller, "Kingship, Torah Obedience, and Prayer," in *Neue Wege der Psalmenforschung*, ed. K. Seybold and E. Zenger (Freiburg: Herder, 1995), 127–42.

4. The term appears almost exclusively in psalm superscriptions. In Hab. 3:19 it appears in a form very similar to a psalm superscription. Otherwise, it occurs three times in 2 Chronicles to refer to "overseers" of Solomon's work on the temple (2:2[1], 18[17]) and of Josiah's repairs to it (34:13). In the superscriptions it is variously translated "choirmaster" (RSV), "choir director" (NASB), "leader" (NRSV), and "director of music" (NIV).

to a barely identifiable mass of voices and a sense that the Psalter, for all its apparent formality of structure, has come to us out of a layered and richly textured history of praise.

It is somewhat paradoxical, therefore, that its dominant voice should be the simple "I." Yet this is what lends it its extraordinary power and opens it radically to interpretation and reception. While the rooting of the Psalms in an actual history ensures that they bear upon the specific realities of human existence, their dislocation from their myriad original settings and relocation in a book make possible the unlimited potential of their utterances for assimilation to the reader's life and world.[5] This assimilation, I have suggested, can be realized in regard to all the spheres of life that we have seen to be contingent upon the concept of humanity as "image of God."

First, and obviously, the language used can be heard simply as the utterance of an individual. The psalmist expresses thoughts and emotions often through the rhetorical device of address to himself, or his "soul" (*nepeš*, Ps. 103:1). And we have seen above (ch. 3) how the Psalms deploy an array of physiological metaphors to evoke the person's inner life. The embodied individual is at the center of human consciousness. Yet it is impossible to conceive of an entirely isolated individual, apart from the communities in which he or she participates, together with their histories and practices. We have attempted to explore these in the intervening chapters (chs. 6–9). The capacity for the royal attribution to express corporateness has already been mentioned. A number of psalms expressly locate the individual in the setting of a group or assembly (Pss. 22:22[23]; 84). The communal aspect of the psalmist's experience has a specifically political quality, evident in the prayers, thanksgivings, and laments concerning Israel. A central theological topic is Yahweh's covenantal promises to David, celebrated in Psalms 2; 46; 48 but threatened by enemies and apparently laid in ruins by the destruction of the Jerusalem temple by the Babylonians (Ps. 74). Psalm 89, positioned at the end of Book 3, comprises a lengthy hymn to Yahweh's faithfulness to that covenant (vv. 1–37[2–38]), in agonized juxtaposition to a lamentation arising from a bewildered experience of abandonment (vv. 38–51[39–52]). A number of psalms in Book 4 then take up the praise of Yahweh's kingship, notably Psalms 93 and 97–99,[6] which seem to put Davidic kingship in the background. Memories of David and Zion continue to feature sporadically in Books 4 and 5, but the final group, Psalms

---

5. In modern interpretation, influenced by canonical criticism, interest rests on the issues addressed by the book in its final form. Because of the nature of the book, however, it is difficult to pin these down with any confidence.

6. These are the so-called *yhwh mālak* psalms identified as a special group by Sigmund Mowinckel as belonging to a festival of the enthronement of Yahweh. See Day, *Psalms*, 67–87.

146–150, brings the Psalter to completion in a crescendo of praise to Yahweh, in which David has no visible presence. The point is unmissable in the line: "Do not put your trust in princes, or human beings [ben-'ādām], in whom there is no salvation" (Ps. 146:3). Not only David but all human resources are subordinated to Yahweh, who alone can come to the aid of Israel. Here, it seems, the historic political institutions of Israel have been transcended in a hope for an entirely new kind of existence for Israel.

For reasons like this, a recent trend in Psalms studies has found the Psalms ultimately oriented toward an eschatological hope, in which all known political arrangements, whether foreign or Israelite, are transformed or transcended. Egbert Ballhorn, among others, thinks that Books 4 and 5 of the Psalter point beyond Davidic kingship to an eschatological kingdom of Yahweh.[7] This identifies a crucial issue in the interpretation of the Psalms—namely, that their extrication from "original" settings and collection in a book allow the significance of major recurrent topics to be subjected perpetually to reconception. What can an ancient promise of Yahweh to David mean to a community that has experienced the loss of king, temple, and land? Even in a restoration to land, and with a temple rebuilt, there is no simple return to a former status quo. Life has been permanently changed. The symbols themselves have a certain ambivalence, well captured in the curious melding of joy and lament on the part of the elders in Jerusalem upon the laying of the foundations for the restored temple (Ezra 3:10–13).

This does not mean that the Psalms lift the spiritual experience out of the concrete life of human interactions and conflicts. Erich Zenger brings out well the indissoluble connection between existence in the present and hope for the future: "The Psalms as praise 'in the midst of the fire of history' are in particular the prayers which give Israel 'al admat nēkār (Ps. 137.4) hope and a home."[8] The point is important when one considers the relationship between the historical matrix of Israel's experience as recorded in the Psalms and the Psalter as a book. While in a sense the collection of individual psalms in a book has detached them from and obscured their original composition and use, the transition from setting in life to setting in a book (*Sitz im Leben* to *Sitz im Buch*) does not mean their removal from what Zenger calls "the fire

---

7. Egbert Ballhorn, *Zum Telos des Psalters: Der Textzusammenhang des Vierten und Fünften Psalmenbuches (Ps 90–150)*, BBB 138 (Berlin: Philo, 2004), 380. Others who find an eschatological orientation in the Psalter include Jamie Grant, *The King as Exemplar: The Function of Deuteronomy's Kingship Law in the Shaping of the Book of Psalms* (Atlanta: Society of Biblical Literature, 2004); and Erich Zenger, who finds "an eschatological–messianic perspective" in Book 5, especially in the collections Pss. 108–112 and 138–145 (Zenger, "The Composition and Theology of the Fifth Book of the Psalms, Psalms 107–145," *JSOT* 80 [1998]: 98).

8. Zenger, "Composition and Theology," 101.

of history." This readiness for the new is not a retreat into radical interiority. The spirituality of the Psalms is thoroughly embedded in the world.

The Psalms and "Happiness"

Having seen that the Psalms have the capacity to express the life of the human in the broadest sense, we turn now to think about the ways in which they speak about the possibilities of transformation. The opening word of the book in most translations is "blessed" or "happy": "Blessed is the one who does not walk in step with the wicked" (Ps. 1:1 NIV). The Hebrew term 'ašrê (lit., "happinesses of"), occurs not only here but, with a range of qualifiers, in a number of other places in Books 1 and 2.[9] Happiness is predicated of those who keep the Torah, who take refuge in Yahweh, whose sin is forgiven; and of the nation whose God is Yahweh (33:12). It is, therefore, a function of a life in active relationship with God. Psalm 1 gives it its abiding image, where the person who keeps Torah is likened to a flourishing tree by streams of water. Happiness is thus declared to be the proper condition of the human in relationship with God. Reciprocity between God and the human is nicely expressed in Psalms 111–112, a pair of corresponding acrostic psalms. The former celebrates God's righteousness, mercy, faithfulness, and the trustworthiness of his "precepts" (v. 7), and Psalm 112 responds with a portrait of one who "fears" God, delights in his laws, and who is righteous, trusting, faithful, and compassionate to the needy. Such a person is said to be "happy" (v. 1).

This foregrounding of happiness as the true human condition is wholly realistic. Following the image of the flourishing person in Psalm 1, the psalmists go on to unfold their acute understanding that the human journey is full of the most painful traumas and setbacks, as well as great joys. Happiness, then, is not understood here in any sentimental way, nor as material prosperity, or what we may think of as security or success. Rather, as J. Clinton McCann puts it, "happiness has to do with the fundamental orientation of the self to God."[10]

In a sense, this can be taken to mean that, in general, a person's happiness is not contingent on their circumstances. It was a theme of Hellenistic philosophy that happiness and freedom depend entirely on the cultivation of wisdom.

9. Pss. 1:1; 2:12; 32:1–2 (2x); 33:12; 34:8[9]; 40:4[5]; 41:1[2]. See J. Clinton McCann, "The Shape of Book I of the Psalter and the Shape of Human Happiness," in *The Book of Psalms*, ed. W. Flint and P. Miller, VTSup 99 (Leiden: Brill, 2005), 340–48.
10. Ibid., 343.

Only the wise are happy and free.[11] The philosophers could find grounds for such a view in the Stoic cosmic theology, which postulated a created harmony (or *logos*) in all things.[12] The Old Testament writers also often express their belief in a basic harmony in things, but for them this derives from Yahweh, the God of creation, who chose Israel as his people and gave them his Torah. Happiness, therefore, is entwined with the specific story of Israel's past with Yahweh, its interpretation of its present, and its expectations for the future. Israel's past is shaped decisively by the exodus from Egypt, an event that is more than an escape, but is charged with moral significance. In the exodus, subjection to the slave-maker Pharaoh is exchanged for service of Yahweh. Liberation from bondage is a liberation into a certain form of life, which is imagined in the possibilities afforded by the "good land" of Israel. At the heart of this life is the Torah, which permanently memorializes the decisive act of liberation and commits Israel to a liberative life commensurate with it. As Israel was a slave in Egypt, so no one in Israel should be permanently poor (Deut. 15:4a); the nation that was conceived in God's forceful repudiation of slave making cannot in turn make slaves, but must live by the same vigorous rejection of structural impoverishment (15:12–15). Happiness, in Old Testament terms, lies in a vision of a community committed to the flourishing of all.

What is entailed in forging such a community, furthermore, is a matter of character, not just strict obedience. This lies behind the most characteristic call to Torah faithfulness in Deuteronomy 6:4–9, in which it penetrates the heart and understanding of individuals, families, and the people as such. With the twin gifts of freedom and Torah, Israel is called to work out what it means to live as God's people. Stanley Hauerwas has noted that the implication of the Old Testament story is that Israel's life is necessarily characterized by growth and development.[13] This fits precisely with what we find in the Psalms. The call to Torah obedience is not the end of the matter, as if it were self-evident what it would entail. The deeper entailments (or the "weightier things of the law" in Jesus' words) need to be plumbed. The psalmists live before God in a permanent engagement with what a life so lived might become. They do so not as philosophers or moralists, but in an attitude of prayer. The point is nowhere clearer than in the Psalter's greatest meditation on the Torah, Psalm

11. The dictum "Only the wise are free" is one of Cicero's six paradoxes, influenced by Greek Stoic philosophy. See Otto Kaiser, *Des Menschen Glück und Gottes Gerechtigkeit* (Tübingen: Mohr Siebeck, 2007), 185–86.

12. Ibid., 14, 76–77.

13. As Hauerwas puts it in *The Peaceable Kingdom: A Primer in Christian Ethics* (London: SCM, 1984): "The Bible is fundamentally a story of a people's journey with their God. A 'biblical ethic' will necessarily be one that portrays life as growth and development" (24).

119 (where "Torah" is meant in the general sense of the instruction of Yahweh). As in Psalm 1, happiness here is a close correlative of Torah keeping (119:1). The meaning of the psalm emerges more strongly, however, from its tone. Its language is pervasively emotive: the psalmist delights in the commandments, treasures them, loves them, and longs for them. And it commits the psalmist's will: "I have sworn an oath . . . to observe" (v. 106); "I do not forget" (v. 109); "I seek you with my whole heart" (v. 10; cf. v. 145).

The psalm is predicated on change and growth. Keeping Torah requires learning, discipline, and understanding. And these are played out against a backdrop of wisdom gained in life experience. There is not only the question, "How can a young man keep his way pure?" (Ps. 119:9), but also familiar themes from the laments in the psalmist's reprobation of the wicked and the enemy (vv. 110, 113), and the unshakable conviction that true maturity is a gift from God to those who look for it (vv. 100, 123). This psalmist lives in no ivory tower. His experience of life echoes the diversity of the Psalter, with a firsthand knowledge of hard-edged reality. In verses 49–56, for example, the "blessing" declared in the final verse of the section comes in spite of the psalmist's distress, derision on the part of others, and his anger when he sees contempt for the Torah. Similar trajectories occur in verses 65–72, 81–88. And he is even brought back from "going astray" by an affliction that apparently comes from God and enables him to "learn your statutes" (vv. 67–71). This psalmist's delight in the Torah, therefore, is grounded in faith in God that has been tested by troubles. It is because of this that it stands as a monument to the human love of God. It not only directs readers in the right way to think; it is itself an instance of the devotion that leads to wholeness.

The Psalms and Transformation

As is already clear in Psalm 119, the model of human happiness through Torah fully reckons with the most disturbing aspects of living life orientated to God. And the psalmists face up to these fearlessly. If the Psalms testify to the possibility of life before God as transformative, the transformations may come along paths of pain and distress. As we have seen, the structure of the Psalter is influenced by the narrative line in which Israel's securities are shaken to their core by the loss of the symbols that gave meaning to its life. The "boundary" psalms in Book 3 (Pss. 73–89) illustrate the point sharply. Psalm 89 closes Book 3 on a note of perplexity because the Davidic promises seem to lie in ruins. Juxtaposed to it is the dreadful Psalm 88, the bleakest of all the Psalter's laments because it runs out in dark and lonely despair, without the lament's expected turn to confidence or petition. Its only redeeming note is that the sufferer is able to address his desperation to God. Corresponding to these two are the two psalms that open Book 3, Psalms 73 and 74. Psalm 74, like 89, faces catastrophic loss, apparently in the destruction of the temple, while Psalm 73 records the inner journey of one who has come within a hair's breadth of abandoning hope in the justice of God.

Curiously, it is these psalms at the opening of Book 3, rather than those at the end, that offer signs of recovery. Psalm 74 proceeds from lament to the hymnic affirmation of Yahweh as creator and king (74:12–17), reminiscent of the polemic in Isaiah 40–55 against the Babylonian royal-creation ideology. But it is Psalm 73 that searches most penetratingly the human capacity to sustain faith in the face of great stress. The stress in this case derives not simply from the psalmist's own suffering from the "usual suspects" of illness or persecution, but from that most disturbing existential question concerning the justice of God itself. The conundrum of the prosperity of the wicked while the innocent suffer is a familiar topic in the Old Testament, shared by the Prophets (Jer. 12:1–4) and Wisdom literature (Job and Ecclesiastes in their different ways), as well as the Psalms. But although the psalmist's problem arises from general observation and not just his own experience, it becomes exceedingly personal for him. His "feet had almost stumbled," that is, he had almost given up his trust in God (Ps. 73:2); he was utterly perplexed (v. 16); he was bitterly, irrationally, brutally angry with God (vv. 21–22).

Psalm 73 stages this extreme experience of spiritual disease as a retrospect, spoken from a position of recovered equilibrium, as already signaled in verse 1. It is also perfectly structured to display the transition from despair to renewed confidence. In the narrative of this dark experience, the turning point comes when the psalmist goes into the "sanctuary of God" (Ps. 73:17). The psalmist does not say whether the decision to go into the temple was itself part of his recovery or whether it was undertaken in some routine way. But the physical act of doing so has the effect of tapping into powerful symbolism and deep memory and becomes a moment of decisive change. The change in the psalmist is not brought about by material alterations in external reality, but entirely inwardly, in a transformed perspective on the nature of things. This involves the realization that the prosperous wicked are not, after all, in an enviable state, but are living dangerously in God's world (vv. 18–20). But it is above all a renewed vision of God, a conviction not only that God is near him (vv. 23–24) but also that for God to be near him is in itself the pearl of greatest price (vv. 25, 28). There is more for the psalmist in this recovery, it seems, than a simple return to the sort of confidence he had before. Rather, there is a sense that he has been taken on to a fuller, more chastened faith, in which his confidence is no longer dependent on preconceived notions of what God's world ought to be like. And this profoundly spiritual experience is also a journey of understanding. The language of Wisdom literature is frequent here,[14] and what is new following the act of prayer in the temple is new understanding (*'ābînâ lĕ'aḥărîtām*, "then I perceived their end") (v. 17). In the psalm, the disciplines of wisdom are married to the passionate desire for justice and for God himself. The psalm is a classic of spiritual growth.

The Psalms and Language

The Psalms testify to the possibility of growth and development in a person's life. In Psalm 73 we focused on a change brought about in the recorded experience of the psalmist. Yet equally important is its capacity to transform the lives of its readers and hearers. Essential to the genius of the Psalms is that they emerge from and are given into the activity of worship. Psalm 73, as well as expressing the poet's own profound experience, has been placed by a believing community at a key juncture in their book of worship. What was true for the psalmist, it is claimed, can be true again for all who make this their own. The Psalms exert a power over the imagination. Their language itself plays a part in this. Walter Brueggemann has recognized this power of the language of the Psalms to bring about something completely new. His model of reorientation does not imply a simple return to a previous state, but allows for the radically new. For example, the "declarative hymns and songs of thanksgiving" (e.g., Ps. 124) understand that "a newness has been given which is not achieved, not automatic, not derived from the old, but is a genuine newness wrought by gift."[15] The Psalms rest on the tacit premise that linguistic acts change things. Writing about the effect of language on the different psychologies of ancient and modern audiences, Brent A. and Brad D. Strawn say that "psychological effects are taking place in the working of the literature itself—in both its writing and its reading."[16] The act of language, in composition and use, is thus a component of the Psalms' capacity to transform.

14. See vv. 7, 11, 16–17, 24.
15. Walter Brueggemann, "Psalms and the Life of Faith: A Suggested Typology of Function," *JSOT* 17 (1980): 9. For his view of language, he refers to Paul Ricoeur, *The Conflict of Interpretations* (Evanston, IL: Northwestern University Press, 1976), e.g., 96.
16. Brent A. Strawn and Brad D. Strawn, "Prophecy and Psychology," in *Dictionary of the Old Testament: The Prophets*, ed. Mark J. Boda and J. Gordon McConville (Downers Grove, IL: IVP Academic, 2012), 618. In the same place they cite N. N. Holland, P. K. Kugler, and M. Grimaud, "Psychological Criticism," in *The New Princeton Encyclopedia of Poetry and Poetics*, ed. A. Preminger and T. G. A. Brogan (Princeton: Princeton University Press, 1993), 1000: "Consciousness is continually being imagined (imaged, in-formed) by the metaphors in

It is yet another caution against a sharp distinction between the inward and the external in a person, as if the performance of ritual acts—including speech acts—could be separate from a truer inward disposition.[17] Such acts, indeed, can produce a change in a person's disposition.[18] The power of utterance, in the context of prayer, may sufficiently explain the "change of mood" in the psalms of lament, that is, without recourse to other special factors (such as a prophetic "word of assurance"). For Gabriel Josipovici, prayer is analogous to speech between human persons, that is, in language that has meaning "in the linguistic and social usages of the community" and is "what mediates between inner and outer"; there is no prayer without words. He goes on to reflect on the significance of uttering the pronoun "I": "By entering language and the community of men I find myself. To speak to God is to acknowledge this, that in speaking I trust that I will find myself."[19] And again, language "[enables] us to outer ourselves and thus become fully alive."[20]

The Psalms, therefore, testify to the possibility of growth and development in individuals and communities. They do not, however, offer an infallible program of self-improvement. There is no all-encompassing trajectory of progress and renewal, but rather a number of trajectories, as many, in the end, as there are psalms in the book. There is untidiness in the achievement of a great high point at the opening of Book 3 (Ps. 73), while the low points of Psalms 88–89 lie still ahead for the reader. The one does not cancel the other out. Rather than being a manual of steady progress, the Psalms work by drawing the reader into worship, by leading them in a way of living before God.

The destination of the journey is praise itself. The point emerges forcefully from the climactic final five psalms, 146–50. Here the "I" speaker virtually disappears from view, yet is inevitably present in the words and acts of praise.

---

the very text it is writing or reading." The creative and transformative power of language has been observed at several points in our study.

17. See the critical remarks of Gabriel Josipovici on Friedrich Heiler, *Prayer* (1918), in which Josipovici resists a distinction between "prayer of the heart" and "formal literary prayers" (*The Book of God: A Response to the Bible* [New Haven: Yale University Press, 1988], 159; cf. 161).

18. This is argued by Jacqueline E. Lapsley, "Feeling Our Way: Love for God in Deuteronomy," *CBQ* 65 (2003): 350–69. She also cites Gary A. Anderson, *A Time to Mourn, a Time to Dance: The Expression of Grief and Joy in Israelite Religion* (University Park: Pennsylvania State University Press, 1991).

19. Josipovici, *Book of God*, 163. He also refers to Samuel Beckett's *Not I* and the character there who cannot say "I." There is in this a kind of refusal of personal responsibility (ibid., 162–63).

20. Ibid., 165. Josipovici deliberately uses "outer" as a verb to reinforce the idea of language as expressive of the self. Iris Murdoch says something similar in her novel *The Black Prince* (Harmondsworth, UK: Penguin, 1973), when she speaks (through her narrator) of "the redemptive role of words in the lives of those without identity" (199).

The "narrative" of the Psalms, with all its particularities of Israel's life, runs
out in the unbridled praise of these "Hallelujah" psalms. Lament has been
left behind here, in ringing notes that seem timeless and pure. A human voice
speaks out of a kind of heavenly vision, having joined the heavenly praise. Yet
the speaker is not airbrushed. It is the same voice that we have encountered
everywhere in the Psalms, in great joys and deep sorrows, the voice that cannot be quite identified with any figure, but who somehow encapsulates the
full range of Israel's—and ordinary human—experience. This "I" is simply
the human being in God's world. It is the bookend echo of the Psalter's opening: "Blessed is the one who does not walk in step with the wicked" (Ps. 1:1
NIV). By this stage we have seen something of what that might mean. The
"endless Hallelujah" that Psalms 146–50 open onto is uttered by one who
has endured all that a human being can endure, but has become wise, and
now, as none other than 'ādām, leads the creation in praise. It is this voice,
possessed by the praise of God, that may be said, in the end, to answer that
other psalmist's question (Ps. 8:4[5]): "What is the human being, that you
should pay attention to them?"

Bibliography

Abma, Richtsje. *Bonds of Love: Methodic Studies of Prophetic Texts with Marriage Imagery (Isaiah 50:1–3 and 54:1–10, Hosea 1–3, and Jeremiah 2–3).* SSN 40. Assen, Neth.: Van Gorcum, 1999.

Alexander, Loveday. "Good Sex, Bad Sex: Reflections on Sexuality and the Bible." In *Conception, Reception, and the Spirit: Essays in Honor of Andrew T. Lincoln,* edited by J. G. McConville and Lloyd K. Pietersen, 253–73. Eugene, OR: Wipf & Stock, 2015.

Allen, Leslie C. *Psalms 101–150.* WBC 21. Waco: Word, 1983.

Alter, Robert. *The Art of Biblical Narrative.* New York: Basic Books, 1981.

———. *The Art of Biblical Poetry.* New York: Basic Books, 1985.

Altmann, Peter. *Festal Meals in Ancient Israel: Deuteronomy's Identity Politics in Their Ancient Near Eastern Context.* BZAW 424. Berlin: de Gruyter, 2011.

Andersen, Francis I., and David Noel Freedman. *Hosea: A New Translation with Introduction and Commentary.* AB 24. Garden City, NY: Doubleday, 1980.

Anderson, Benedict. *Imagined Communities: Reflections on the Origins and Spread of Nationalism.* London: Verso, 2006.

Anderson, Gary A. *A Time to Mourn, a Time to Dance: The Expression of Grief and Joy in Israelite Religion.* University Park: Pennsylvania State University Press, 1991.

Arnold, Bill T. "Deuteronomy 12 and the Law of the Central Sanctuary *noch einmal.*" VT 64 (2014): 246–48.

Assmann, Jan. *Das kulturelle Gedächtnis: Schrift, Erinnerung und politische Identität in frühen Hochkulturen.* Munich: Beck, 1997.

———. *Moses the Egyptian: The Memory of Egypt in Western Monotheism.* Cambridge, MA: Harvard University Press, 1997.

———. *Religion und kulturelles Gedächtnis.* Munich: Beck, 2000.

Atkins, Peter. "The Limitless Power of Science." In *The Frontiers of Scientific Vision*, edited by John Cornwell, 122–33. Oxford: Oxford University Press, 1995.

Bahrani, Zainab. *The Graven Image: Representation in Babylonia and Assyria*. Philadelphia: University of Pennsylvania Press, 2003.

Balentine, Samuel E. *The Hidden God: The Hiding of the Face of God in the Old Testament*. OTM. Oxford: Oxford University Press, 1983.

Ballhorn, Egbert. *Zum Telos des Psalters: Der Textzusammenhang des Vierten und Fünften Psalmenbuches (Ps 90–150)*. BBB 138. Berlin: Philo, 2004.

Barr, James. *The Garden of Eden and the Hope of Immortality*. Minneapolis: Fortress, 1993.

Barstad, Hans M. *The Myth of the Empty Land: A Study in the History and Archaeology of Judah in the "Exilic" Period*. Oslo: Scandinavian University Press, 1996.

Barth, Karl, *Church Dogmatics* III/1. Edited by G. W. Bromiley and T. F. Torrance. Edinburgh: T&T Clark, 1958.

Bartholomew, Craig. *Where Mortals Dwell: A Christian View of Place Today*. Grand Rapids: Baker Academic, 2011.

Barton, John. *Understanding Old Testament Ethics: Approaches and Explorations*. Louisville: Westminster John Knox, 2003.

Bauckham, Richard. *The Bible in Politics: How to Read the Bible Politically*. 2nd ed. London: SPCK, 2010.

Bechtel, Lyn M. "Genesis 2.4b–3.24: A Myth about Human Maturation." *JSOT* 67 (1995): 3–26.

Blenkinsopp, Joseph. *The Pentateuch: An Introduction to the First Five Books of the Bible*. London: SCM, 1992.

Block, Daniel I. *Judges, Ruth*. NAC 6. Nashville: Broadman & Holman, 1999.

Bodner, Keith. *David Observed: A King in the Eyes of His Court*. HBM 5. Sheffield, UK: Sheffield Phoenix, 2008.

Bragg, Melvyn. *The Book of Books: The Radical Impact of the King James Bible 1611–2011*. London: Sceptre, 2011.

Braulik, Georg A. *Die Mittel deuteronomischer Rhetorik: Erhoben aus Deuteronomium 40,1–40*. AnBib 68. Rome: Biblical Institute Press, 1978.

Brown, William P. *The Ethos of the Cosmos: The Genesis of Moral Imagination in the Bible*. Grand Rapids: Eerdmans, 1999.

———. *Seeing the Psalms: Theology of Metaphor*. Louisville: Westminster John Knox, 2002.

Brueggemann, Walter. *The Land: Place as Gift, Promise, and Challenge in Biblical Faith*. 2nd ed. OBT. Minneapolis: Fortress, 2002.

———. "Psalms and the Life of Faith: A Suggested Typology of Function." *JSOT* 17 (1980): 3–32.

———. *Theology of the Old Testament*. Minneapolis: Fortress, 1997.

Burnside, Jonathan. *God, Justice and Society: Aspects of Law and Legality in the Bible.* Oxford: Oxford University Press, 2011.

Calvin, John. *Genesis.* 1554. Translated and edited by John King. Calvin Translation Society, 1847. Reprint, Edinburgh: Banner of Truth Trust, 1965.

Carasik, Michael. *Theologies of the Mind in Biblical Israel.* StBibLit 85. New York: Lang, 2006.

Carrière, Jean-Marie. *Théorie du politique dans le Deutéronome: Analyse des unités, des structures et des concepts de Dt 16,18–18,22.* ÖBS 18. Frankfurt: Lang, 1997.

Carruthers, Jo. "Literature." In *The Blackwell Companion to the Bible and Culture,* edited by John F. A. Sawyer, 253–67. Oxford: Blackwell, 2006.

Carson, D. A. *Christ and Culture Revisited.* Grand Rapids: Eerdmans, 2012.

Carson, Rachel. *Silent Spring.* Boston: Houghton Mifflin, 1962.

Carter, Dee. "Unholy Alliances: Religion, Science, and Environment." *Zygon* 36, no. 2 (2011): 357–72.

Childs, Brevard S. *Introduction to the Old Testament as Scripture.* London: SCM, 1979.

———. *Isaiah: A Commentary.* OTL. Louisville: Westminster John Knox, 2001.

———. *The Struggle to Understand Isaiah as Christian Scripture.* Grand Rapids: Eerdmans, 2004.

Clines, David J. A. *The Theme of the Pentateuch.* JSOTSup 10. Sheffield, UK: JSOT Press, 1978.

———. *What Does Eve Do to Help? And Other Readerly Questions to the Old Testament.* JSOTSup 94. 1990. Reprint, Sheffield, UK: JSOT Press, 1994.

Cloninger, C. Robert. *Feeling Good: The Science of Well-Being.* Oxford: Oxford University Press, 2004.

Coakley, Sarah. *God, Sexuality, and the Self: An Essay 'On the Trinity.'* Cambridge: Cambridge University Press, 2013.

Collaud, Thierry. "Beyond the Solitude for Two: Justice, Theology, and General Practice." In Cox, Campbell, and Fulford, *Medicine of the Person,* 156–70.

Collins, Francis. *The Language of God: A Scientist Presents Evidence for Belief.* London: Pocket Books, 2007.

Connerton, Paul. *How Societies Remember.* Cambridge: Cambridge University Press, 1989.

Cox, John, Alastair V. Campbell, and Bill (K. W. M.) Fulford, eds. *Medicine of the Person: Faith, Science and Values.* London: Kingsley, 2007.

Cross, Frank Moore. *Canaanite Myth and Hebrew Epic.* Cambridge, MA: Harvard University Press, 1973.

Crüsemann, Frank. *Der Widerstand gegen das Königtum: Die antiköniglichen Texte des Alten Testaments und der Kampf um den frühen israelitischen Staat.* WMANT 49. Neukirchen-Vluyn: Neukirchener Verlag, 1987.

Curthoys, Ann, and John Docker. *Is History Fiction?* Sydney: University of New South Wales Press, 2006.

Curtis, Edward M. "Image of God (OT)." *ABD* 3:389–91.

———. "Man as the Image of God in Genesis in the Light of Ancient Near Eastern Parallels." PhD diss., University of Pennsylvania, 1984.

Dalley, Stephanie. *Myths from Mesopotamia.* Oxford: Oxford University Press, 1991.

Davies, Philip R. *In Search of "Ancient Israel."* JSOTSup 148. 1992. Reprint, Sheffield, UK: Sheffield Academic, 1995.

Davis, Ellen. *Getting Involved with God: Rediscovering the Old Testament.* Cambridge, MA: Cowley, 2001.

———. *Proverbs, Ecclesiastes, and the Song of Songs.* Westminster Bible Companion. Louisville: Westminster John Knox, 2000.

———. *Scripture, Culture, and Agriculture: An Agrarian Reading of the Bible.* Cambridge: Cambridge University Press, 2009.

Dawkins, Richard. *The God Delusion.* London: Bantam, 2006.

———. *The Selfish Gene.* London: Granada, 1976.

Day, John. *Psalms.* OTG. Sheffield, UK: JSOT Press, 1990.

Dijk-Hemmes, Fokkelien van. "The Imagination of Power and the Power of Imagination: An Intertextual Analysis of Two Biblical Love Songs: The Song of Songs and Hosea 2." *JSOT* 44 (1989): 75–88.

Dolan, Jill. "The Dynamics of Desire: Sexuality and Gender in Pornography and Performance." *Theatre Journal* 89 (1987): 156–74.

Durham, J. I. *Exodus.* WBC 3. Nashville: Nelson, 1987.

Eagleton, Terry. *The Event of Literature.* New Haven: Yale University Press, 2012.

———. *Reason, Faith, and Revolution: Reflections on the God Debate.* New Haven: Yale University Press, 2009.

Eaton, John. *Kingship and the Psalms.* London: SCM, 1976.

Eliot, George. *Adam Bede.* 1859. London: Collins, 1965.

Elliott, Mark W. "Human Embodiment." In *The Dynamics of Human Life*, edited by Mark Elliott, 67–116. Carlisle, UK: Paternoster, 2001.

———. *The Song of Songs and Christology in the Early Church 381–451.* Tübingen: Mohr Siebeck, 2000.

Esler, Philip. *Sex, Wives, and Warriors: Reading Biblical Narrative with the Ancient Audience.* Eugene, OR: Cascade, 2011.

Exum, Cheryl. "Prophetic Pornography." In *Plotted, Shot, and Painted: Cultural Representations of Biblical Women*, 101–28. JSOTSup 215. Sheffield, UK: Sheffield Academic, 1996.

Fewell, Danna Nolan, and David M. Gunn. *Compromising Redemption: Relating Characters in the Book of Ruth.* Louisville: Westminster John Knox, 1990.

Finsterbusch, Karin. "Die kollektive Identität und die Kinder: Bemerkungen zu einem Programm im Buch Deuteronomium." *JBTh* 17 (2002): 99–120.

Fischer, Georg. "Die Josephsgeschichte als Modell für Versöhnung." In *Studies in the Book of Genesis: Literature, Redaction, and History*, edited by A. Wénin, 243–71. BETL 155. Leuven: Peeters, 2001.

Ford, David F. *Christian Wisdom: Desiring God and Learning in Love*. Cambridge: Cambridge University Press, 2007.

———. *Self and Salvation: Being Transformed*. Cambridge: Cambridge University Press, 1999.

Fox, Michael. *Proverbs 1–9*. AB 18a. New Haven: Yale University Press, 2000.

Fretheim, Terence E. *God and World in the Old Testament: A Relational Theology of Creation*. Nashville: Abingdon, 2005.

Frye, Northrop. *The Great Code: The Bible and Literature*. San Diego: Harcourt Brace Jovanovich, 1982.

Galambush, Julie. *Jerusalem in the Book of Ezekiel: The City as Yahweh's Wife*. SBLDS 130. Atlanta: Scholars Press, 1992.

Garrard, Greg. *Ecocriticism*. Oxford: Routledge, 2012.

Geiger, Michaela. *Gottesräume: Die literarische und theologische Konzeption von Raum im Deuteronomium*. BWANT 183. Stuttgart: Kohlhammer, 2010.

George, Mark K. "Yhwh's Own Heart." *CBQ* 64 (2002): 442–59.

Gibson, John C. L., ed. *Canaanite Myths and Legends*. 2nd ed. Edinburgh: T&T Clark, 1978.

Goldingay, John. *Old Testament Theology*. Vol. 1, *Israel's Gospel*. Downers Grove, IL: IVP Academic, 2003.

Good, Edwin M. *Irony in the Old Testament*. London: SPCK, 1965.

Gordis, Robert. *The Book of God and Man: A Study of Job*. Chicago: University of Chicago Press, 1965.

Gordon, Robert P. *I and II Samuel: A Commentary*. 1986. Reprint, Carlisle, UK: Paternoster, 2004.

———. "The Week That Made the World: Reflections on the First Pages of the Bible." In *Reading the Law: Studies in Honour of Gordon J. Wenham*, edited by J. G. McConville and Karl Möller, 228–41. New York: T&T Clark, 2007.

Gorringe, Tim. *The Education of Desire*. London: SCM, 2001.

Grant, Jamie. *The King as Exemplar: The Function of Deuteronomy's Kingship Law in the Shaping of the Book of Psalms*. Atlanta: Society of Biblical Literature, 2004.

Green, Barbara. *What Profit for Us? Remembering the Story of Joseph*. Lanham, MD: University Press of America, 1996.

Grenz, Stanley. *The Social God and the Relational Self: A Trinitarian Theology of the Imago Dei*. Louisville: Westminster John Knox, 2001.

Gunn, David M. *Judges through the Centuries*. BBC. Oxford: Blackwell, 2005.

Hadot, Pierre. *Veil of Isis: An Essay on the History of the Idea of Nature*. Cambridge, MA: The Belknap Press of Harvard University Press, 2006.

Halpern, Baruch. "Jerusalem and the Lineages in the Seventh Century BCE: Kinship and the Rise of Individual Moral Liability." In *Law and Ideology in Monarchic Israel*, edited by Baruch Halpern and D. Hobson, 11–107. JSOTSup 124. Sheffield, UK: Sheffield Academic, 1991.

Hampson, Daphne. *Pure Lust: Elemental Feminist Philosophy*. London: Women's Press, 1984.

Hauerwas, Stanley. *The Peaceable Kingdom: A Primer in Christian Ethics*. London: SCM, 1984.

Hepworth, Barbara. *Drawings from a Sculptor's Landscape*. New York: Praeger, 1967.

Herring, Stephen. *Divine Substitution: Humanity as the Manifestation of Deity in the Hebrew Bible and the Ancient Near East*. FRLANT 247. Göttingen: Vandenhoeck & Ruprecht, 2013.

Hitchens, Christopher. *God Is Not Great: How Religion Poisons Everything*. London: Atlantic, 2008.

Hobbes, Thomas. *Leviathan*. 1651. Reprint, London: Dent, 1931.

Holland, N. N., P. K. Kugler, and M. Grimaud. "Psychological Criticism." In *The New Princeton Encyclopedia of Poetry and Poetics*, edited by A. Preminger and T. G. A. Brogan, 997–1002. Princeton: Princeton University Press, 1993.

Houghton, Sir John. *Does God Play Dice?* Leicester, UK: Inter-Varsity, 1988.

———. *Global Warming: The Complete Briefing*. 3rd ed. Cambridge: Cambridge University Press, 2004.

Houston, Walter J. "Rejoicing before the Lord: The Function of the Festal Gathering in Deuteronomy." In *Feasts and Festivals*, edited by C. Tuckett, 1–14. CBET 53. Leuven: Peeters, 2009.

Ishida, Tomoo. *The Royal Dynasties in Ancient Israel*. BZAW 142. Berlin: de Gruyter, 1977.

Janowski, Bernd. *Gottes Gegenwart in Israel*. BTAT 1. Neukirchen-Vluyn: Neukirchener Verlag, 1993.

Jeffrey, David Lyle, ed. *Dictionary of Biblical Tradition in English Literature*. Grand Rapids: Eerdmans, 1992.

Josipovici, Gabriel. *The Book of God: A Response to the Bible*. New Haven: Yale University Press, 1988.

Kaiser, Otto. *Des Menschen Glück und Gottes Gerechtigkeit*. Tübingen: Mohr Siebeck, 2007.

Kang, J. J. *The Persuasive Portrayal of Solomon in 1 Kings 1–11*. Bern: Lang, 2003.

Kaufman, Gordon D. *God the Problem*. Cambridge, MA: Harvard University Press, 1972.

———. *In Face of Mystery: A Constructive Theology*. Cambridge, MA: Harvard University Press, 1991.

Keefe, Alice A. *Woman's Body and the Social Body in Hosea*. JSOTSup 338. London: Sheffield Academic, 2001.

Kelsey, David H. *Eccentric Existence: A Theological Anthropology*. 2 vols. Louisville: Westminster John Knox, 2009.

Kennedy, G. A. *New Testament Interpretation through Rhetorical Criticism*. Chapel Hill: University of North Carolina Press, 1984.

King, Ursula. "Can Spirituality Transform Our World?" *Journal for the Study of Spirituality* 1 (2011): 17–34.

———. *The Search for Spirituality: Our Global Quest for Meaning and Fulfillment*. Norwich, UK: Canterbury Press, 2009.

Kline, Meredith G. *The Treaty of the Great King: The Covenant Structure of Deuteronomy*. Grand Rapids: Eerdmans, 1963.

Kraus, Hans-Joachim. *Psalms 60–150*. Translated by Hilton C. Oswald. Minneapolis: Fortress, 1989. Translation of *Psalmen 60–150*. BKAT 15.2. Neukirchen-Vluyn: Neukirchener Verlag, 1978.

Kugel, James L. *The Idea of Biblical Poetry*. New Haven: Yale University Press, 1981.

Kuhn, Karl Allen. *The Heart of Biblical Narrative: Rediscovering Biblical Appeal to the Emotions*. Minneapolis: Fortress, 2009.

Küng, Hans, and Karl-Josef Kuschel, eds. *A Global Ethic: The Declaration of the Parliament of the World's Religions*. London: SCM, 1993.

Lapsley, Jacqueline E. "Feeling Our Way: Love for God in Deuteronomy." *CBQ* 65 (2003): 350–69.

Lefebvre, Henri. *The Production of Space*. Translated by Donald Nicholson-Smith. Oxford: Blackwell, 1991.

Levenson, Jon D. *Creation and the Persistence of Evil: The Jewish Drama of Divine Omnipotence*. Princeton: Princeton University Press, 1988.

Levinson, Bernard. *Deuteronomy and the Hermeneutics of Legal Innovation*. New York: Oxford University Press, 1997.

Lincoln, Andrew T. "Spirituality in a Secular Age: From Charles Taylor to Study of the Bible and Spirituality." In *The Spirit That Inspires: Perspectives on Biblical Spirituality*, edited by Pieter de Villiers and Lloyd K. Pietersen, 61–80. Acta Theologica Supplementum 15. Bloemfontein, South Africa: University of the Free State Press, 2011.

Lincoln, Andrew T., J. G. McConville, and Lloyd K. Pietersen, eds. *The Bible and Spirituality: Exploratory Essays in Reading Scripture Spiritually*. Eugene, OR: Cascade, 2013.

Lo, Alison. *Job 28 as Rhetoric: An Analysis of Job 28 in the Context of Job 22–31*. VTSup 97. Leiden: Brill, 2003.

Lohfink, Norbert. "God the Creator and the Stability of Heaven and Earth." In *Theology of the Pentateuch: Themes of the Priestly Narrative and Deuteronomy*, 116–35. Translated by Linda M. Maloney. Minneapolis: Fortress; Edinburgh: T&T Clark, 1994.

Longman, Tremper, III. *Proverbs*. BCOTWP. Grand Rapids: Baker Academic, 2006.

Lovelock, James. *Gaia: A New Look at Life on Earth*. Oxford: Oxford University Press, 2000.

Lubac, Henri de. *Medieval Exegesis: The Four Senses of Scripture*. Vol. 1 translated by M. Sebanc; vols. 2 and 3 translated by E. M. Macierowski. Grand Rapids: Eerdmans, 1998–2009. Translation of *Exégèse médiévale: Les quatre sens de l'Écriture*. Paris: Aubier, 1959–64.

MacDonald, Nathan. *Not Bread Alone: The Uses of Food in the Old Testament*. Oxford: Oxford University Press, 2008.

Macquarrie, John. *In Search of Humanity: A Theological and Philosophical Approach*. London: SCM, 1982.

Malthus, Robert. *An Essay on the Principle of Population*. 1798. Reprint, Oxford: Oxford Paperbacks, 2008.

Marlow, Hilary. *Biblical Prophets and Contemporary Environmental Ethics*. Oxford: Oxford University Press, 2009.

Matthews, Victor H., and Don C. Benjamin. *Old Testament Parallels: Laws and Stories from the Ancient Near East*. 3rd ed. New York: Paulist Press, 2006.

Mayes, A. D. H. *Deuteronomy*. NCB. London: Oliphants, 1979.

———. "Deuteronomy 4 and the Literary Criticism of Deuteronomy." *JBL* 100 (1981): 23–51.

Mays, James Luther. *Hosea*. OTL. London: SCM, 1969.

McCann, J. Clinton. "The Shape of Book I of the Psalter and the Shape of Human Happiness." In *The Book of Psalms*, edited by W. Flint and P. Miller, 340–48. VTSup 99. Leiden: Brill, 2005.

McCarter, P. Kyle. *I Samuel*. AB 8. New York: Doubleday, 1980.

———. *II Samuel*. AB 9. New York: Doubleday, 1984.

McCarthy, Dennis J. *Treaty and Covenant: A Study in Form in the Ancient Oriental Documents and in the Old Testament*. AnBib 21. Rome: Biblical Institute Press, 1978.

McConville, J. Gordon. "Biblical Law and Human Formation." *Political Theology* 14, no. 5 (2013): 628–40.

———. *Deuteronomy*. ApOTC 5. Leicester, UK: Apollos; Downers Grove, IL: Inter-Varsity, 2002.

———. "Forgiveness as Private and Public Act: A Reading of the Biblical Joseph Narrative." *CBQ* 75 (2013): 635–48.

———. *God and Earthly Power: An Old Testament Political Theology, Genesis–Kings*. 2006. Reprint, London: T&T Clark, 2008.

———. "Human 'Dominion' and Being 'Like God': An Exploration of Peace, Violence, and Truth in the Old Testament." In *Encountering Violence in the Bible*, edited by Markus Zehnder and Hallvard Hagelia, 194–206. Sheffield, UK: Sheffield Phoenix, 2013.

———. "'I Am like a Luxuriant Juniper': Language about God in Hosea." In *Let Us Go Up to Zion: Essays in Honour of H. G. M. Williamson on His 65th Birthday*, edited by M. Boda and I. Provan, 181–92. VTSup 153. Leiden: Brill, 2012.

———. *Joshua: Crossing Divides*. PGOT. Sheffield, UK: Sheffield Phoenix, 2013.

———. "'Keep These Words in Your Heart' (Deut 6:6): A Spirituality of Torah in the Context of the Shema." In *For Our Good Always: Studies on the Message and Influence of Deuteronomy in Honor of Daniel I. Block*, edited by Jason S. de Rouchie, Jason Gile, and Kenneth J. Turner, 127–44. Winona Lake, IN: Eisenbrauns, 2013.

———. "Metaphor, Symbol, and Interpretation in Deuteronomy." In *After Pentecost: Language and Biblical Interpretation*, edited by Craig G. Bartholomew, Colin J. D. Greene, and Karl Möller, 321–51. SHS 2. Grand Rapids: Zondervan, 2002.

———. "Singular Address in the Deuteronomic Law and the Politics of Legal Administration." *JSOT* 97 (2002): 19–36.

McConville, J. G., and J. G. Millar. *Time and Place in Deuteronomy*. JSOTSup 179. Sheffield, UK: Sheffield Academic, 1994.

McConville, J. G., and S. N. Williams. *Joshua*. THOTC. Grand Rapids: Eerdmans, 2010.

McDowell, Catherine L. (formerly Beckerleg). "The Image of God in Eden: The Creation of Mankind in Genesis 2:5–3:24 in Light of the *mīs pî*, *pit pî* and *wpt-r* Rituals of Mesopotamia and Ancient Egypt." PhD diss., Harvard University, 2009. Published as *The Image of God in the Garden of Eden: The Creation of Humankind in Genesis 2:5–3:24 in Light of* mīs pî, pīt pî *and* wpt-r *Rituals of Mesopotamia and Ancient Egypt*. Siphrut: Literature and Theology of the Hebrew Scriptures 15. Winona Lake, IN: Eisenbrauns, 2015.

McKeown, James. *Ruth*. THOTC. Grand Rapids: Eerdmans, 2015.

McKeown, John. *God's Babies: Natalism and Bible Interpretation in Modern America*. Cambridge, UK: Open Book, 2014.

Meinhold, A. "Theologische Erwägungen zum Buch Esther." *TZ* 34 (1978): 321–33.

Meyers, Carol. *Discovering Eve: Ancient Israelite Women in Context*. New York: Oxford University Press, 1988.

Middleton, J. Richard. *The Liberating Image: The* Imago Dei *in Genesis 1*. Grand Rapids: Brazos, 2005.

Midgley, Mary. *The Myths We Live By*. London: Routledge, 2011.

———. *Science and Poetry*. London: Routledge, 2001.

———. *The Solitary Self*. Durham, UK: Acumen, 2010.

Miller, Patrick D. "Kingship, Torah Obedience, and Prayer." In *Neue Wege der Psalmenforschung*, edited by K. Seybold and E. Zenger, 127–42. Freiburg: Herder, 1995.

Minette de Tillesse, Georges. "Sections 'vous' et sections 'tu' dans le Deutéronome." *VT* 12 (1962): 56–63.

Moberly, R. W. L. "Did the Serpent Get It Right?" *JTS* 39 (1988): 1–27.

Möller, Karl. "Images of God and Creation in Genesis 1–2." In *A God of Faithfulness: Essays in Honour of J. Gordon McConville on His Sixtieth Birthday*, edited by Jamie Grant, Alison Lo, and Gordon J. Wenham, 3–29. New York: T&T Clark, 2011.

Moltmann, Jürgen. *Ethics of Hope*. Translated by Margaret Kohl. Minneapolis: Fortress, 2012. Translation of *Ethik der Hoffnung*. Gütersloh: Gütersloher Verlagshaus, 2010.

Moore, Thomas. *Care of the Soul: A Guide for Cultivating Depth and Sacredness in Everyday Life*. New York: Harper Collins, 1992.

Moran, William L. "The Ancient Near Eastern Background of the Love of God in Deuteronomy." *CBQ* 25 (1963): 77–87.

Morgenstern, Mira. *Conceiving a Nation: The Development of Political Discourse in the Hebrew Bible*. University Park: Pennsylvania State University Press, 2009.

Moughtin-Mumby, Sharon. *Sexual and Marital Metaphors in Hosea, Jeremiah, Isaiah, and Ezekiel*. OTM. Oxford: Oxford University Press, 2008.

Murdoch, Iris. *The Black Prince*. Harmondsworth, UK: Penguin, 1973.

Nelson, Richard D. *Joshua: A Commentary*. OTL. Louisville: Westminster John Knox, 1997.

———. "Josiah in the Book of Joshua." *JBL* 100 (1981): 531–40.

Niebuhr, H. Richard. *Christ and Culture*. London: Faber & Faber, 1951.

Nielsen, Kirsten. *Ruth*. Translated by Edward Broadbridge. OTL. London: SCM, 1997.

Nietzsche, Friedrich. *The Gay Science*. Translated by Josefine Nauckhoff. Cambridge: Cambridge University Press, 2001.

Nussbaum, Martha. *Upheavals of Thought: The Intelligence of Emotions*. New York: Cambridge University Press, 2001.

O'Donovan, Oliver. "Reflections on Work." In *On Rock or Sand? Firm Foundations for Britain's Future*, edited by John Sentamu, 111–31. London: SPCK, 2015.

O'Dowd, Ryan. *The Wisdom of Torah: Epistemology in Deuteronomy and the Wisdom Literature*. FRLANT 225. Göttingen: Vandenhoeck & Ruprecht, 2009.

O'Keefe, John J., and Russell R. Reno. *Sanctified Vision: An Introduction to Early Christian Interpretation of the Bible*. Baltimore: Johns Hopkins University Press, 2005.

Olsen, Glenn W. "The Spiritual Sense(s) Today." In *The Bible and the University*, edited by David Lyle Jeffrey and Stephen Evans, 117–38. Grand Rapids: Zondervan; Carlisle, UK: Paternoster, 2007.

Olson, Dennis T. *Deuteronomy and the Death of Moses: A Theological Reading.* OBT. Minneapolis: Fortress, 1994.

Otto, Eckart. *Krieg und Frieden in der Hebräischen Bibel und im Alten Orient: Aspekte für eine Friedensordnung in der Moderne.* Stuttgart: Kohlhammer, 1999.

———. *Theologische Ethik des Alten Testaments.* Stuttgart: Kohlhammer, 1994.

Pascal, Blaise. *Pensées.* Edited by L. Lafuma. Paris: Garnier-Flammarion, 1973.

Patrick, Dale, and Allen M. Scult. *Rhetoric and Biblical Interpretation.* JSOTSup 82. Sheffield, UK: Almond Press, 1990.

Peplau, Hildegard E. *Interpersonal Relations in Nursing.* New York: Putnam's Sons, 1952.

Polkinghorne, John. *Reason and Reality: The Relationship between Science and Theology.* London: SPCK, 1991.

Polzin, Robert. *David and the Deuteronomist: A Literary Study of the Deuteronomic History; Part Three: 2 Samuel.* Bloomington: Indiana University Press, 1993.

———. *Moses and the Deuteronomist: A Literary Study of the Deuteronomic History; Part One: Deuteronomy, Joshua, Judges.* New York: Seabury, 1980.

Rad, Gerhard von. *Old Testament Theology.* Vol. 1, *The Theology of Israel's Historical Traditions.* Translated by D. M. G. Stalker. London: Oliver & Boyd, 1962.

———. "Vom Menschenbild des Alten Testaments." In *Der alte und der neue Mensch: Aufsätze zur theologischen Anthropologie,* by G. von Rad, H. Schlier, E. Wolf, and E. Schlink, 5–23. BEvT 8. Munich: Lempp, 1942.

Rand, Ayn. *The Fountainhead.* New York: Signet, 1943.

Raphael, Melissa. *Judaism and the Visual Image: A Jewish Theology of Art.* London: Continuum, 2009.

Richter, Sandra. "Environmental Law in Deuteronomy: One Lens on a Biblical Theology of Creation Care." *BBR* 20, no. 3 (2010): 355–76.

Ricoeur, Paul. *The Conflict of Interpretations.* Evanston, IL: Northwestern University Press, 1976.

———. *Discourse and the Surplus of Meaning.* Fort Worth: Texas Christian University Press, 1976.

———. "The Nuptial Metaphor." In *Thinking Biblically: Exegetical and Hermeneutical Studies,* edited by André Lacocque and Paul Ricoeur, 265–303. Chicago: University of Chicago Press, 1988.

———. *Oneself as Another.* Chicago: University of Chicago Press, 1995.

Robinson, Marilynne. "Austerity as Ideology." In *When I Was a Child I Read Books,* 35–58.

———. "Darwinism." In *The Death of Adam: Essays on Modern Thought,* 28–75. 1998. Reprint, New York: Picador, 2005.

———. *Gilead.* New York: Farrar, Straus and Giroux, 2004.

———. *Home.* New York: Farrar, Straus and Giroux, 2008.

———. *Housekeeping.* New York: Farrar, Straus and Giroux, 1980.

———. "When I Was a Child." In *When I Was a Child I Read Books*, 85–94.

———. *When I Was a Child I Read Books*. London: Virago, 2012.

Rogerson, John W. *Anthropology and the Old Testament*. Oxford: Blackwell, 1978.

———. *A Theology of the Old Testament: Cultural Memory, Communication, and Being Human*. London: SPCK, 2009.

———. "Towards a Communicative Theology of the Old Testament." In *Reading the Law: Essays in Honour of Gordon J. Wenham*, edited by J. G. McConville and Karl Möller, 283–96. London: T&T Clark, 2007.

Rogerson, John, Christopher Rowland, and Barnabas Lindars, eds. *The Study and Use of the Bible*. Basingstoke, UK: Pickering; Grand Rapids: Eerdmans, 1988.

Rosenberg, Joel. *King and Kin: Political Allegory in the Hebrew Bible*. Bloomington: Indiana University Press, 1986.

Santmire, H. P. *Brother Earth: Nature, God, and Ecology in Time of Crisis*. New York: Nelson, 1970.

Schäfer-Lichtenberger, Christa. *Josua und Salomo: Eine Studie zu Autorität und Legitimität des Nachfolgers im Alten Testament*. VTSup 58. Leiden: Brill, 1995.

Schellenberg, Annette. *Der Mensch, das Bild Gottes? Zum Gedanken einer Sonderstellung des Menschen im Alten Testament und in weiteren altorientalischen Quellen*. ATANT 101. Zurich: Theologischer Verlag, 2011.

Schmid, Konrad. *Erzväter und Exodus: Untersuchungen zur doppelten Begründung der Ursprünge Israels innerhalb der Geschichtsbücher des Alten Testaments*. WMANT 81. Neukirchen-Vluyn: Neukirchener Verlag, 1999. Published in English as *Genesis and the Moses Story: Israel's Dual Origins in the Hebrew Bible*. Translated by James D. Nogalski. Siphrut: Literature and Theology of the Hebrew Scriptures 3. Winona Lake, IN: Eisenbrauns, 2010.

Schmidt, W. H. *Die Schöpfungsgeschichte in der Priesterschrift*. 2nd ed. Neukirchen-Vluyn: Neukirchener Verlag, 1967.

Schneiders, Sandra. "Christian Spirituality: Definition, Methods, and Types." In *The New Westminster Dictionary of Christian Spirituality*, edited by P. Sheldrake, 1–6. Louisville: Westminster John Knox, 2005.

———. *The Revelatory Text: Interpreting the New Testament as Sacred Scripture*. 2nd ed. Collegeville, MN: Liturgical Press, 1999.

Schüle, Andreas. "Made in the 'Image of God': The Concepts of Divine Images in Gen 1–3." ZAW 117 (2005): 1–20.

Schwartz, Regina. *The Curse of Cain: The Violent Legacy of Monotheism*. Chicago: University of Chicago Press, 1997.

Seligman, Martin. *Flourish*. London: Brealey, 2011.

Setel, T. Drorah. "Prophets and Pornography: Female Sexual Imagery in Hosea." In *Feminist Interpretation of the Bible*, edited by Letty Russell, 86–95. Philadelphia: Westminster, 1985.

Shakespeare, William. *Hamlet: An Authoritative Text, Intellectual Backgrounds, Extracts from Sources, Essays in Criticism.* Edited by Cyrus Hoy. Norton Critical Editions. 1963. 2nd ed. New York: Norton, 1992.

Sherwood, Yvonne. *The Prostitute and the Prophet: Hosea's Marriage in Literary-Theoretical Perspective.* JSOTSup 212. Sheffield, UK: Sheffield Academic, 1996.

Skinner, John. *Prophecy and Religion.* Cambridge: Cambridge University Press, 1922.

Smith, Henry P. *A Critical and Exegetical Commentary on the Books of Samuel.* ICC. Edinburgh: T&T Clark, 1899.

Smith, James K. A. *Imagining the Kingdom: How Worship Works.* Grand Rapids: Baker Academic, 2013.

Song, Robert. *Covenant Calling: Towards a Theology of Same-Sex Relationships.* London: SCM, 2014.

Sophocles. *Antigone.* Edited by Mark Griffith. CGLC. Cambridge: Cambridge University Press, 1999.

Soskice, Janet Martin. *Metaphor and Religious Language.* Oxford: Oxford University Press, 1985.

Sternberg, Meir. *The Poetics of Biblical Narrative.* Bloomington: Indiana University Press, 1985.

Strawn, Brent A., and Brad D. Strawn. "Prophecy and Psychology." In *Dictionary of the Old Testament: The Prophets*, edited by Mark J. Boda and J. Gordon McConville, 610–23. Downers Grove, IL: IVP Academic, 2012.

Strong, John T. "Israel as a Testimony to Yhwh's Power: The Priests' Definition of Israel." In *Constituting the Community: Studies in Honor of S. Dean McBride*, edited by John T. Strong and Steven S. Tuell, 89–106. Winona Lake, IN: Eisenbrauns, 2005.

Swinton, John. *Spirituality and Mental Health Care: Recovering a "Forgotten" Dimension.* London: Kingsley, 2001.

Taylor, Charles. *A Secular Age.* Cambridge, MA: The Belknap Press of Harvard University Press, 2007.

Taylor, Lyrica, ed. *Still Small Voice: British Biblical Art in a Secular Age (1850–2014) from the Ahmanson Collection.* Irvine, CA: Pinatubo Press, 2015.

Tigay, Jeffrey. *Deuteronomy.* JPS Torah Commentary. Philadelphia: Jewish Publication Society, 1996.

Tournier, Paul. *Médecine de la personne.* Neuchâtel: Delachaud et Niestlé, 1940.

Trible, Phyllis. *God and the Rhetoric of Sexuality.* OBT. 1978. Reprint, Philadelphia: Fortress, 1992.

———. *Texts of Terror: Literary Feminist Readings of Biblical Narratives.* OBT. Philadelphia: Fortress, 1984.

Vanier, Jean. *Drawn into the Mystery of Jesus through the Gospel of John.* London: Darton, Longman & Todd, 2004.

———. *Man and Woman He Made Them*. London: Darton, Longman & Todd, 1985.

Van Leeuwen, Raymond. "The Book of Proverbs." *NIB* 5:19–264.

Villiers, Pieter de, and Lloyd K. Pietersen, eds. *The Spirit That Inspires: Perspectives on Biblical Spirituality*. Acta Theologica Supplementum 15. Bloemfontein, South Africa: University of the Free State Press, 2011.

Volf, Miroslav. *Work in the Spirit: Toward a Theology of Work*. New York: Oxford University Press, 1991.

Vos, Jacobus Cornelis de. *Das Los Judas: Über Entstehung und Ziele der Landbeschreibung in Josua 15*. VTSup 95. Leiden: Brill, 2003.

Waaijman, Kees. *Spirituality: Forms, Foundations, Methods*. Leuven: Peeters, 2002.

Walker, Christopher, and Michael B. Dick. *The Induction of the Cult Image in Ancient Mesopotamia: The Mesopotamian Mīs Pî Ritual*. State Archives of Assyria Literary Texts. Helsinki: Neo-Assyrian Corpus Project, 2001.

Walker-Jones, Arthur. *The Green Psalter: Resources for an Ecological Spirituality*. Minneapolis: Fortress, 2009.

Walzer, Michael. *In God's Shadow: Politics in the Hebrew Bible*. New Haven: Yale University Press, 2012.

Ward, Keith. *Why There Almost Certainly Is a God*. Oxford: Lion, 2008.

Weeks, S. *Instruction and Wisdom in Proverbs 1–9*. New York: Oxford University Press, 2007.

Weinfeld, Moshe. *Deuteronomy 1–11*. AB 5. New York: Doubleday, 1991.

Wenham, Gordon J. *Genesis 1–15*. WBC 1. Nashville: Nelson, 1987.

Westermann, Claus. *Genesis 1–11*. Translated by John J. Scullion. London: SPCK; Minneapolis: Augsburg, 1984. Translation of *Genesis 1–11*. BKAT 1.2. Neukirchen-Vluyn: Neukirchener Verlag, 1974.

———. *Praise and Lament in the Psalms*. Translated by Keith R. Crim and Richard N. Soulen. Edinburgh: T&T Clark, 1981. Translation of *Lob und Klage in den Psalmen*. Göttingen: Vandenhoeck & Ruprecht, 1977.

White, Lynn, Jr. "The Historical Roots of Our Ecologic Crisis." *Science* 155, no. 3767 (1967): 1203–7.

Wig, N. N. Mary Hemingway Rees Memorial Lecture. World Federation of Mental Health, Trinity College, Dublin, 1995.

Wildavsky, Aaron. "What Is Permissible So That This People May Survive? Joseph the Administrator." *PS: Political Science and Politics* 22 (1989): 779–88.

Wildberger, Hans. "Das Abbild Gottes: Gen. 1,26–30." *TZ* 21 (1965): 245–59, 481–501.

Williams, Rowan. "The Body's Grace." In *Theology and Sexuality: Classic and Contemporary Readings*, edited by Eugene F. Rogers Jr., 309–21. Malden, MA: Wiley-Blackwell, 2001.

Williamson, H. G. M. *Variations on a Theme: King, Messiah, and Servant in the Book of Isaiah*. Carlisle, UK: Paternoster, 1998.

Wilson, Alan. *More Perfect Union? Understanding Same-Sex Marriage*. London: Darton, Longman & Todd, 2014.

Winterson, Jeanette. *Oranges Are Not the Only Fruit*. London: Pandora Press, 1985.

Wolde, Ellen van. *Ruth and Naomi*. Translated by John Bowden. London: SCM, 1997.

———. *A Semiotic Analysis of Genesis 2–3: A Semiotic Theory and Method of Analysis Applied to the Story of the Garden of Eden*. Assen, Neth.: Van Gorcum, 1989.

———. *Stories of the Beginning: Genesis 1–11 and Other Creation Stories*. Translated by John Bowden. London: SCM, 1995.

Wolff, Hans Walter. *Anthropology of the Old Testament*. Translated by Margaret Kohl. London: SCM, 1974.

———. *Hosea: A Commentary on the Book of Hosea*. Translated by G. Stanstell. Hermeneia. Philadelphia: Fortress, 1974.

Wolterstorff, Nicholas. *Art in Action*. Grand Rapids: Eerdmans, 1980.

Zenger, Erich. "The Composition and Theology of the Fifth Book of the Psalms, Psalms 107–145." *JSOT* 80 (1998): 77–102.

Subject Index

218

Author Index

221

Scripture Index

224